Leadership for

ACTIVE CREATIVE ENGAGED

communities

Leadership for

ACTIVE CREATIVE ENGAGED

communities

Brenda Herchmer

iUniverse, Inc.
Bloomington

Leadership
For Active Creative Engaged Communities

iUniverse books may be ordered through booksellers or by contacting:

iUniverse
1663 Liberty Drive
Bloomington, IN 47403
www.iuniverse.com
1-800-Authors (1-800-288-4677)

Because of the dynamic nature of the Internet, any web addresses or links contained in this book may have changed since publication and may no longer be valid. The views expressed in this work are solely those of the author and do not necessarily reflect the views of the publisher, and the publisher hereby disclaims any responsibility for them.

ISBN: 978-1-4620-6399-4 (sc)
ISBN: 978-1-4620-6400-7 (ebk)

Also by the same author:
A Planning Toolkit for Community Leaders
Creating Community: A Handbook for Recreation Practitioners

Printed in the United States of America

iUniverse rev. date: 01/04/2012

Table of Contents

Competency 2:
Commitment to Continuous Improvement 105

Foreword by Ian Hill

I have been involved in some 250 plus community-based projects across Canada and the United States over the past five years. I have been in community halls, schools, parks and churches, meetings with elected officials, collaborating with business leaders, talking with public employees, working with quality of life sector professionals, building playgrounds with thousands of parents, and listening to our kids.

As a result of these experiences, I've come to three conclusions:

1) Communities get better as soon as leaders do.
2) Who is "really" getting things done in communities has changed.
3) Our approach to "community leadership" no longer works.

In short, we need a "game changer"!

I first heard the term game changer when I was coaching track. It was used to refer to an individual whose unique attributes and abilities transcended the athletic endeavor. Then I heard the term used again when I was an executive in the Casino industry. There, the term was used to describe an approach to doing business that would take a company to the next level. Finally, as partner in a boutique venture capital fund, the term was used to refer to technology that was on the transformational edge.

I have read numerous books about leadership and "community". Most have interesting theories; a few had practical tools, but none have changed the "game".

This book is a game changer.

I first met Brenda Herchmer some fifteen years ago when I was asked to speak to a group of recreation and parks professionals who were holding a national conference. Brenda was one of the attendees and presenters. When I was finished speaking she approached me and we chatted. Little did I know that in those indefinable split seconds, I had met a person who I have now come to realize is a game changer whose work, and now writings, hold the keys to the improvement of our communities in these changing times.

Much like the gifted athlete, Brenda's abilities, attributes, and life experiences make her uniquely equipped to write the "game chang-ing" book about community leadership and how to effectively do it.

She began as a community-based recreation professional, working at the Boys and Girls Club and later for a municipal recreation department, seeing firsthand the power and potential of the quality of life sector. She then moved to the world of academics, teaching at the college level and heading up a first of its kind community leadership institute that was a catalyst for the development of programs, activities, and educational opportunities for community leaders. Brenda then took her life's work and applied it to the role of social entrepreneur in creating the leading edge, community-improving Active, Creative, and Engaged (ACE) Communities initiative.

The convergence of the practical and academic, along with an entrepreneurial spirit, a sincere heart, and a desire to lighten the burden of her fellow citizens, result in making her the only person I have encountered who has the background, and proven leadership track record to write a book of this kind. You can trust that you are hearing from a tour guide (a person that has actually been where you want to go) as opposed to a travel agent (someone who has only studied where you want to go).

Much like game changers in industry, this book puts forward a new way of doing business in community leadership—a holistic, practical, and proven approach to effective community leadership today. The core competencies discussed, and the tangible tools found within, will transform the way communities and their leaders get things done.

Just as I saw innovative technology transform, I have seen the transformational effects of the concepts within this book put into practice. In every one of the community projects where I was involved, we used the concepts that you will read about in the coming pages. One only has to look across Alberta, and in fact across the country, to see community after community transformed by applying the ACE Communities process.

Really, this book is a handbook. Brenda puts forth a compelling case for the ACE way, as well as practical tools to give the reader everything they need to put the ACE Community Leadership approach into practice.

I believe this is a book whose time has come, penned by a person uniquely equipped to write it. The material is proven well beyond the theoretical. And most importantly, there is no doubt — it works. However, the book will only be a game changer if you do something with it.

Use the game changing material within this book to improve your leadership capacity and to lighten the burden of your fellow citizens. Use it to go out and be a world changer, or at the very least, improve your little corner of it.

Ian Hill
Award Winning Humanitarian and Innovator
www.thechangingpoint.com

About the Author

Brenda Herchmer has a diverse background gained in a variety of business, government, education, and social profit settings. Owner of Grassroots Enterprises, a company specializing in community development and community leadership, she is now serving as the director of ACE Communities for Alberta Recreation and Parks Association (ARPA).

Previously she taught in the Recreation and Leisure Services Program at Niagara College in Welland, Ontario and also worked with others to found and then manage the Niagara Centre for Community Leadership. The Centre was acknowledged by the Association of Canadian Community Colleges as an "exemplary practice in community development" and was a finalist for the prestigious national Peter F. Drucker Innovation Award.

Brenda is an avid writer and blogger (see http://brenda.herchmer. net/) and produces a weekly column for the Welland Tribune. In addition to this publication, she is the author of a textbook entitled *Creating Communities: A Handbook for Recreation Practitioners,* and *A Toolkit for Community Leaders.* Brenda has been acknowledged as a YWCA Woman of Distinction in Training and Education, and as winner of the Toastmasters Communication and Leadership Award.

Previously Brenda has been employed by the City of Niagara Falls, the Boys and Girls Club, The Investors Group, and Bell Canada. She has also owned three retail outlets and with her husband co-owned the Village Gallery—winner of the Welland Small Business of the Year Award.

Brenda and her husband Vince raised their blended family of three active sons in Ontario, but are now enjoying their adventures in Edmonton as official empty nesters.

While Brenda's experience is diverse, there is a common thread throughout—as a community builder she is committed to, and believes in, the importance and strength of our communities.

Acknowledgements

This book was written for the many caring and concerned individuals who want to make a difference in their communities and are looking for practical advice and direction on how to do it. It is for those who understand that the quality of life in a community is impacted as much by the public benefit economy as it is by the market economy. Even if one doesn't consider themselves to be a leader, it is my hope that after reading this book they will have a better understanding of their own leadership abilities, how they can be enhanced, and why they themselves might just be more of what the world needs.

In large part, this book reflects learnings that were the result of the Alberta Recreation and Parks Association's (ARPA) ACE Communities initiative and my role as Director. None of that would have been possible without the vision of their CEO Rick Curtis and Board of Directors, and the significant funding provided by Rural Alberta Development Fund, Encana, Cenovus Energy, and Canwest (now Postmedia Network Inc.).

The current and former ACE Communities core team, Carol Petersen, Dianne Renton Clark (Trendspire Canada Inc.), Janet Naclia, Rose Carmichael, Byron Walker, Heather O'Hearn, and Carolyn Mead are extraordinarily talented and are simply as good as a team can get. ACE Communities has been further blessed by assistance from the ARPA staff, a team of talented contractors, including our gifted ACE Ambassador Ian Hill, and local community leaders who have taught us so much. The most valuable and consistent learning they have reinforced has been the wisdom, intelligence, and passion that exists at the grassroots of our communities.

On a personal note, I need to acknowledge Bob Burger who many years ago took a chance in giving me a job at the Niagara Falls Boys and Girls Club, modeled shared leadership, and started me on such a meaningful career path; Robert Sones Jr. who first taught me about community building when I worked for the City of Niagara Falls; Alison Burgoyne at Niagara College who so believed in our community leadership work; Carol Petersen who made it possible for me to work with the mavericks in Alberta, and especially the brilliant, and hardworking Dianne Renton Clark with whom I have shared so many community building adventures over the years. Both the Niagara Falls and the Welland Tribune encouraged me as a writer by supporting me as a columnist. Believe me there is nothing like a weekly deadline to keep a writer writing. The talent and patience of Jen Stevenson, who is responsible for the book design, is also very much appreciated. Thanks to those who have provided so much encouragement along the way especially my family and my mother Wilma Berswick who is the nicest and kindest cheerleader one could ever hope to have in their corner, and my father from whom I seem to have inherited the system-thinking gene.

Last, but always first in my heart, I am grateful to my husband Vince for his unwavering and unconditional love and support, and our amazing three sons Jason and Chris Herchmer and William Mowat.

 **Chapter 1**

Introduction

I never set out to write a book about leadership. For most of my life I never equated either myself, or the work I did, as having anything to do with leadership.

While my career path first took me into the corporate world, I was attracted to the field of recreation leadership because of its focus on outcomes—helping people grow and be healthy, building strong families and communities, working with those who were disadvantaged, protecting the environment, and adding to the quality of life in our communities.

I subsequently worked in a variety of settings including a Boys and Girls Club, municipal recreation, Niagara College, consulting, and then with the Alberta Recreation and Parks Association (ARPA) and the Active, Creative, Engaged (ACE) Communities initiative.

While my work was driven by wanting to make a difference, thinking of it as leadership was something that, for the longest time, wasn't even part of my vocabulary. Along with many others, I instead saw leadership as something that took place in a corporate setting utilizing a command and control, top down direction usually provided by more men than women.

Over a period of time, three distinct moments occurred that made the need for a particular type of leadership much more clear. It was like the very first time I tried on a pair of glasses and my view of the world became sharper and more finely tuned.

The first moment of clarity occurred during a meeting that took place a number of years ago. Along with about fifteen others from the social profit[1] sector, I was invited to be part of an effort to identify solutions that could strengthen the capacity of organizations across the country.

My work at that time focused on managing a centre at Niagara College whose mandate was capacity building for communities and social-profit organizations, so I attended that meeting with some confidence. However, I remember feeling annoyed with the woman who chaired the meeting because she insisted we focus on leadership while ignoring the issues myself and others felt were significantly more relevant to capacity building. Our concerns focused on areas such as generating resources, managing staff and volunteers, board governance, marketing, technology, planning, and ensuring relevant programs.

However, as the discussion evolved, we all came around, albeit grudgingly, to the idea that we needed to focus on leadership development.

Most of us left that meeting better attuned to the idea that a focus on leadership would mean highlighting solutions rather than simply reacting to the problems.

From that point on, I started to see working with my community as more akin to dealing with a leaky faucet. Instead of running and trying to catch the drips, strong leaders would help us keep the faucet from leaking in the first place. While it was still important to respond to the symptoms of social, health, and environmental challenges in our community and deal with the preoccupation with bottom line financial results that has too often overridden "public good" outcomes, we would also be able to tackle root causes by addressing leadership.

The second moment of clarity happened during yet another meeting several months later. As the daylong discussion circled, swooped, and looped, it struck me that despite the passionate and energetic conversation, we were simply not making any progress. Although the meeting participants had shared values and noble intentions, the majority simply lacked, through no fault of their own, the knowledge and skills necessary to engage and involve those in the room in a synergistic movement forward.

---

1 Also referred to as non-profit, voluntary, or not-for-profit sector (as opposed to the private or government sectors).

The third instance was a meeting several years ago that took place in Canmore, Alberta. Carol Petersen, a manager at Alberta Recreation and Parks Association (ARPA), had arranged for me, along with two other consultants, to meet with her to discuss an initiative that had received funding to impact the quality of life across the province.

Despite having the funding in place, it was a daunting task. After all, where and how does one begin to improve the quality of life across an entire community, never mind an entire province? As Carol said it isn't as if one could just walk into a community, knock on a door, and say "Hi we're here to improve your quality of life!"

Regardless, we jumped in and found ourselves brainstorming and analyzing for several hours before having a breakthrough moment. That moment was when we realized there was one common denominator among all of the communities that *were* doing well. All of the communities that had a strong quality of life also had *strong local leadership*. That was when we knew the most significant impact and the greatest legacy would occur as the result of investing in the development of local leaders.

For me, those three defining moments culminated in an understanding of a new kind of work that needed to be done. The work would involve defining, describing, and providing tools, resources, and support for a new and emerging kind of leadership. Not corporate or business leadership, but instead a kind of leadership that would impact the quality of life for each and every one of us—the *community leadership* that would ensure collective impact and the kind of communities where we all want to live, work, and play—leadership for active, creative, and engaged communities—ACE Communities.

 **Chapter 2**

What is an
ACE Community?

The original initiative discussed at that first meeting in the beautiful mountains of Canmore grew to become a multi million dollar initiative known as ACE Communities—ACE being the acronym for active, creative, and engaged. But what exactly is an ACE Community?

The truth is that when we first started it wasn't all that clear. We did know that an ACE Community would have high levels of citizens who are physically and socially active and engaged, and an emphasis would be placed on creativity, social capital, and social cohesion. We believed it was this that would ensure quality of life and communities where people would want to live and visit.

Additional characteristics of ACE Communities would include a sense of belonging, citizens involved in decision-making, diverse recreation, cultural and active living opportunities, high levels of volunteer involvement, and inviting, sustainable design.

While we weren't exactly sure how to go about doing it at the time, we also knew the work of ACE Communities would need to support six key shifts:

1) Leadership would need to shift from traditional, business, or hierarchical leadership to a form of community leadership that was more shared and distributed.
2) We would need to encourage community leaders to move away from traditional ways of working that had them focused on single outcomes. Instead they would need to become more

comfortable dealing with the complexity of multiple outcomes.

3) Power would need to move from being driven top-down and become more about a bottom-up or grassroots approach.

4) There needed to be far more collaboration—not only within silos or sectors (e.g. health, social services, education, recreation, business) but also across the many that make up our communities.

5) Community involvement would need to be citizen-driven rather than professionally-driven.

6) No longer could timing be about short term cautious fixes, it was time to focus on long term courageous change.[2]

While we knew we were in for a challenge, we also knew we had something of a "secret sauce". Our secret sauce was in knowing the odds of success would be far greater if we used a community development approach. Using community development we would be able to strengthen the community leadership, collaboration, and innovation that would ensure there was a high quality of life available and accessible to all.

2   Alberta Recreation and Parks Association (2006). *Foundations for action*. ARPA: Edmonton.

 **Chapter 3**

What is Community Development?

The simplest way to understand the meaning of community development may be to break down the two words—community and development. If *community* is about sharing, connecting, and belonging, and *development* means improvement or growth, then community development is simply "helping people to help themselves".[3] A more academic definition defines community development "as local empowerment through organized groups of people acting collectively to control decisions, projects, programs, and policies that affect them as a community".[4]

A deeper understanding of community development and what it means also results when there is (1) a better understanding of communities—how to find them and why they are often difficult to describe, and (2) why communities are so important.

About Communities

Like many baby boomers, I grew up in a neighbourhood that was a community where everybody knew our names.

Not only did they know our names, they knew exactly where we lived, the names of our parents and pets, and probably what we had for dinner the night before. We played tag and hide and seek until the street lights went on, organized lavish theatre productions in our

---

3 Herchmer, B. (1996). *Creating community: A community development handbook for the recreation practitioner.* Edmonton: Grassroots Enterprises.

4 Rubin, H.J. & Rubin, I.S. (1992). *Community organising and developing.* NY: MacMillan.

backyards, skated on ice rinks that stretched across several backyards, and delivered casseroles baked by our mothers to those who were sick or had lost a loved one.

While most of us were second or third generation Canadians, our cultural backgrounds were varied and reflected in the accents of our parents or grandparents—Ukrainian, Italian, Russian, English, French, German, and more. Like many others at the time, we couldn't have told you that someone like Gilles was in a wheelchair as the result of cerebral palsy. However, we did know that when he gestured and waved to the kids too enthusiastically and as a result moved himself too close to the road, we needed to push him back up his driveway to keep him safe. And, although we didn't know much about dementia at the time, we did know that when Gail's grandma got confused and forgot where she lived, we needed to walk her back to her house. All in all, it was a good place to grow up.

Although most people think about community from this geographic or neighbourhood perspective, there are other ways of thinking about community.

As I write this, my husband and I have just enjoyed a lovely barbecue dinner on our back patio. Afterward, sitting in the beautiful late evening sun, we watched kids, adults, and their pets walk by or play in the park across the street. As beautiful as it was, and as much as we enjoy living where we do, the truth is that even after living here three years, we only know our neighbours well enough to wave to them.

> " If you look at the cause of so many of the challenges facing our society, most center on the loss of a sense of community and the common good."
>
> — Peter Block

I must admit it led to a sense of nostalgia for the community where I grew up. On this same kind of evening, kids would have been running and playing in everyone's yards while the adults sat on their porches or stood chatting in clusters on the sidewalk. However, my nostalgia was relatively short-lived as I realized that these days both my husband and I, like many others, have simply found community in a different way.

Sometimes community is about the space where we connect physically or even virtually via the Internet to share common interests, ideas, values, or beliefs. My husband connects with his fellow curlers, my sister connects with her flag football team, my brother-in-law through his scout troop. Others find their communities through support groups for addicts, clubs for gardeners, leagues for bowlers, or even as owners of Harley-Davidson motorcycles.

It may also be that we find community as identity. That's likely why I often refer to myself as coming from a long line of healthy Ukrainian peasant stock. Somehow I just identify myself with the image of those hardworking, sturdy, and strong women. For others it might be identifying as an Italian, Francophone, feminist, gay, or Catholic.

Today, however, it does seem we are more likely to define community by our experience. After all, while everyone lives in a place or a space, it ultimately is the *feeling* of community—the experience of being connected, accepted, and part of something larger than oneself—that is most important.

In my case I've found community through a network of colleagues who share a passion for community building and making positive change. Although we have diverse backgrounds and talents, our group is indicative of how we often gravitate to others who share a space, interests, or situations similar to our own.

Although in our case we often meet via phone and video chats, occasionally my community of colleagues gets together in noisy and productive face-to-face meetings. It becomes clear that despite the diversity and difference of our experiences, there is a growing sense of community. While we are connected primarily by our work, we also share values and a growing emotional attachment. So while we aren't living in the same community, we definitely are all part of one and have the experience of community. This experience is the result of participating in a nurturing, responsive environment that encourages us to be our authentic selves while contributing to the mutual good.

So, as I spent that evening watching my neighbours connect in our local park, it also struck me that it doesn't matter how we define community or what we call it. What really matters is that we have it and know how it feels.

Benefits of Community

A while back our team met in a stuffy, windowless room to explore the sometimes dry, but essential, world of evaluation and its application to our initiative. Others in the building were startled and somewhat surprised to hear boisterous enthusiastic voices and a lot of raucous laughter.

A colleague walked by the doorway and remarked that it sounded like we were having a party. One woman within our group—we're definitely not a group of shrinking violets—raised her voice and said to him, "You're just not used to it… *this* is the sound of productivity"!

She was so very right. We were, and continue to be, incredibly productive.

However, what is becoming even clearer is that we are productive because in addition to being connected to the larger whole of meaningful work, we are experiencing the unity and synergy that is the result of becoming a community.

Real community is more likely to be about what our team was experiencing—the acceptance, a sureness that our individual contributions were valued, a sense of belonging, and a knowing that we were connected to something greater than our individual selves.

For those who have been fortunate enough to work with a tightly knit group of coworkers or volunteers, or have been part of a successful service club, organization, sports team, or self-help group, there is likely already an understanding of what community is all about.

If you haven't experienced community, chances are you're searching for it even though you may not be aware of it.

These days community is too often rare and my guess is that people are hungry for it. There are many who live in relative isolation, often not even knowing the names of their neighbours. Some believe this is an indication that the very concept of community may be at-risk in North American society.

For our team, community is about being able to communicate honestly with each other. It's about working together on challenges that are so complex they require all of our respective experiences and competencies. It means pushing each other to learn and grow, and celebrating together when we get it right.

Sometimes the synergy is downright magical. M. Scott Peck[5] compares community to electricity and concluded there are questions about community that can't be answered just as there are questions about electricity that even the most knowledgeable scientists can't answer.

Regardless, what we need to know and understand is that community is important.

In a community there is an understanding and acceptance of the importance of each member and their capacity to contribute. Communities are also about collective effort—people working together, assuming shared responsibility, and utilizing their many talents. And, even though it often looks loud and messy from the outside, there is still an order even though it may not always be obvious.

Communities incorporate celebration, stories, parties, and social events into their activities. The line between work and play is fuzzy and laughter and singing is often heard.

Food is also an important part of connecting and celebrating so it is no accident that our team members often bring snacks or homemade baked goods.

While our typical managed and structured businesses and bureaucracies too often leave little room for fun and celebration they can, and should be, places to build communities where people can share, work, play, and grow together.

Increasing Importance of Community

Even though we may find an individual sense of community, many of us are sensing that the geographical communities in which we live are breaking down and, just as importantly, want to do something about it.

In fact, Robert Putnam[6] suggests a significant 75–80% of us believe there should be more emphasis on community even if it puts more demands on us. Putnam was also able to demonstrate that

---

5   Peck, M. S. 1987. *The different drum: Community making and peace.* New York: Simon and Schuster.

6   Putnam, R. (2000). *Bowling alone: The collapse and revival of American community.* New York: Simon and Schuster.

when a community has a strong level of social capital, it will also have increased educational performance, decreased crime, and improved physical and mental health. Those are sound reasons for investing in community building.

It has become more obvious that a sense of community is not just a nice-to-have but rather something essential that we all long for and need to have. And, it's not just about what community does for the public good. As it turns out, research confirms what we've always known on some level about the importance of community—people are nourished by other people.

Research has labeled this nourishing as "The Roseto Effect"[7] as the result of a study that examined the importance of social networks to health and longevity in a close-knit Italian-American community in Roseto, Pennsylvania.

Over thirty years ago, medical researchers were intrigued by statistics that showed Roseto seemed almost immune to the most common causes of death. Their rate of heart attacks was forty percent below that of neighbouring towns despite the fact they didn't have an especially healthy lifestyle, smoked as much, consumed as much fat in their diets, and were just as overweight and sedentary.

Additionally, both the crime rate and the applications for public assistance were zero.

The only distinguishing feature in Roseto was a much higher level of social cohesiveness and a greater sense of community.

All of the houses contained three generations of family who took care of one another. Turns out their kitchen tables, as well as other community rituals that included evening strolls and many social clubs and church events, nourished the spirit as well as the bodies of the local citizens.

The work ethic in Roseto, together with their working toward a common goal of ensuring a better life for their children, reduced the division between the haves and have-nots and the stress of material achievements into the 1960's. However, life changed in Roseto when, as the result of placing a priority on education, their children began to graduate from college at a higher than average rate. By the 70's,

---

7   Shaffer, C. & Anundsen, K. The healing powers of community. *Utne Reader* September-October, 1995.

materialism replaced their traditional community values and in 1971 the first heart attack death of a person less than forty five years of age occurred. As their sense of community eroded so too did their health, and over the years that followed their rate rose to the national average. Consequently, Roseto lost their unique statistical advantage.

In addition to changing community values, there is also a growing movement, inspired in part by Ed Everett,[8] suggesting that the changing roles of municipal government may have influenced our feelings about community.

Everett has suggested that while the role of local government with the public in our early history utilized more of a "townhall" approach with the public active as citizens, we moved to one he characterizes as "political bosses" during the 1800s to 1930s, to "city fathers" during the 1940s to 1960s, and to our current format which he characterizes as a "vending machine". He believes we are stuck in the vending machine form of government with the public viewing themselves as customers who put in their tax dollars and pull a lever to get the exact service they want.

He instead suggests the ideal approach is one where everyone, including the municipality, views the community as a partner and the people who live there as citizens rather than customers.

When people who live in a community see themselves as citizens, there is a greater commitment and accountability to the well-being of the entire community. Working in partnership with the municipality, there is the ability to create the future rather than wait for it, a choice to utilize our collective power rather than defer it to others, and a greater understanding that sustainable change in a community can only happen when citizens step up to the plate.

For sure, engaging citizens rather than customers is harder work for everyone involved. Ultimately though, it is work that will make a difference in whatever you define as your corner of the world. It is work that will build the capacity of the community while bringing passion, joy, challenge, and excitement. It will touch your heart, your soul, and your spirit.

---

8   Everett, E. Ibid.

 **Chapter 4**

Developing as an ACE Community

What Makes a Community Successful?

My work with ACE Communities has provided me with the opportunity to travel to a number of diverse communities across the province of Alberta and beyond. It struck me recently that even though the communities are diverse, they are struggling with many of the same complex and ambiguous issues. Not only are they being challenged to find ways to do more with less, they are trying to do it while maintaining high quality and achieving results faster. However, while the challenges may be the same, the responses from the communities are not.

While some communities stay stuck with their heads in the sand, others have risen to the challenges with some wonderfully resourceful and creative responses.

But why is it that some communities are successful in generating innovative solutions while others get stuck?

It could be, as Alice Major, former Poet Laureate for the City of Edmonton suggests, that communities are like fractals.[9] Fractals are described as irregular, infinitely complex structures that are different even though they may look the same. Clouds, snowflakes, lightning bolts, coastlines, and river networks are examples of fractals. Even though we might think of communities as fractals that look the same, they are in fact quite different and should be treated that

---

9   Major, A. (Oct 2006). *Communities as fractals.* Creative Cities Conference Plenary Session. Edmonton, AB.

way. Rather than being a river system where one community is connected to another, it may be that we need to be somewhat separate in order to build on our own uniqueness and authenticity. "More", Major mused, "Like a slow-moving swamp that nurtures and grows its inhabitants".[10]

Ultimately, communities that are the most successful are those that find and magnify their distinctiveness. Each community needs to know what makes their community special and unique and then to say it simply, and say it over and over again.

This distinctiveness is becoming more and more critical today in part because we are more mobile than ever before in history.

Communities will have to work harder to attract and retain talent. "Place", for those who are relatively new to the workforce, is paramount in their decisions about where they locate. Most typically, they will choose the place first, and then find a job. Retirees also have choices about where they will live. For leaders, this translates to a need to improve a community's livability by using and building on the assets that will attract new residents and young talent.

> " A community that lives only for greed and commerce and consumption does not enjoy itself and does not enjoy life. It has no great passions and dreams only small dreams. We need to rediscover how to make the communities where we live able to raise our passions and move our hearts."
>
> — T. Bender

What is it they're looking for? Likely what we're all looking for—communities that are clean, green, safe, with attractive, affordable housing, good schools, jobs, and a vibrancy reflected in energetic and distinctive neighbourhoods, recreation, and social opportunities.

We are also typically seeking what many smaller communities may already have. We want communities that understand the importance of community. Whereas in larger communities it is not considered unusual if you don't know your neighbours, in smaller communities, the odds are greater that you do. Knowing one another is essential for caring, connected communities. Residents in smaller communities also seem to do a better job of taking care of one another. Maybe it's the result of having fewer health and social service departments and agencies headquartered in their midst, or perhaps because there

---

10   Major, A. Ibid.

simply aren't a lot of services to rely on. Regardless, the end result is that they are more apt to turn to one another.

And, although they don't always think of it as volunteerism, the spirit of volunteerism is often stronger in small communities. Residents typically rally when one of their own needs help whether it's a fundraiser for a family who lost everything in a fire or coming together as a community to grieve when a young life is lost in a car accident. In addition to reacting, residents often take the initiative to organize themselves. In a big city it is more typical to assume someone else will step up to the plate.

Smaller communities also tend to be less entrenched within silos and less partial to turf protection. Perhaps because of the smaller population, there aren't as many silos or subsectors to connect, and, it is easier to find them. It seems easier to get to where you need to go. Even more importantly, you know who to go to, as well as where you'll find them.

Generally it is much easier for small communities to know their communities and their issues. As a result, community leaders are generally knowledgeable about their communities and better able to prioritize their energies and resources. It makes it easier to practice systems-thinking and to maximize resources by converging disciplines and sectors.

Smaller and rural communities often seem to have a better grasp on the importance of community development. They reflect an understanding that leadership is about helping people to help themselves—to teach people to fish rather than just giving them fish to eat. Citizens in smaller communities don't generally appear to be looking for a knight in shining armour or a magic solution. They seem to know intuitively that the wisdom is within their collective midst and not likely to come from an outsider.

And, perhaps because smaller communities have to change with the times to survive, many have worked to establish a vision for their future. They're pretty smart about where it is they want to go because in large part they've learned that if you just take the time to ask people, they will tell you what is good about their community, what needs some work, and most importantly, how it can be fixed.

Smaller communities also may have more of the sense of peace and quiet, fresh air, and green space we're seeking. Additionally there seems to be much more character, atmosphere, and charm. I love that the real estate is varied and cookie cutter neighbourhoods aren't as common as they are in many larger communities.

Living in a small town is like traveling back in a time machine to an era where life is less complicated, less stressed, and people know their neighbours. Despite the challenging times, people know and care about one another. With that comes a sense of belonging and a feeling of home.

Maybe its not that complicated after all? Perhaps successful communities are those that value and nurture the qualities we typically associate with small towns.

Finding a Community Personality

I recently had brief conversation with a woman who, with good reason, is very unhappy with her job. In addition to clearly being underpaid and too often treated unfairly by her employer, she isn't in a place that allows her to utilize her creativity or pursue her long-time dream of interior decorating.

Knowing my husband and I had recently moved across the country to pursue our careers, Susan said rather wistfully that we were very brave. She then went on to say that while she knew she had to make a move, she also knew she wasn't a risk taker and didn't really like change.

Rather than let her beat herself up anymore, I suggested that perhaps it wasn't about her not being brave but rather more about the fact that we just happened to be wired in a different way.

After all, in my case, both sets of grandparents left all they knew when they immigrated to Canada. My maternal grandparents first settled in Toronto where my grandfather eventually owned a successful wholesale fruit distribution company. My paternal grandparents were drawn to the west and the promise of free farm land.

I'm quite convinced I inherited their genes—especially the one that reflects their openness to new experience.

Best selling author, Richard Florida, suspected that happiness might be impacted by psychological as well as the economic and sociological factors he had been studying for years. In his book, *Who's Your City*,[11] he explores this connection between personality and where we live.

Florida summarizes the five dimensions to personality that psychologists have verified. These five traits, rooted in our biology, include openness to experience, conscientiousness, extroversion, agreeableness, and neuroticism.

No one just fits into any one category as it is clear that each of our personalities is made up of a unique combination of all five.

I suspect my husband's and my dimension of openness to experience is high. Open types are curious and have a tendency to enjoy change, creativity, the arts, and anything that exposes them to new facts, ideas, and experiences.

Susan is likely high in conscientiousness as it describes those who work hard, are responsible, detail-oriented, and strive for achievement.

The third type is extroversion or those who are talkative, outgoing, assertive, and enthusiastic. They enjoy meeting new people and tend to maintain a consistent, positive mood. I think my husband and I both also fit here.

Agreeableness is the fourth type and describes those who are warm, friendly, compassionate, and concerned about others. They typically trust others and expect others to trust them.

The fifth type is neuroticism or those who are emotionally unstable and likely to experience anxiety, hostility, depression, self-consciousness, and impulsiveness.

Using this proven research about personalities, Florida to his surprise, was able to determine that there are clusters of places with distinct personalities. In fact, cities may even be able to attract and energize certain types of personality.

Although his research was American-based he was able to draw some conclusions that may also be applicable to Canada. For instance, Florida was able to show that openness to experience was highest in the northeast and west coast states and was related to the proportion

---

11 Florida. R. (2008). *Who's your city?: How the creative economy is making where to live the most important decision of your life.* Toronto: Random House Canada.

19

of artists and entertainers working there, the percentage of votes cast for liberal candidates, support for same sex marriage, and patent production. In addition to these creative or experiential regions, he also found clusters of outgoing or extroverted regions (think Chicago or Atlanta), and conventional or dutiful regions (think Detroit).

What's beginning to emerge is that communities as well as individuals have personality. Not only that, personality may play a key role in regional innovation, talent, and economic growth.

Of the five personality factors, openness to experience is clearly the most important not only for our own growth, but also for the creative class that every community needs for the innovation, human capital, and economic growth necessary for our knowledge economy.

> ❝ ❝ In the landscape of the 21st century, nothing looms larger than culture. It is the new infrastructure, the civic bedrock on which the most successful modern metropolises are built. Culture is to the contemporary city what roads, sewers and bridges were in the 19th and early 20th centuries."
>
> — Christopher Hume, *The Toronto Star*

Consequently, just as Susan wants to strengthen her own openness to experience, so too should our communities. And, even if we know we don't like change and need security, we can still explore and enjoy on a more gradual basis that doesn't necessarily involve packing up and moving across the country.

As for our communities, perhaps instead of focusing all our energies on attracting jobs, we should think about the personality our community reflects. If it isn't an energetic, open-minded, vibrant place where people feel free to express themselves and cultivate their identity, we've got work to do.

Embracing the Concept of Being a Creative Community

The bottom line shaping my core belief in the importance of community leadership and quality of life is that we are living during a time of a fundamental shift. Just as our world was rocked over a century ago when we transitioned from being an *agricultural* based society to *manufacturing*, we are now moving through a *knowledge* or *information age*, and into what some futurists are referring to as the *organic* or *creative* molecular economy.

Whereas the engine of national, regional, and local growth used to be an economy driven by the availability of manufacturing jobs, today the driver is much more likely about what Florida has described as being a 'creative city'.[12]

A growing number of people today are mobile because their work is focused on knowledge rather than machines. This 'creative class'—artists, designers, writers, scientists, innovators, entrepreneurs, those in media and communications etc.—earn their money by means of creative thinking, designing, and producing. Because they can work from anywhere, these innovators are looking for places and conditions in creative cities that combine the three T's—tolerance, talent and technology. This has meant that economic prosperity is no longer as straightforward as attracting a factory and new jobs but instead more about attracting creative talent to a community that nurtures active, creative, and engaged living. It means a strong business climate as well as a vibrant people climate.

Ultimately it means we need authentic communities that include art galleries, music, an exciting nightlife, great restaurants, parks, greenspace, and trails. We also need to ensure support for entrepreneurs and a strong and healthy social-profit sector. In other words, these communities need attractive amenities and a quality of life that draws the creative class.

> ❝ Participants agreed that creative cities express their uniqueness and authenticity in three principal settings: the arts, commerce, and community. Further, it is the quality and intensity of the connections among the three that influence most strongly the city's creative capacities and achievements. More broadly, there was consensus that the creative city excels in bringing together "place, people, and investment."
>
> — Bradford, N. (2004). Creative Cities Structured Policy Dialogue (Research Report F46, *Family Network*). Ottawa, Ontario: Canadian Policy Research Networks

This creative class in turn brings with them the creativity that is essential for innovation and economic growth. It could be likened to planting flowers to attract bees even though it's really the production of honey that is the priority. You don't start by building beehives, you start by attracting the bees with the flowers.

---

12   Florida, R. (2002). *The rise of the creative class: And how it's transforming work, leisure, community and everyday life.* New York: Perseus Book Group.

As the late writer and activist Jane Jacobs[13] has pointed out, the built community also plays a key role, particularly in the need for diversity of buildings, people, and their economic activities. She also suggested creative people look for authentic places that aren't finished yet, places where you can add something of your own, "New ideas often require old buildings." Office towers, shopping malls, large-scale conference centres, and multifunctional stadiums are boring as they're already finished and therefore don't stimulate creativity.

Jacobs saw streets as the vital organs of the creative city as people meet in the streets and it is there that human contact occurs and unexpected encounters and business life takes place. She believed neighbourhoods should have several functions so that streets are filled with activity at all times of the day so entrepreneurs can benefit from the cross fertilization that happens when there is a variety of knowledge, skills, and attitudes readily available. The mix of old and new buildings is especially important for creativity because it gives innovation a chance to emerge.

Of course, even once a community embraces the idea of becoming more active, creative, and engaged, the challenge will be ensuring the right kind of leadership is in place, and that there is an understanding of how to nurture change and growth in a community.

Nurturing Creative Communities

Personally I think my hometown of Welland, Ontario is a pretty special place but when I travel and someone asks, "Where are you from?" I've learned that answering "Niagara" gets a much more enthusiastic and head-nodding response. Welland is, after all, only one of twelve municipalities within the Region of Niagara.

So, while I might be clear about my roots, there really isn't a collective identity for the region of Niagara and what makes it special, except of course the major tourist draw of Niagara Falls. Very few have even heard of the city of Welland, never mind assigned it an identity.

Recent efforts have focused on the idea of transforming Niagara through cultural initiatives given their potential to vitalize commu-

---

13   Jacobs, J. (1961). *The death and life of great American cities*. New York: Random House.

nities. Glen Murray, a former mayor of Winnipeg, Manitoba, now working as an urban management consultant, is an advocate of this approach.[14]

Murray spent his first years as a mayor of Winnipeg focusing on what most people said were the priorities—reducing debt, property taxes, crimes, and potholes, and dealing with the uniquely Winnipeg issue of menacing mosquitoes.

Despite his success with the typical municipal responsibilities, he still kept hearing that Winnipeg was a boring place to live. And, with young people still continuing to leave, he decided that if Winnipeg was going to generate wealth, it would have to invest in itself. He also saw that while emphasis needs to be placed on economic, social, and environmental development, an investment in cultural vitality was just as essential. "Pride, passion and place", he discovered, were ultimately as important as "Police, pavement, and pipes".[15]

Winnipeg needed to nurture creativity, innovation, and their local culture. Silos needed to be broken down and cultural organizations needed to sit at every planning table.

Murray built on what he had learned in his first years as a councilor while addressing a run down neighbourhood. In that case, they had spent money on landscaping the streets to create atmosphere—streets were widened, interesting street furniture was installed, and a public art program was initiated. The once run-down neighbourhood became an attractive place to visit, cafes and

❝ … there is an increasing awareness and understanding of the importance of the cultural dimension to a community's identity and prosperity. This report also suggests that festivals and celebrations are pivotal to community engagement, identity, and cohesiveness." Also, "built cultural form – museums, heritage districts, galleries, performing arts centres, visual arts spaces, libraries, and academic institutions" – were seen as pivotal to a community's identity and as place markers for interaction, connection, inspiration, and engagement."

— Bradford, N. (2004). Creative Cities Structured Policy Dialogue (Research Report F46, *Family Network*). Ottawa, Ontario: Canadian Policy Research Networks

---

14   Murray, G. (2006). Keynote address: *Transforming Niagara through cultural initiatives.* Niagara Falls: Venture Niagara.

15   Murray, G. Ibid.

restaurants opened, and it ultimately became a gathering place. The street is now blocks of cafes, small shops, and all kinds of interesting knowledge workers in design and creativity. And, the tax assessments and the city's revenue increased far beyond what they had originally invested.

With a clear focus on investing more in cultural initiatives, Winnipeg began with an inventory of their existing cultural assets. Among other assets, they found a budding film and graphics arts industry working, but also living illegally, in old commercial buildings in downtown Winnipeg. The city nurtured it, and other arts related industries, by granting tax holidays to landlords. They started planning for 24/7 use of the area. A library designed as a knowledge centre anchored the area and captured the sunlight. The districts became people-magnets and flourished.

Erin, Ontario is an example of another community that is successful because of its cultural initiatives. A small community of artists, it closes their Main Street and offers a variety of festivals. People go there because they can see authentic and real things they don't see anywhere else. It is an interesting place.

Prince Edward County, an area of Ontario has levered their assets of farms, roadside fruit stands, wineries, artists, and bed and breakfasts into a cultural experience that increased their tourism 74% between 1999 and 2004 from approximately 253,000 to 440,000 annually, while spending by these visitors increased 168% from approximately $24.4 million to $65.4 million annually. Their goal now is to raise that to 600,000 visitors and $100 million.[16]

It is clear that communities doing well are doing so because they are vibrant, exciting, and beautiful places to live. As such, they attract and retain the global, highly mobile, and well paid knowledge workers. Their creativity drives the design and innovation necessary for the services, experiences, and products a community produces.

The communities not doing well are those doing the opposite—becoming boring places with big-box stores, sprawl, and chain-store sameness and blandness. Having safe and well-maintained infrastruc-

16   Prince Edward County Tourism, (July 2006). *Tourism development strategy final report.* Retrieved http://www.pecounty.on.ca/pdf/PrinceEdwardCountyTourismDevelopmentStrategyFinalReportJuly302006.pdf.

ture is no longer enough. Communities must offer extraordinary cultural experiences, high-quality public spaces, and authentic, unique neighbourhoods and amenities.

Preserving and enhancing each community's uniqueness and historical character is what draws people together and make outsiders want to visit.

The downtown factor is especially important as an emerging trend in that many young people, particularly those holding jobs in creative areas, are moving back into the central areas of communities. Additional common traits of successful communities include vibrant recreation, arts, culture, and heritage sectors as well as social diversity. Parks and open spaces, including places to be physically active and outdoor gathering places, are also key.

One enterprising city—Paducah, Kentucky, is now thriving having reaped the rewards of recent artist-led economic development.[17] They did it by providing an extraordinary incentive program for artists that allowed them to own properties and set up living, studio, and gallery spaces in a formally blighted, downwardly spiraling neighbourhood.

Successful communities also have strong connections. Smart, creative people need to connect with other smart creative people. Particularly for industry, this proximity to clusters is fundamental for building creativity. And it is this intentional creativity that results in innovation.

Becoming an ACE Community

Becoming an ACE Community will never be simply about finding and emulating best practices. It is instead about focusing and building on what it is that makes one's community a special place and, making sure we have community leaders who can facilitate the journey of making that a reality. But, it's not just the responsibility of elected officials and corporate leaders. It's also our job. A job for citizens. It's up to each of us to be more vocal about the kind of communities we want to have, and then to get involved to make it happen.

---

17   Paducah Arts. *Artists relocation program*. Retrieved September, 2010 http://www.paducaharts.com/about_the_program.php.

The desire for a sense of belonging and community is deep and the time has never been riper for each of us to be part of that change. Together we can be catalysts for building a culture that is open and responsive to the power and possibility of bold and imaginative thinking.

There isn't a magic bullet or a cookie-cutter solution. Instead, active, creative, engaged communities happen when community leaders and citizens make it a priority.

It doesn't happen "top down" it happens "bottom up". It takes leaders who understand community development as well as the importance of engaging citizens to develop a vision and values for strong, healthy, and vibrant communities. Community leadership skills will also be required to bring diverse disciplines together to work collaboratively on the community's agreed upon outcomes.

It will also take funding and funders that are flexible enough to go where a community needs to go. And, while government policy is important, it needs to engage those who will be impacted by the policy and be viewed as a work-in-progress rather than something carved in stone.

Along the way, a priority will need to be placed on working together for collective impact and for making success travel.

It will be complicated and chaotic and the underlying multiple root causes within each community will require cross domain boundary work, astute political leadership and decision-making, compromise, negotiation, knowledge-building, and experimentation.

66 We carry within us the wonders we seek without us."

— Sir Thomas Browne

The reality is that we will need to be brave and stop trying to change reality by pretending it isn't complicated because it is. However if we don't change it, it will ultimately be very costly in the future.

Somehow I think a lot of communities might be just like Oz. Just as Dorothy always had the red shoes and the power, so too do the residents have it within them to create their own destiny. And, even when caught up in a storm, they will just need to do what Dorothy did—keep their heads, gather information, and watch the skies!

 **Chapter 5**

Leadership for ACE Communities

About Leadership

I was introduced to leadership at the age of sixteen. At the time, our local YMCA identified youth leadership as a priority. To involve teens, a number of sororities and fraternities were developed. I was one of eighteen Delta Chi members when I suddenly and unexpectedly, found myself elected president.

In addition to our own social and fundraising events, we made and delivered Christmas gifts at a nearby seniors' home and served as volunteers for a number of children's recreation programs. It was a busy year.

Working in my new leadership capacity, empowered by YMCA staff, I learned skills that included planning, time management, organizing, budgeting, marketing, fundraising, and problem solving. I learned to prepare agendas, chair productive meetings, resolve conflicts, communicate effectively, and motivate others. I became more disciplined and organized, more effective at working with groups, and better able to contribute to team building.

That valuable learning experience, combined with a wonderful sense of community among an amazing group of young women, impacted my life in an unanticipated and extraordinarily positive way.

Somewhat ironically, I'm now in a position to support and coach emerging leaders just as I was empowered by YMCA staff all those years ago.

Along the way, I've learned and grown in ways I could never have anticipated. While much of the learning has focused on communities and the kind of leadership they need, I've also learned that leadership means different things to different people.

> " " ... the need for new leaders is urgent. We need new leadership in communities everywhere. We need leaders who know how to nourish and rely on the innate creativity, freedom, generosity, and caring of people. We need leaders who are life-affirming rather than life destroying. Unless we quickly figure out how to nurture and support this new leadership, we can't hope for peaceful change. We will, instead, be confronted by increasing anarchy and societal meltdowns."
>
> — Margaret Wheatley

The variance in the interpretation of leadership may be the result of age, education, experience, or perhaps it may be about genetics or gender. Likely there isn't ever a right or wrong—there is just different—and that's okay.

For example, under my current contract I'm working for a wonderful CEO for whom leadership is very much about logic. It occurred to me after getting caught up in a tug of war conversation with him, that for me leadership isn't always about logic, research, facts, and figures. It is instead much more about emotion and heart.

Ultimately of course, leadership needs to be about both emotion and logic so one isn't necessarily better than the other. However, acknowledging and understanding the underlying differences in our approach make them much easier to accept and appreciate.

Anyway, that understanding also got me thinking about what else it is I value that might be different from those of other leaders. At its very core, what do I think leaders should do?

One of my favourite leadership quotes, and one that is especially relevant to community leadership is from Lao Tzu: "A leader is best when people barely know he exists, not so good when people obey and acclaim him, worse when they despise him. But of a good leader who talks little when his work is done, his aim fulfilled, they will say: "we did it ourselves."

To get to that kind of success, I think leadership will need to be about emotion and inspiration and is therefore about heart—our own heart as well as the hearts of others. It is about understanding and recognizing that each and every one of us has gifts and talents to contribute. A leader's job is to provide an environment that will empower everyone to envision a better way and to help them tap their passions, talents, skills, and creativity to move toward that vision.

Part of that challenge is finding an appropriate balance of flexibility to harness those talents. None of that will happen without a clear understanding of the overall vision and values. Once the vision and values are embraced, clear frameworks will be essential. Then of course a good leader will be the one who just gets out of the way.

When a person puts leadership into practice they are really engaging in an activity—not focusing on one person leading the way while the rest follow. This means leadership can, and needs to happen, at all levels of a community, organization, or business. When an issue or trend surfaces and an individual acts to address it, that's leadership.

Today's organizations and communities need to create the space and environment to encourage and foster leadership. When the space is created, individuals can take part in the conversations and be the catalysts for responding to challenging and complex issues. They can ask the tough questions, surface underlying root causes, and ultimately become change agents in their homes, organizations, and communities.

Being a leader is also about having a vision and moving toward it even when the resources aren't available. So perhaps being a leader may essentially be about courage. Courage to dream, courage to challenge existing paradigms, courage to work with others who's view of the world is different from our own, courage to be honest about what we may intuitively know to be true as well as honest about what we don't know, and courage to do what's best for the greater good—even when it's just plain hard.

About Community Leadership

There's nothing like challenging times to bring out new books and blogs about leadership.

Being something of a junkie when it comes to information about community leadership and change, I am passionate about following the newest theories, written works, and ideas as best I can.

29

> " Without collective intelligence and wise, effective action, the future of our organizations, our communities, and our planet remain imperiled."
>
> — Thomas J. Hurley and Juanita Brown

Unfortunately, it's become an increasingly frustrating exercise as most of them seem to be written by an academic or someone in a corporate setting sitting at, or near, the top of the hierarchy. Although there's nothing wrong with that distinct point of view, too often it does not resonate with the realities of what I'm seeing. Nor does it provide many meaningful solutions for the complex issues and challenges that communities across North America and beyond are facing.

Most books and blogs miss the point that meaningful leadership in communities is usually unrelated to hierarchies. In fact, much of the leadership I see is not coming from those at the top of the hierarchy but rather from those who intuitively understand you can lead without being in charge or having the official title.

Nowhere is this more evident than among the Internet generation who use technology to influence and shape their surroundings.

Take for example, Chris Hughes who, in addition to helping create the phenomena of Facebook, put the online campaign in place that is credited with getting Barack Obama elected as president. While those involved in Obama's campaign may not have paid much attention to baby-faced Hughes in the beginning, when he speaks these days, everyone listens. That by itself should be a key leadership learning for a CEO, academic, or elected official anywhere. "Grass-roots" leadership from someone like Hughes is just as critical as the "grass-tops" leadership provided by Obama.

Additionally, most leadership and management books seem to provide a lot of information about the specific traits and behaviours needed. And while there's no doubt that is important, perhaps what is more crucial, is a greater awareness of what each of us lacks as a potential leader.

This know-how of what we're missing can lead to building collaborative efforts and teams that will make a difference in achieving greater success.

It is a lesson reinforced for me on a regular basis. For instance, while I can and have focused on detailed work such as written and implemented policies and procedures, budgets, and action plans, it just isn't something I like or am good at doing. It takes me more time than it should and truly saps my energy.

Many experts either identify the traits or behaviours of a leader that should be emulated or suggest that if I am to be a leader I need to work at strengthening and enhancing my weaker skills. However, I am instead more and more of the opinion that I'm better off knowing my strengths and using them more. For instance, I now know I'm simply much more wired to be a big picture thinker. Focusing on details more than I already do, might not make a lot of sense.

A better use of time and energy for any leader would seem to be that of paying more attention to vision and values and to building a team that collectively reflects a lot of different leadership strengths to drive it forward.

Far more important than trying to be one leader who can do everything is accepting that it will never happen. It's better to know how to build a leadership team that is aware of the context within which they are operating, and to appreciate that each leader is partly in charge of the situation as a whole.

Leaders today need to understand how to gather and build a team that is honest and comfortable enough with one another to have authentic, brave conversations, to trust one another, and to provide opportunities for each member to tap into and utilize their respective strengths and passions.

This in turn will lead to the shared meaning, and aligned and coherent action that will be clearly viewed by all stakeholders as leadership.

It won't mean everyone will always agree with one another but there will be enough shared meaning and commitment to take action. In fact, the important part of a leadership team is that they do push each other's buttons. As painful as that will be, it is within these conflicts and stumbles that real leadership growth and learning will take place.

It doesn't happen "top down" it happens "bottom up". It takes leaders who understand community development as well as the importance of engaging citizens to develop a vision and values for strong, healthy, and vibrant communities. Community leadership skills will

31

> " "A social leader is born when one ponders such questions as, "What is the highest and best use of my talents and passions? What can I do that will have the most positive impact on society? How will the world be better because of my life and my contribution? What was I born to become and accomplish?"
>
> — Centre for Social Leadership

also be required to bring diverse disciplines together to work collaboratively on the community's agreed upon outcomes.

It will also take funding and funders that are flexible enough to go where a community needs to go. And, while policy is important, it needs to engage those who will be impacted by the policy and be viewed as a work-in-progress rather than something carved in stone. Along the way, a priority will need to be placed on making success travel.

In some cases, communities will simply need some fine tuning to be the best they can be. As American ethicist, Josephson has said, "You don't have to be sick to get better". However, fixing communities that may be more broken is technically and socially complex.

It will be complicated and chaotic and multiple root causes will require work across silos, astute political leadership and decision-making, compromise, negotiation, knowledge-building, and experimentation.

We will need to acknowledge that these complexities will require serious leadership efforts to find and implement the long term community-specific solutions that will ensure collective impact. But, if we don't work collectively to implement change, there will be a much steeper price to pay in the future.

 **Chapter 6**

What Does it Take to be a Community Leader?

The late American business guru Peter F. Drucker once said, "Every few hundred years in Western history there occurs a sharp transformation. Within a few short decades, society rearranges itself—its worldview; its basic values; its social and political structure; its arts; its key institutions. Fifty years later, there is a new world. And the people born then cannot even imagine the world in which their grandparents lived and into which their own parents were born. We are currently living through just such a transformation."[18]

Think of it as the equivalent of being a flapper and trying to relate to the Victorian era into which your parents were born. The changes would have had been mind-boggling.

Today we're living through that same kind of transformation albeit at an even faster pace.

Clearly a new world requires new leadership. But what exactly is it that we're looking for from our leaders?

One of the things I am hearing much more often these days when it comes to describing an unsuccessful leader, is the phrase, "They don't get it".

And, while it does seem that most people nod and agree when someone says it, at a recent lunch with my colleagues, we stopped to question it. After all, when one says, "they don't get it", what exactly is "it"? It's a phrase usually uttered when someone in charge is making bad decisions. So for us at least, "it" is about having the right

---

18   Mazarr, M. (1999). Global trends 2005: An owners manual for the next decade. New York: St Martins Press.

stuff, and doing the right thing. We also concluded that in a time of rapidly accelerating change, having the right stuff and doing the right thing is becoming even more important.

We do know we want to see less of a command-and-control leadership style and a new, more collaborative kind of leadership.

Maybe we are also looking for leaders who can provide direction when people don't know what to do. Rather than leaders who *require*, we're looking for leaders who *inspire*.

"As models of leadership shift from organizational hierarchies with leaders at the top to more distributed, shared networks, a lot changes... That's why I think that cultivation, 'becoming a real human being,' really is the primary leadership issue of our time, but on a scale never required before. It's a very old idea that may actually hold the key to a new age of 'global democracy.'"

— Betty Sue Flowers

That means it is not about the influence that results from formal positions of authority. Today it is more about influence that comes as the result of someone who conveys vision, passion, and commitment.

Part of that will be the result of paying attention and responding to the trends and issues impacting our communities. In other words, being able to sense possibilities while others are stuck in outdated thinking.

Maybe it is also about leaders who flatten the hierarchy by seeking and valuing feedback from all sources and being comfortable sharing control and empowering others.

A good friend of mine recently left a work environment where those in charge spoke publicly about the importance of engaging their staff and the broader community in the decision making process. However, the reality was that those in charge didn't trust their stakeholders and were not willing to give up control and power.

Those who do get "it" seem far more likely to put "everyone in charge" by engaging them in developing and ultimately owning a collective vision for the future. When there is a collective vision and direction for the future, the result will be more of the collaborative relationships and partnerships that are necessary for creative and effective solutions.

Probably though, when we talk about those who get "it", we are also talking about those who are authentic, honest, direct, and comfortable in their own skins. Additionally, those who get "it" are always known as being those who genuinely care about others and do what's best for the broader good even when it hurts.

While it may seem simplistic, perhaps that kind of leadership does not need to be all that complicated. It may just be a six-pack of competencies.

First of all, we want our leaders to be **agents of change** who can exert influence by building and nurturing trusting relationships. We are hungry for leaders who have the passion and motivation that is respected by others so that barriers can be addressed and overcome.

We also want leaders who are committed to **continuous improvement** both for themselves and others. That of course doesn't happen without strong values, a moral compass, and a code of conduct that reflects those values.

Next we want leaders who are optimistic, proactive, **big picture thinkers**. That big picture or system approach is essential because the issues in our country and our communities are too complicated to be solved by any one sector or silo. While they are examining that big picture we would also like them to pay attention to, and apply some creative responses to the social, economic, environmental, and technology trends and issues that have the potential to impact our communities.

We don't expect community leaders to do it by themselves either because we want them instead to be **catalysts for encouraging citizen responsibility** and for engaging and cultivating community ownership. That means that while we want to see leaders who understand the need to facilitate change, we also want them to believe in the power and possibilities of individual contributions.

As citizens, we understand the importance of supporting businesses but we also want leaders to be **advocates for quality of life** who understand that the most important investments we can ever make will be in our children, our families, our health, our environment, and our social infrastructure.

Lastly, we want leaders who know how to **plan effectively**. This typically will mean using a community development approach that engages others in a process that will result in visionary yet pragmatic plans that resonate because they are an innovative response to real community needs and priorities.

An interest in this particular book likely indicates a reader who already has many of the above competencies. If not, it may be that you are seeking a new kind of leadership. By exploring these competencies in upcoming chapters with additional indicators, stories, and explanations, the intent is to reinforce what you're already doing and/ or providing a path to becoming a stronger community leader.

Competencies for Community Leaders

Our work suggests that those able to steward the development of active, creative, and engaged communities will ideally be able to reliably demonstrate the ability to deliver the following core competencies:

1) **Agent of Change**
   Understands, demonstrates, and exerts influence by building trusting relationships.
2) **Commitment to Continuous Improvement**
   Practices ongoing personal and professional growth and development.
3) **Big Picture Thinking**
   Utilizes a proactive system thinking/holistic approach.
4) **Catalyst for Citizen Responsibility**
   Places a priority on engaging and cultivating community ownership and responsibility.
5) **Quality of Life Advocacy**
   Has the ability to work proactively to promote recreation, parks, sport, arts, culture and heritage as services that deliver essential benefits.
6) **Community Development Planning**
   Applies community development planning strategies.

Before delving into these more deeply, it is important to understand more about competencies.

Do any of these scenarios sound familiar?

Debra is part of a conference planning committee but is concerned because there doesn't seem to be any way to prioritize the many potential sessions that have been submitted for consideration.

Susan is keen to continue her self-directed learning and growth but isn't sure where she should be directing her efforts.

Tom's organization has been contracted to develop training materials for a specific list of topics but he doesn't have a clue as to where he should begin.

Fortunately, I've learned—often the hard way—that all of these situations can be effectively addressed when those involved have the benefit of working from a set of competencies or learning outcomes.

I first learned about competencies a number of years ago when I was seconded from my teaching position at Niagara College to the Ministry of Training, Colleges and Universities. My job was to facilitate the development of a program standard for all of the recreation-related programs within Ontario Community Colleges.

No small task, the idea was part of an inspired movement designed by the Government of Ontario to ensure students graduated with the entry-level skills needed to become successfully employed. The intent was to bring a greater degree of consistency to college programming and provide public accountability for the quality and relevance of college programs.

Within each program standard there are typically about ten to fifteen vocational learning outcomes or competencies. Each college is required to ensure their programs and program delivery are consistent with these as minimum standards, and must assist students to achieve them.

In addition to seeing competencies or outcomes at the post secondary level, many professional associations in Canada have developed their own standards. I've been involved with the development of competencies for entry-level recreation practitioners as well as the more advanced competencies required for community leadership previously referenced.

While it all sounds relatively straightforward, the process of getting consensus for competencies for an entire field or practice can be quite complicated and time consuming. This is in large part due to the fact that ideally, the process should involve a cross-section of practitioners, employers, and academics who may not always agree on what is essential.

Additionally, there is the matter of grasping the concept of a competency. It's not, as many think, simply a list of discrete skills. Instead, competencies describe a culminating demonstration of learning and achievement that typically reflects a combination of skills, knowledge, and attitudes.

To clarify each competency, they are typically accompanied by additional descriptions, elements, or indicators. These further define the level and quality of performance necessary to meet the requirements of an individual competency or learning outcome.

Identifying and agreeing to a foundational set of vocational competencies allows a field or practice to work with post secondary institutions to develop strategies for working together. They are also useful when it comes to promoting the profession, writing position descriptions, and developing evaluation strategies.

Additionally the competencies would serve as a framework to help Debra's committee develop a meaningful and relevant conference program, direct Susan to the most appropriate learning and skill development, and help Tom develop appropriate training materials.

From here on in we'll use the competencies, additional indicators, and stories related to each indicator to further an understanding of what it takes to be effective as a community leader. Each of the six competency discussions begins with a self-assessment chart.

 **Chapter 7**

Competency 1:
Agent of Change

*Understands, demonstrates,
and exerts influence by building
trusting relationships*

COMPETENCY AREA		INDICATORS TO HELP YOU UNDERSTAND WHAT ENCOMPASSES THIS COMPETENCY	1 = I AM NOT AT ALL LIKE THAT						10 = I AM 100% LIKE THAT			
1 Agent of Change	1.1	I believe I can make a difference to others, in my community, and the world.	1 2 3 4 5 6 7 8 9 10
	1.2	I demonstrate awareness that people communicate in a variety of ways.	1 2 3 4 5 6 7 8 9 10
	1.3	I can adapt my communication style to meet the needs of others.	1 2 3 4 5 6 7 8 9 10
	1.4	I demonstrate awareness that people learn in a variety of ways.	1 2 3 4 5 6 7 8 9 10
	1.5	I understand there are different kinds of individual intelligence.	1 2 3 4 5 6 7 8 9 10
	1.6	I can facilitate the removal of attitudinal barriers to change.	1 2 3 4 5 6 7 8 9 10
	1.7	I understand the process of change in individuals, organizations, and communities.	1 2 3 4 5 6 7 8 9 10
	1.8	I can apply strategies for building trust.	1 2 3 4 5 6 7 8 9 10
	1.9	I understand political governance at local, regional, provincial, and national levels.	1 2 3 4 5 6 7 8 9 10
	1.10	I nurture positive relationships with elected officials and community and corporate leaders.	1 2 3 4 5 6 7 8 9 10
	1.11	I apply effective media strategies.	1 2 3 4 5 6 7 8 9 10
	1.12	I utilize the power of storytelling.	1 2 3 4 5 6 7 8 9 10
	1.13	I apply appropriate social media strategies.	1 2 3 4 5 6 7 8 9 10
	1.14	I enable groups and organizations to collaborate and achieve synergy.	1 2 3 4 5 6 7 8 9 10
	1.15	I apply diverse facilitation models, skills, and techniques.	1 2 3 4 5 6 7 8 9 10
	1.16	I value both fact-based and intuitive knowing.	1 2 3 4 5 6 7 8 9 10
	1.17	I model a commitment to optimism and hope.	1 2 3 4 5 6 7 8 9 10

Believe You Can Make a Difference

It is disconcerting to walk into stores and see clothes that look so much like those I wore in my younger years. Fortunately most of them are pretty unattractive and are clothes I would never wear again even if I could. On the other hand, they bring back memories of an era and of a generation that staged protests and raised their voices in an endeavor to make the world a better place.

I like that I often see that same desire in today's youth.

While my generation may like to think they invented the concept of social action, I recently heard the remarkable story of a relatively unknown activist who predated the flower children by several decades.

Some fifty-plus years ago a forty-four year-old American woman, Mildred Lisette Norman Ryder, known by most as Peace Pilgrim, initiated her first cross-country walk for peace.

It was 1953, and time she felt, for a pilgrim to step forward. The war in Korea was raging and the McCarthy era had created fear and a sense among many that it was safest to be apathetic. Perhaps, Ryder thought, a pilgrim could make people think.

> " When we change ourselves, we change how people see us and they respond to us. When we change ourselves, we change the world."
>
> — R. Quinn, *Building the Bridge as You Walk on It*

Between 1953 and 1981 Peace walked over 25,000 miles crossing the United States seven times and making trips to Mexico and Canada.

She walked on her own, penniless, her only possessions—a toothbrush, comb, pen, and later, her pamphlets. She carried all of this in the pockets of a tunic she wore that had "Peace Pilgrim" painted on the front and "Walking Coast to Coast for Peace" on the back. She walked until someone offered her shelter or food. Most often she was given both but she sometimes slept in fields or missed meals.

Her message along the way was a simple one: overcome evil with good, hatred with love, and falsehood with truth. Her definition of peace included peace among nations, among people and individuals, and the most important peace, peace within oneself.

Setting out she carried three petitions—one was to end the war in Korea, the second to establish a U.S. Peace Department, and a third petition directed at the United Nations, urging world disarmament and the redirection of arms spending toward funding for human needs. She delivered all three upon her arrival on the east coast eleven months later.

Throughout a journey that spanned almost three decades, she never approached anyone, instead waiting for people to approach her.

When they did, she talked tirelessly. For those who asked, she gave out her "Steps Toward Inner Peace" pamphlet.

She had a magnetism that was instantly felt and became a spellbinding, forceful speaker with a consistent message that included powerful stories and inspiring one-liners that were easy for people to understand, apply, and remember.

She claimed people needed two things for life to be meaningful. Something to lift them up spiritually and inspire them to awaken to their higher nature such as religion, art, or nature, and a calling, a path of service or something to do that would help someone else because, in this world, she said, "You are given as you give."

Her message was a personal one, directed at the individual, and delivered in a simple, understandable way, one-on-one. Her brilliance was in a message and a manner of delivery that changed people, one person at a time, to empower and release their individual potential.

And that perhaps is the most important lesson—everyone can make a difference.

Peace Pilgrim wasn't all that different from anyone else. She grew up on a small farm in a loving family. She was at one point married, albeit not happily. Throughout her life she searched diligently for the service she felt she was called to undertake, working with senior citizens, those with emotional problems, and volunteering with peace organizations.

Prior to her pilgrimage, she simplified her life getting rid of unnecessary possessions and activities. She took up hiking to increase her physical strength and as a way to experience and appreciate the freedom of simplicity.

Through trial and error Peace worked out her own steps to inner peace, walking daily, appreciating nature, and putting into practice the inspirations that came to her. After she had attained inner peace she had a compulsion to share it. That became the impetus for what became a pilgrimage of almost thirty years.

She walked until July 7, 1981 when she was struck by an oncoming car that crossed the median. She died shortly thereafter as perhaps one of the most underrated and least known spiritual leaders and peace activists of our time.

What was her legacy?

Perhaps the greatest testament to her influence is that her story, teachings, and writings have endured and continue to be distributed long after her death mostly now via a web-site at http://www.peacepilgrim.com.

Her message continues to be shared.

This same understanding—that one person can make a difference—occurred for Ian Hill, a good friend of mine, and the ambassador for ACE Communities, several years ago. His changing point came one day as he drove by and saw kids splashing about in a puddle in the parking lot of a rundown motel. Despite cool weather, the kids were shoeless and dressed in ill-fitting, grungy clothes that had seen better days. For some unknown reason, Ian felt compelled to stop and talk.

> ❝ Here is the test to find whether your mission on earth is finished: If you're alive, it isn't."
>
> — Richard Bach

He learned that although the kids lived with their mother in one of the dismal motel rooms, they were alone because she was at work. They were without shoes because they had outgrown the ones they had and their mother couldn't afford to replace them.

Moved by their story, he handed them all the cash he had with him and told the kids to give it to their mother when she got home from work. He continued on to his well-paid, high profile job, thinking he had done a good deed and that was the end of it.

But, it was not to be. Haunted by the images of those kids, fueled by memories of his own challenging childhood, he started to get angry. How could it be, given the resources in his city, that kids could be shoeless? As the anger simmered so did his recognition that shoeless kids reflected on both himself and the community he loved. As such, it was up to him to do something about it.

Shortly thereafter, my amazing friend Ian began calling every school in his hometown and asked each principal to estimate the number of kids who needed shoes. Within two weeks he had raised $20,000 in shoes and gift certificates—enough to ensure every child in need had a new pair of shoes.

So while he didn't save the world, and of course couldn't single-handedly eliminate poverty given its inherent complexity, he did demonstrate what can happen when one person believes they can make a difference.

From this beginning, my friend Ian has gone on to do some powerful work as a change agent. He has been recognized for his commitment to positive change by the National Council for Community and Justice and the Martin Luther King Jr. Commission, which both named him Humanitarian of the Year. The Stand for Children Organization named him its Child Advocate of the Year, the World Leisure Congress named his Let Them Be Kids initiative one of the four most innovative social leisure programs in the world. Most recently he was the recipient of the first ever Harry Rosen Community Leadership Award.

However, his most significant work is what he does to inspire change. He makes you feel you can do better, makes you believe you can do it, and somehow motivates you to do it.

While Ian works as a change agent on a fairly large scale across North America, he also makes it less intimidating by suggesting that everyone has the potential to make a difference on a smaller scale by changing their own corner of the world.

Chances are each of us has been impacted by someone like Ian or the Peace Pilgrim who has made a difference in our lives. For me it happened at Christmas a number of years ago. A single mother at the time, I was working as a frontline staff member at the Boys and Girls Club. It had been a roller coaster of a year—good, bad, and downright ugly. While I had found a rewarding career running programs that integrated children with special needs, my marriage had dissolved midway through the year, and as Christmas approached, it was clear I was running on empty. With no vacation time left, I knew that despite being overwhelmed, I would just have to buckle down and do the best I could to deal with the hustle and bustle of the season. However, it seemed Bob Burger, the Executive Director at the Club had other plans.

Calling me into his office, he sat me down, thanked me for the good work I was doing and told me to go home. He told me to go home, come back ten days later, and not to worry because I'd be paid for the time off.

It was an incredible act of kindness that, in addition to reflecting empathy and compassion, made me feel recognized and valued at a time when my fragile self-esteem needed it most.

I've often thought since then that while simple kindness may too often be dismissed as something soft and fuzzy, the reality is that it might just be what the world needs most.

We should never underestimate the impact we can have with even the tiniest act of caring, a smile, a kind word, or an honest compliment. All have the power to change a life—your own included. They say you can't smile without cheering yourself up a little. Likewise, you can't commit an act of kindness without feeling as if your own troubles have been lightened, if only because you know you've helped the world become a slightly better place.

This same belief is what has continued to power a worldwide movement based on the phrase, "practice random acts of kindness and senseless acts of beauty" that was initiated over twenty years ago.

> 66 I want to put a ding in the universe."
>
> — Steve Jobs

What does it mean? It is actually pretty simple. Think about the things you think we need more of and then do them…randomly. It doesn't have to be anything major. Just do it, be kind.

The movement started when a Californian, Judy Foreman, spotted the phrase spray painted on a warehouse wall a hundred miles from her home.[19] It stayed on her mind for days until she finally gave up and drove all the way back to copy it down.

Her husband, Frank, liked the phrase so much that he put it up on the wall for his students, one of whom was the daughter of a local columnist. The columnist put it in the paper, admitting that although she liked it, she didn't really know where it came from or what it really meant.

Two days later she heard from peace activist Anne Herbert, the woman who had coined the phrase.[20] Herbert explained that the phrase had evolved from her belief that kindness can build on itself as much as violence can. She had turned the phrase around in her mind for days before eventually jotting the phrase down on a paper placemat while sitting in a restaurant. Her own fantasy random acts of kindness include: breaking into depressing-looking schools to paint the classrooms; leaving hot meals on kitchen tables in the poor

---

19   Canfield, J. & Hansen, J. *Chicken soup for the soul.* Deerfield Beach, FL: Health Communications.

20   http://en.wikipedia.org/wiki/Anne_Herbert_(writer).

> "How wonderful it is that nobody need wait a single moment before starting to improve the world."
>
> — Anne Frank

parts of town; slipping money into a proud old woman's purse.

Your own "random acts of kindness" don't necessarily have to be anything grandiose. Sometimes the best way to change the world is to start with your own small corner.

- Pay a compliment at least once a day.
- Give another driver your parking spot.
- Offer to return a shopping cart to the store for someone loading a car.
- Let the person behind you in the grocery store go ahead of you in line.
- When drivers try to merge into your lane, let them in with a wave and a smile.
- Open the door for another person.
- Bring your coworkers a special treat.
- Call or visit a homebound person.
- Say something nice to everyone you meet today.
- Shovel someone's sidewalk.
- Send home a note telling parents something their child did well.
- Tell your children why you love them.
- Write a note to your mother/father telling them why they are special.
- Tell your boss that you think he or she does a good job.
- Tell your employees how much you appreciate their work.
- Let your staff leave work an hour early.
- Laugh out loud often and share your smile generously.

Do any of the above and in addition to brightening someone else's day, you'll brighten your own.

Embracing and believing you can make a difference is an essential component of community leadership.

Demonstrate Awareness that People Communicate in a Variety of Ways

A number of years ago, as the result of working with others to find the secret sauce for strengthening community leadership, collaboration, and innovation, I ended up as the lead writer on the proposal for what became ACE Communities. You can just imagine the excitement when we learned that significant corporate and government funding was approved thereby clearing the way. Bubbling with excitement we fully expected the national organization with whom we had submitted the original proposal to be equally so.

Truth be told, it took them just a little while longer to wrap their heads around it.

Unfortunately, as the result of their recent staff and board changes, and the less than desired internal communications that are often the result of so much change, key players had been left out of the loop and knew nothing at all about the proposal. Quite understandably, the initial meeting between our respective organizations wasn't quite the celebratory event we had envisioned. However, several weeks later, things started to come together—largely in part because of some clear, forthright, and honest conversations among the principal players.

All of this reinforced the key role of communications and how, when it's lacking, things are at risk of falling apart even when all the planets seem to be aligned.

Ultimately, it is communication that brings people together and establishes a team environment of congeniality, support, and understanding.

Communication helps ideas move more efficiently and effectively from concept to application, and ensure sound decisions, ideas, and approaches. Without it, the relationships and trust that will determine success or failure won't be in place.

The other reminder for me was the importance of openness and transparency in our communications. Those at the table didn't play any games. The dialogue was authentic and real. Challenges were acknowledged and put on the table. And while some might question being as honest as we were, in the end it was this honesty that

47

strengthened the relationship. While such honesty sometimes takes courage, it is also liberating for those involved to put it out there.

Somehow it seems that when you speak the truth—and others know it's the truth—it is typical for people to respond appropriately.

My experience shows that this openness or transparency in sharing successes, failures, ideas, and thinking is an important factor in gathering support from others, as is a demonstrated willingness to listen. People are just more likely to engage when they feel they are being heard and if there is honesty about what's going on. And, just as we respond to authenticity, it's also clear people are pretty good at spotting and turning away from a phoney.

An open and inclusive communication style also results in a culture of acceptance and flexibility, one that promotes warmth, support, and a willingness to listen.

Although it may sound pretty straightforward, establishing open and healthy communication is not always an easy endeavor. When pushed by other priorities, communication too often gets put on the backburner.

Leaders need to make conscious efforts to continually ask themselves, "Who else needs to know about this" and then to make sure it is communicated. Regular updates via face-to-face and virtual meetings, conference calls, emails, newsletters, and other forms of social media need to be made a priority. Even informal social events can further communication. After all, if we don't work together to fill in the blanks, there is a human tendency to fill them in on our own. And, the inaccuracies of a do-it-yourself-fill-in-the-blanks approach often results in something we might do well to avoid.

In addition to placing an emphasis on communication, it is essential to understand that effective community leadership requires adapting our listening and verbal, written, and graphic or pictorial communications to meeting the needs of others.

Adapting Your Communication Style to Meet the Needs of Others

Each of us has a leadership style that influences how we prefer to communicate. Knowing our own as well as those of others can help us to adapt and strengthen the effectiveness of our communication.

While it is impossible to categorize the entire population, generally it seems our style is based on two elements of interpersonal communication. The first is whether we are *introverted* (private) or *extroverted* (public), and the second is whether or not we are more *task/goal-focused* or *people-focused*.

These elements translate into four leadership and communication styles: ***Organizers, Energizers, Researchers***, and ***Nurturers***.[21]

None of us is exclusively one style or the other. Instead, we each reflect characteristics of all four.

Organizers (extroverted and task oriented) are fast thinkers who want the outcomes first. While back up information will be important, they'll be looking for the executive summary and an understanding of how this will have a positive impact on the bottom line. Confident, competitive, decisive, and known for taking charge and getting things done, Organizers can be known to intimidate others in a group with their direct, action-oriented style of communication. They won't be afraid to take charge even if it's someone else's show, in order to ensure things get done.

Energizers (extroverted and people-oriented) will want to know how an idea or project will position you for the future. Confident, optimistic, and enthusiastic, Energizers care about innovation and being on the leading edge. As a result, communication needs to stress new thinking and new ways of doing things. While they like data, they use it to project or connect ideas. While their intensity and enthusiasm may be annoying to some, their qualities are valued particularly during times of change and upheaval.

Researchers (introverted and task-oriented) are seeking "the facts". Those who reflect the strengths of a Researcher won't be looking for a lot of small talk up front or getting too personal. When communicating with them, prepare by gathering research that shows the logic in your idea or proposal. They want to know, "How much will it cost? What will I gain? When will it be done?" Researchers are described as being serious and analytical people who thrive on details and dis-

---

21   http://www.acecommunities.ca/downloads/.

cipline. They often prefer to communicate in writing in order to be allowed time to think and reason. Provide detailed information and documentation whenever possible but understand the inherent possibilities of analysis paralysis. Know that the quiet Researcher will produce excellent results, but may sometimes appear aloof or distant to others.

Nurturers (extroverted and people-oriented) will want to know how others feel about the idea. As those who care deeply about relationships with others, these are the team players who can generate support for a new idea and smooth the sometimes rough waters of change. While their informal chatty style may at times appear unbusinesslike, they are the ones who will build consensus and get the group working together. When communicating with a nurturer, make time for friendly conversations and let them know you're concerned about how this might impact people. Also ask for their help to ensure others will see how this will make things better for everyone.

In addition to better understanding one's self, recognizing and adjusting to *Organizers*, *Energizers*, *Researchers*, and *Nurturers* will help community leaders maximize their communication efforts and ultimately their impact.

Male vs. Female Communication

Good communication also requires an understanding that men and women may communicate and lead differently.

Although I'd like to think I'm a good communicator, a recent and somewhat tense meeting made me realize I may have some work to do. However, the fact that I shouldered the responsibility for the tension in that meeting was also probably a typical female reaction.

Until recently, the team I had been working with was predominantly female, albeit quite diverse in terms of personalities and skills. Their passion for the work we were doing in community leadership, in combination with shared values and strong communication skills, had resulted in a rare team that was harmonious, productive, and innovative.

This particular meeting was focused on the daunting task of integrating two initiatives and figuring out how they all fit together within the organization. Of course all of this needed to be accomplished while keeping everything moving at its normal breakneck speed.

The first clue should have been our differing ideas about the agenda for the meeting. As it turned out the men approached this as being about the need for a business plan that would prioritize tasks and timelines for the first three months. On the other hand, the women saw the first priority as the need to build trusted relationships among those on the expanded team by discussing our respective backgrounds and values. Only then did they see the team collectively determining next steps.

This emphasis on tasks versus relationships is a key difference between men and women. Since women generally have a tendency to be more relationship oriented, they accomplish tasks by building relationships first. Once the relationships are in place, they are comfortable involving others and asking others to help get things done. Men often tend to be more task focused and jump right in, building their relationships as they work on the actual tasks.

In our case, I must say the men were quite patient as the women shared their experiences in order to build the common ground. However, I also sensed they were anxious to get down to what they saw as the real business. Perhaps next time it will be clearer that when women tell a story, they are building a team. As for the women, their compromise could perhaps be that of being more succinct.

Our focus on inclusion and building relationships also meant we spent a lot of time talking about problems and solving them collaboratively. Often the female emphasis was on feelings and communications whereas the guys, perhaps because their values were more heavily weighted to results, moved to solutions right away. Also, whereas much of our processing was out loud, theirs seemed to be internal. Because of this, the women in our group sometimes thought the men were being unresponsive to suggestions. On the flip side, the men probably thought the women don't know what they were doing or were looking for approval because they processed out loud. Some men may even think that a woman's way of processing is a sign of weakness.

There were also some differences in actual communication styles. Although the women were quick to acknowledge good ideas, regardless of the source, the men remained much more neutral, rarely acknowledging anyone's good ideas.

That same neutrality created some confusion for me. Even though I know I put good ideas on the table, I honestly wasn't sure if they were understood or received. I may have even repeated myself several times because I wasn't sure my ideas were being heard. Probably not a good idea, as men may be more likely to interpret that as me talking too much or being insecure.

So what did all of this tell me?

Like most things in life, there is no one best way to ensure effective communication among men and women. We can't stereotype all men or all women and of course not everyone fits these generalizations. However, both men and women need to be aware of each other's style of communication, both verbal and non-verbal, in order to avoid miscommunication and to work better together.

Being aware of our respective stereotypes and bias is perhaps the first step. We will also have to recognize that many different styles of both communication and leadership can be effective. By learning about and using both male and female styles, we will all be better equipped to deal with the complexity and diversity of situations in today's world.

Speaking in Public

Adapting communication styles to meet the needs of others also means community leaders will need to take responsibility for being able to speak confidently and persuasively in public situations. This may be especially challenging for some, as public speaking is our number one fear[22] even topping the fear of heights, being closed in small spaces, spiders and insects, and flying.

Like many others, my introduction to public speaking took place in a classroom setting.

It was one of the most stressful events of life. An absolute wreck, I hadn't slept all night, my stomach insisted on doing belly flops, my

---

22   Retrieved September 2010. http://faceyourfearstoday.com/Top_10_Fears.html.

palms were clammy, and every time I even thought about what it was I was about to do, my heart started pounding in my ears.

I was ten years old at the time and delivering my very first speech. Fortunately I survived and my grade five classmates learned a little about one of my heroines—Florence Nightingale.

Although I've done a lot of presentations since then, it really isn't something I truly enjoy even though I do know presenting in public settings is essential for community leadership. Even when teaching at Niagara College I preferred to describe myself as a "guide on the side" rather than a "sage on the stage"[23]. And, while I knew there were organizations like Toastmasters that could help, I never did join.

One can imagine my surprise then, when a number of years ago I found I was to be honoured with a Communications and Leadership Award from Toastmasters International at their annual conference. It was especially surprising because I had never been a member of their organization. Part of the award was the opportunity to speak to their audience. You'd think after all these years, a ten minute speech would be a piece of cake. However, I stressed about it for weeks because I knew I would have to deliver it to a roomful of about 250 Toastmasters from across the province.

On the plus side, I have learned enough over the years to understand the value of preparation. I did my homework and actually wrote out the full speech and revised it a number of times. After that I summarized the speech in bullet points and practiced it out loud. I even did a run-through of it with a colleague of mine, Dianne Bolton, who just happened to be an international award-winning toastmaster and the woman who nominated me for the award.

When I finally did get to the podium and forced my dry lips into something resembling a smile, I found myself looking out at a group of bright and attentive people who somehow managed to convey that they were with me. Right then and there, I knew it was going to be okay.

And that, I think, is the secret of Toastmasters. It isn't so much a club as it is a "community" of individuals who genuinely care about one another, want each other to succeed, and celebrate one another's success.

---

23   King, A. (1993). From sage on the stage to guide on the side. *College Teaching*. Vol 41, p.30-35.

Bottom line is that if you need to hone your communication and public speaking skills and are looking for a mutually supportive and positive learning environment, Toastmasters might be a good place to start.

Communicating Concisely

Another key aspect of communication is learning to do it effectively and succinctly.

Although I am an admitted information junkie I must confess that recently I've suffered from a bit of data overload. Although normally I can handle it and even enjoy it, I think data is like food—best when served in reasonably-sized portions from several food groups leaving one satisfied but not stuffed.

Today it seems the amount of information is enough to choke the heartiest of eaters, even when chewed properly. The constant spew of email, voice mail, social media, phone calls, meetings, newspapers, and magazines is overwhelming.

While there are experts giving us lots of information on how to manage information (ironic isn't it?), there are those who are simply rebelling by reducing and simplifying how they communicate. By way of example, *Fast Company,* a magazine primarily focused on business trends and forward thinking, published an article a number of years ago called "The Napkin Sketch".[24] It shows how large companies like Walmart and Microsoft are distilling complicated concepts by using simple pictures. These primitive graphics seem better able to counteract the information overload and complexity facing us all.

With a napkin sketch as an inspirational jumping off point, our team has worked to convey ACE Communities as a one page rendering. While we didn't use stick figures like Walmart and Microsoft, I must admit there's something non-threatening and even comforting about the Fisher-Price-like little people in our drawing.

Another movement, involving a presentation technique called Pecha Kucha,[25] is spreading to hundreds of cities around the world. Using Pecha Kucha (generally pronounced "pet-sha coot-sha") people

---

24   Bonamici Flaim, K., (Mar 20, 2008). The napkin sketch. *Fast Company Magazine.* Retrieved http://www.fastcompany.com/magazine/124/the-napkin-sketch.html.

25   Retrieved http://www.pecha-kucha.org.

are meeting monthly to present creations and ideas using a strategy that totally rejects the idea that more is better.

What is Pecha Kucha? Pecha Kucha, the Japanese word for chit-chat, was originally devised by two architects in Tokyo as a way for young designers to meet, network, and show their work in public. The idea behind Pecha Kucha is to keep presentations concise, the interest level up, and to have many presenters share their ideas within the course of one meeting. In other words, get to the main point quickly, concisely, and creatively, and then sit the heck down.

The Pecha Kucha format allows each presenter a slide show made up of twenty images of their choice—usually photographs, graphics, or video with limited text. The catch is that each of the images is set to automatically show for only twenty seconds resulting in a total on-stage time of six minutes forty seconds for each presenter. While most presentations include an over-arching narrative to pull the work together, the speaker has no control over the advancement of the images.

When done well, Pecha Kucha presentations are fast, furious, fun, and somehow combine the best of meetings, poetry slams, and performance art.

Experts recommend a number of steps for building a Pecha Kucha presentation. For that matter, they probably are steps that should be considered for any good presentation.

Begin by choosing a theme. Tell a story. Don't just describe what is on the screen; reveal your thought process, your mistakes, and your breakthrough learnings. By being authentic, the audience is much more likely to care and relate to your topic.

Crafting a presentation takes time. Dumping twenty images into Power Point won't cut it. It takes time to determine a theme, gather material, work out the script, and adjust rhythm and pace. Count on at least six hours of preparation spread over a few days.

Completing the slides doesn't mean you are ready to present them. Even twenty seconds will drag for both you and the audience if you don't know the material. Rehearse until you feel a rhythm and cadence starting to emerge.

Do a test run through with a friendly audience. Pay attention to your body language and the tone of your voice. Make sure you stand straight and relaxed, smile, and look interested. Try to put yourself in the audience and ask yourself whether or not you would enjoy the presentation. If not, keep working at it.

While there is no doubt that communicating the essentials in a concise and interesting manner is hard work, community leaders have a responsibility to do their part to reduce data overload.

People Learn in a Variety of Ways

On condition that I promise not to come back, my grade twelve math teacher gave me the gift of a passing mark. Truth be told, I don't think she was a very good math teacher. It certainly didn't help that my brain isn't, and never has been, wired for numbers.

While I've improved somewhat over the years, numbers and accounting remain the least favourite part of my job. While I now do manage to cope with budgets, financial statements, and expense claims, it always takes me much longer than I think it should, and, I usually end up with a headache. On the plus side, I think the pained expressions on my face during budget reviews do provide some entertainment value for the accountants. They, unlike me, think math is fun.

The reality is that everyone has an inborn thinking style. The concept of right brain or holistic and left brain or analytic thinking developed from research in the late 1960s of American psychobiologist Roger W. Sperry.[26]

One thing I'm quite sure of is that I'm definitely not an **analytic.** Analytics are those who tend to use their left brain hemisphere. Like the number crunchers in our accounting department, these people enjoy logic, order, facts, and details. Theirs is a black and white world where sequential steps are followed and the present and past is important. I'm also guessing that in addition to enjoying math, they're probably good at word games. For them it is primarily about *what* is said not *how* it is said.

Strong **holistics** or right brain processors like me tend to be more artistic, creative, big picture thinkers, and much more about feelings

---

26   Bogen, J. E., (September 1999). Roger Wolcott Sperry. *Proceedings of the American Philosophical Society* 143 (3): 491–500.

than facts. For us it won't be about *what* is said but *how* it is said. Unlike the analytics or left brain thinkers who tend to dive immediately into the details, holistics need to have the overall picture before the facts can make sense. We need to understand why something is important before we can assemble the data. However we're also more impetuous risk-takers who think more about the present and the future.

Not surprisingly, left brain thinkers learn quite differently from us right brainers. Analytics with a left brain style of processing, learn sequentially, building details into their understanding. They often prefer a quiet place to learn, bright light, formal seating, and continuing uninterrupted until their task is complete.

On the other hand, until they understand the concept, holistics or right brainers will find it difficult to focus on the details. My accounting experience is a good example. As the big picture of budgets and operations becomes clear, I do find it easier to focus on the details.

And, unlike those left brainers who are often easily distracted, we right-brainers can work quite comfortably in an environment that has music playing and people talking and walking around. We will also often be the ones who work on many things simultaneously, unlike the left-brainers who like to stay focused on one thing from start to finish.

Knowing what I know now about learning, it's not surprising that I wasn't always a great student. Most of my education took place in an environment that stressed analytical teaching methods. In fact, I think every one of my teachers was probably analytical. And, with me being so strongly holistic, I'm sure I often had them scratching their heads. Unfortunately I don't recall ever having a teacher who taught using a variety of methods.

I'm not saying it is easy to teach using a style that is diametrically opposed to one's own but, left brained community leaders are often in a position where they need to facilitate learning among holistics as well as analytics. Here's what the left brainers need to know about what works for holistics.

Provide an overview of the concept and explain the purpose of the learning. Vary the time of day for the heavy learning (mornings aren't always the best). Use more hands-on activities, and variety rather than routines and patterns. Role play, games, quizzes, panel discussions will all make learning easier and more appealing for us. Lessons related to experience are helpful as are using humorous or practical examples. Please don't recite facts, it works better if we're allowed to discover them. Positive feedback is good, even for small achievements. Last but not least, please recognize that focusing and sitting still is extraordinarily difficult for us. You'll need to get over that because it's definitely not personal.

Preferred Learning Styles

In addition to understanding analytics and holistics and what that means for learning, it is also important to know about preferred learning styles.

I have a good friend who I've always thought would make a fabulous teacher. When Alison finally made the leap into teaching courses at Niagara College, I volunteered to help in any way I could. While I was able to review her lesson plans, in hindsight I wish I had also thought to pass on my greatest learning about teaching. My learning was understanding that people don't necessarily learn the same way I do. Of course, they don't. In the context of learning, people have different ways of responding to and using information. As a teacher, or a community leader, you need to learn to adopt a variety of styles to accommodate all learners.

A fair bit of research has been done, so while there are a variety of instruments that can be used to determine an individual's learning style, there isn't universal agreement that any one of them is totally accurate.

However, even if there is agreement that you can't really divide the entire population into distinct learning categories, the tools do convey an understanding that people learn in different ways. Of course no one falls neatly into any one category, so it is also important to understand we can't pigeonhole people. Also, even if we prefer one style, it doesn't mean the other styles don't do us any good as we are all capable of learning in different ways.

The most popular model, likely because it is so simplistic, is VAK—an acronym for **visual, auditory,** and **kinesthetic.** The VAK concept, theories and methods (initially also referred to as VAKT, for Visual-

Auditory-Kinesthetic-Tactile) were first developed by psychologists and teaching specialists beginning in the 1920s.[27]

I'm mainly a visual learner but kinesthetic is also important for me. Kindergarten to grade three included a lot of kinesthetic learning so that worked out well for me as did grades four to eight which provided more opportunities for visual learning. High school and university were more about auditory learning so for me they were definitely more of a challenge.

As a *visual learner,* I learn best through two conduits—linguistic and spatial. As a visual-linguistic I learn through written language and remember what is written down. I need to write down directions and I pay better attention to lectures if I watch them. As a visual-spatial learner I also do better with charts, demonstrations, videos, and other visual materials. I find it easy to visualize faces and places by using my imagination and, unlike my husband, seldom get lost in new surroundings.

The best strategies for teaching visual learners include using graphs, diagrams, illustrations or other visual aids, using outlines, agendas, and handouts for reading and taking notes, flip charts, emphasizing key points, inviting questions, and role play.

Auditory learners, like my husband, are quite different. They often talk to themselves, may move their lips, and read out loud. He often does better talking to a colleague or hearing what was said.

In a learning environment, he likes it best when he is told what he is going to learn, is taught, and is then told what he has just learned. Unlike me, he likes lectures, dialogues, and being asked questions to test his learning and to make connections between what he has learned and how it applies.

Kinesthetic learners do best while touching and moving. It also has two conduits—kinesthetic or movement, and tactile or touch. They tend to lose concentration if there is little or no external stimulation or movement. When listening to lectures they may want to take notes. When reading, they like to scan the material first to get the big picture and then focus in on the details.

These are the learners most likely to use highlighters and take notes by drawing pictures, diagrams, or doodling. Teachers wanting

---

27   Gardner, H. (1983). *Frames of mind: The theory of multiple intelligences.* New York: Basic Books.

to accommodate kinesthetic learners should give them something specific to do or use activities that get them up and moving. Transferring information from one medium to another is also helpful such as recording notes onto a computer or a flipchart.

Once both my students and I had a better understanding of these learning styles, I was able to incorporate a variety of learning activities into my daily lesson plans rather than simply teach the way I preferred to learn—which is what I did when I first started. In hindsight, I'm sure I made all the auditory learners absolutely crazy.

Regardless, when all is said and done, understanding learning styles will make you a better leader.

There are Different Kinds of Individual Intelligence

There is, or at least there used to be, a television show called, "Are you smarter than a fifth grader?" Quite honestly, I've never watched it. The truth is that while I'd like to think I'm smarter than a fifth grader, I'm afraid to find out that I might not be.

When I was in grade five, I was a good student although it wasn't always easy. Virtually the entire curriculum was based on being able to demonstrate knowledge by memorizing and regurgitating information.

There weren't a lot of opportunities to do something with that knowledge that would require imagination and critical thinking skills—areas where I was more comfortable.

Additionally, while I am normally undaunted by creative or literary challenges, I remember the panic I felt when called upon in math class. The mere sight of a row of numbers still sends me into a panic. I've had to accept the fact that when it comes to mathematical or technological intelligence, I am severely deprived. According to the theories advanced by Dr. Howard Gardner of Harvard University,[28] these differences shouldn't be surprising as people are often smart in different ways.

Rather than a single, generalized intelligence that can be described by an IQ score, Gardner believes we have multiple intelligences (MISs). He believes there are seven different types of intelligence;

---

28   Gardner, H. (1993). *Frames of mind: The theory of multiple intelligences.* New York: Basic Books.

musical, interpersonal, logico-mathematical, linguistic, spatial, intraper-sonal, and *bodily-kinesthetic.*

Not surprisingly, these intelligences go beyond the two forms of intelligence generally measured in our school systems—the two dealing with words and numbers.

Sadly, because most school systems focus on the intelligence dealing with words and numbers, the different areas of intelligence of a child may not be recognized or rewarded. A child's musical ability, mechanical skills, or talent for leadership may go unnoticed.

A child with *musical intelligence* will be sensitive to the essential elements of music—pitch or melody, rhythm, and timbre or quality of tone. One of the earliest talents to emerge, a child with musical talent will be able to sing on key, keep a beat, compose his or her own songs, and remember music just heard.

Interpersonal intelligence is the ability to distinguish differences among people, to pick up on their vibes and perceive their different moods, temperaments,, and motivations.

Logico-mathematical intelligence—the one I definitely do not have—is the intelligence necessary to work in the world of logic, computers, or mathematics. This would include the ability to think conceptually, to investigate relationships in the physical world by experimenting, and to explore more abstract relationships.

Not surprisingly, *linguistic intelligence* is the talent for using language to express verbal and written meaning. Reading and writing, and therefore school in general, will be much more appealing for the student with this type of intelligence.

Spatial intelligence deals with good visual memory—the ability to recognize shapes and to mentally modify a visual image. This kind of intelligence is important for architects, inventors, painters, and sculptors.

Intrapersonal intelligence is the ability to recognize and sort out one's own feelings. Young children with this type of intelligence will be able to talk insightfully about their own experience and feelings and can later translate this intelligence into roles as poets or artists. Although they may prefer to work alone, some choose to use their understanding of themselves to work with others as a therapist or counselor.

Bodily-kinesthetic intelligence relates to the capacity for using one's body. It isn't your imagination; some people simply are more coordinated and have better motor skills. Potential athletes, actors, and dancers will need this kind of ability.

Gardner has also suggested there could be additional intelligences worthy of inclusion within the model such as *Naturalist intelligence* (perception of and relationship with the natural environment); *Spiritual or Existential intelligence* (as would concern one's relationship with the universe or God, depending on one's personal philosophy); and *Moral intelligence* (one's relationship with other living things and their well-being).[29]

The upshot is that everyone has their own unique combination of smarts. While I will never be a whiz at math, it's reassuring to know there are other stronger types of intelligence within me. While they may not be forms of intelligence that would have helped me out as a fifth grader, they've certainly been useful in real life.

Emotional Intelligence

There's yet another form of intelligence that is essential to understand and utilize as a community leader.

Several years ago I participated in an exceptional conference that provided some wonderful learning opportunities. An hour and a half into one of the full day sessions, a participant entered somewhat noisily, stated that she was late, even though it was rather obvious, and proceeded to announce that she didn't really even have a reason.

When we broke for lunch, this same woman went up to the presenter and asked her for the five-minute version of what she missed as the result of having been late. The presenter, a talented and seasoned former university professor and now consultant, took the time from her own well-deserved break, and provided the requested overview.

As their conversation concluded, the participant also volunteered that she herself was taking a course on facilitating, had made notes on the presenter's style, and would be happy to provide her with feedback.

---

29   http://www.businessballs.com/howardgardnermultipleintelligences.htm (*Living things and their well-being*).

While the consultant took it all graciously, it was apparent that both she and everyone else who overheard the exchange, were appalled by the woman's behaviour. And yet, even though her behaviour was clearly inappropriate, this was not an unintelligent woman. She was spirited, passionate, and energetic about her work. Regardless, it was clear she was lacking in emotional intelligence.

According to Daniel Goleman,[30] "Emotional Intelligence is the capacity for recognizing our own feelings and those of others around us, for motivating ourselves, and for managing emotions well in ourselves and others." As such, emotional intelligence just might be the largest single predictor of success as a community leader.

Emotional intelligence or EQ is not the opposite of intellectual intelligence or IQ, although some people are blessed with a lot of both, some may not have a lot of either. What researchers are trying to understand is how they complement each other. It now appears that one's intelligence or IQ only accounts for up to twenty five percent of the variance in professional success and job performance[31] whereas social and emotional abilities are four times more important than IQ in determining success.[32]

So exactly what is EQ? The term encompasses five characteristics and abilities. The first is knowing your feelings and using them to make effective life decisions. It is also about being able to manage your emotional life without being immobilized by depression or worry, or swept away by anger. Persisting in the face of setbacks and channeling one's impulses in order to pursue one's goals is important, as is handling feelings in relationships with skill and harmony.

But perhaps the most important are the visible emotional or people skills of empathy. It is these skills that allow one to recognize feelings in others by tuning in to both their verbal and non-verbal clues without them having to tell you what it is they are feeling.

My guess is that the woman from my session isn't having a lot of success in the workplace, or in her personal life if her typical interactions are as inappropriate as what she demonstrated. If she lacks

30   Goleman, D. (1996). *Emotional intelligence: Why it can matter more than IQ.* New York: Bantam Books.

31   Hunter, J. E., & Hunter, R. F. (1984). Validity and utility of alternative predictors of job performance. *Psychological Bulletin, 76*(1), 72-93.

32   Sternberg, R. (1996). *Successful intelligence.* New York: Simon & Schuster.

empathy, graciousness, and the ability to read a social situation, she will no doubt be ruffling a lot of feathers. I do hope that somewhere along the line, someone will invest the time in helping her to develop and grow her emotional intelligence.

So too will community leaders be far more successful if they understand and grow their EQs.

Identify and Facilitate the Removal of Attitudinal Barriers to Change

In the end all leadership comes down to being able to facilitate changed behavior. That change begins with addressing attitudinal barriers. As such, it is perhaps one of the greatest challenges facing community leaders.

My first real thinking about change happened a long time ago but it is a memory that never fails to make me smile. I was seventeen years old and in my second year of serious competition in track. With some of my key contenders competing elsewhere, I managed to win gold at the Eastern Canadian meet in the 400 metres and to everyone's surprise, including my own, qualified for the national championships in Winnipeg.

I knew I was in over my head even though my coach was positive and never really said so. The pre-printed program listed qualifying times for the other competitors whereas mine was blank. One look at the times of the competitors and I knew the coach had omitted my time to save me from being embarrassed.

Nervous but not ready to give up and motivated by the very real possibility of finishing last, I blasted out of the starting blocks in the semi-final, led the pack for the first 300 metres, then tensed up, died in the final stretch, and barely hung on to qualify for the final.

Downplaying expectations but pleased that I had qualified for the final, my coach stressed the importance of the race as "experience" telling me to go out and do the best I could. I figured that was a nice way of telling me there wasn't much hope of me winning the race! Disappointed with my near choke finish in the semi-finals, but not really giving up hope, I figured it was time for a change.

Knowing I couldn't handle the pressure of leading the pack, I opted instead for another strategy.

This time when the starting pistol blasted, instead of going all out, I began a strong, steady, and very relaxed run, settling in at the rear of the pack. I cruised, cool and calm down the backstretch before starting to dig in. I drove into the final turn and motored into the homestretch picking up speed as I went.

To this day, I have never forgotten the wonderful disbelief I felt, as having passed all other runners, I suddenly realized I was in the lead. A goofy grin on my face, I flew down the last stretch to win an upset gold medal at the Canada Games in by far the best time I had ever run.

Although I know that in the big picture of life, it was, after all, simply a race, it taught me two extraordinarily important life lessons.

First of all, I learned I could do what I set my mind to doing. Having beat the odds and proven the experts wrong in obtaining a dream, I knew it could be done again. I learned that if I knew what I wanted, stayed focused, and worked hard, dreams do come true. What an incredibly important lesson for a seventeen year-old to learn.

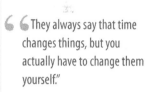
❝❝They always say that time changes things, but you actually have to change them yourself."

— Andy Warhol

The second and just as powerful lesson—always change a losing game.

The logic of sport can be applied to everyday situations. If you aren't winning anyway, what have you got to lose by changing? That goes for our communities as well. If our community isn't doing well, why not try doing something different?

Easy to say but the reality is that change is much harder for some than others.

Community leaders need to understand there really is only a tiny percentage of the population who like and embrace change. Also, despite conventional thinking that says the older you are the more resistant to change you are, resistance actually has nothing to do with age.

In a recent study done by the Center for Creative Leadership, a survey of 3,200 workers of all ages showed that a mere twelve people

> 66 It's never too late to be what you might have been."
>
> — George Eliot

said they liked change at work.[33] The study concluded that resistance to change isn't about age. Instead it is about how much you stand to gain or lose.

People typically dislike or resist change because they believe it will increase their workload, decrease their authority or power, or make getting their job done more difficult.

Fundamentally it seems people want the same things regardless of their age. According to the study, regardless of whether you are a Veteran, Boomer, Gen Xer, or a member of Generation Y, you likely share a number of values—no one really likes change, everyone wants leaders who are credible and trustworthy, organizational politics are a problem for everyone, almost everyone wants a coach, and loyalty depends on the context, not on the generation.

So it follows that if we acknowledge we live in a world that is constantly changing—and that change is also essential for innovative and successful government, businesses, organizations and communities—how on earth do we support a greater receptiveness to change?

Ultimately, a lot of it will come down to understanding how we can support individual behavioural change.

Understanding the Process of Change in Individuals, Organizations, and Communities

Supporting Individual Change

A long time ago I worked for a guy who was something of a leadership junkie. Every time he got back from a conference or read a new book, we would brace ourselves for what we referred to as his new flavour-of-the-week management theory.

Inspired by his enthusiasm, we would initially adopt a gung-ho approach to implementing some new thinking or approach. Without fail, it would die a slow death and we would then hold our collective breath waiting for the next new great idea to be sent our way.

---

33   Centre for Creative Leadership (October, 2008). *Emerging leaders research survey summary report*. Retrieved http://www.ccl.org/leadership/enewsletter/2008/OCTissue.aspx.

Unfortunately, when my old boss attempted change he was trying to improve strategies, structure, culture or the system without fully understanding how to support individual behavioural change.

I think my former boss especially would appreciate the book entitled *Change or Die* by Alan Deutschman.[34]

Change or Die began as a magazine article Deutschman wrote that was prompted by statistics from the American health care industry.

He learned that despite conventional wisdom that says people change when there is a crisis—they don't. He cites the example of cardiac patients for whom it is indeed a case of 'change or die'. In their case it meant changing diet, decreasing stress, and increasing exercise after critical and expensive by-pass surgery. Even knowing they were facing the ultimate crisis and could die if they didn't, an astonishing nine out of ten were simply not able to change. And yet, it is estimated that 70–80% of all chronic diseases are preventable by dietary and lifestyle.[35]

Learning that, Deutschman instead began to focus on what he could learn from the cardiac patients as well as others in different situations who *had* been able to change.

What he learned, and went on to write more about in his book, is that the secret of those who were able to change their behaviour amounted to three keys. The first key was them being able to form a new relationship with a person or community that helped them change. Secondly, this new relationship then helped them to practice new skills and habits, thus learning to think as if they had already changed. And, doing that, allowed them to reframe their experiences—key three.

The first key speaks to the importance of an emotional relationship with a person or community that inspires and restores your hope. It is not willpower that gets one unstuck, it is a relationship that makes you believe you can, and are expected, to change. In essence, the individual or community imparts a belief that you have the ability to change. Additionally, those involved in this relationship sell you on themselves as your partners, mentors, role models, or source of new

---

34   Deutschman, A. (2008). *Change or die.* New York: Harper Collins.

35   Kiberstis, P. & Roberts, L. (2002). *It's not just the genes. Science* 296 (5568): 685.

knowledge and the specific methods or strategies that they, and now you, need to employ.

If that doesn't make sense, then just think about any time you've changed significantly in the past. Chances are there has been a good teacher, coach, or mentor jumpstarting your change by providing guidance, encouragement, and direction to show you the way.

The second key is that this new relationship, which is much more about heart and emotion than facts, helps you learn, practice, and master the new skills, knowledge, and attitudes that you need. In essence this speaks to the importance of training to ensure the new behaviours become automatic.

The third key is about reframing. Your new relationship helps you learn ways to think about your situation, your life, your organization, or your community. In the end you view the situation in a whole new way that would have been foreign to you before you changed.

So, the three keys to change are three new R's that are well worth learning—*relate, repeat, reframe*. All in all what this could mean is new hope, new skills, and a new way of thinking not only for individuals but for entire communities.

Supporting Community Change

Barriers to change in communities can be broken down by community leaders when they use these same three R's—*relate, repeat, reframe*—at a broader level. *Relate* will be about facilitating the development of trusted relationships among community leaders. Typically this will be a cohort of local leaders from a variety of sectors including business, social profits, and governments who see the advantage of working together for collective impact. *Repeat* will mean a focus on working alongside these leaders and community stakeholders to help everyone learn, practice, and master the new skills, knowledge, and attitudes required for change. Thirdly, *reframe* and learn ways to work together to make the community a better place to live, work, and play by inviting discussion, feedback, and ownership of the reasons for change as well as new solutions.

Community change will also require an *investment of resources, strong communication, making it safe to change, managing expectations, transferring knowledge, speaking to people's emotions, focusing on com-*

prehensive change, framing change for success, and *adding an element of fun.*

Change requires an investment and community leaders will need to work hard to ensure that adequate *resources* of time and money are allocated for training, resources, and ongoing support and development.

When everything is done by the book, people may still end up being confused by change, especially if they don't fully understand the technology or process being introduced. They may be afraid to ask questions and may act with only a partial understanding. As a result, ongoing *communication* will be essential.

We also need to make it *safe to change.* Generally, we need to assure stakeholders that according to the The Pareto principle[36] (also known as the 80-20 rule), roughly eighty percent of the effects come from twenty percent of the causes. Typically that means the change that needs to happen in our lives, organizations, businesses, and communities is less than twenty percent. Knowing that eighty percent of what we're doing is probably okay, and that only we're talking about addressing twenty percent makes the idea of change much less intimidating.

Managing expectations will be critical. As my friend Ian Hill puts it, we need to think like the pilot on the plane who tells us to put our seatbelts on because we're about to enter some turbulence. In other words, we need to be clear up front that we're in for a bumpy ride when change is anticipated. If we are told to expect it to be rough, it never seems quite as bad as we anticipated.

Leaders can also facilitate the process of change by *transferring the knowledge* that will help others believe, unlearn, and relearn new things. This can be done by working at gathering and sharing new resources, promising practices, and inspirational stories.

We also know that behaviour is more likely to change if we *speak to people's feelings.*[37] Consequently, we can support change more effectively if we find ways to help others see challenges or solutions in ways that will influence their emotions as well as their thoughts.

---

36 Bunkley, N. (March 3, 2008), Joseph Juran, 103, Pioneer in Quality Control, Dies, *New York Times.*

37 Kotter, J. (2002). *The heart of change.* Boston: Harvard Business Press.

For example, in the case of cardiac patients, providing information about healthier lifestyles is important but motivating by fear of death doesn't work. By the same token, a new and inspiring vision for a community will be a far more powerful motivator than the fear of a lack of economic growth. Facts alone can't change the concepts or frames that we hold. On the other hand, getting people to exchange one frame for another is tough. What works most effectively are "stories that are simple, easy to identify with, emotionally resonant, and evocative of positive experiences".[38]

However, even if we manage to reframe our thinking, it isn't enough. It will be important to understand yet another recent finding. "Radical, sweeping, *comprehensive changes* are often easier for some people than small incremental ones."[39] For example, my brother-in-law recently convinced my mother-in-law to fly to Florida for a holiday. While the preparation and the unknown factors of being away in a strange place created a great deal of angst, her thinking was reframed to the point that she now understands that while change may be hard, it can also bring great joy. It was a short-term win that has nourished her faith that the effort to change is worthwhile.

Most importantly, we all need to embrace the idea that if we don't like what's going on in our life or in our communities, or perhaps not going on, it is up to us to change it.

Once the need for change has been embraced, it is important to *frame it for success.* This is a challenge for all community leaders especially as it seems inevitable that the need for change always seems to occur at the busiest, most stressful times when emotions are running close to the surface. Community leaders must stay focused and convey a positive message. It may also mean continuing to restate something that you see as implicit or quite obvious because for many it won't even appear as a blip on their radar. I have learned to be explicit even when I don't think there is a need to be. For instance, I used to think that some on our team were simply refusing to see the need for change and the vision and advantages of being entrepreneurial and innovative. It wasn't. It was more about me not being clear enough about why we needed to change and how that change was linked

---

38   Kotter, J. (2002) Ibid.

39   Deutschman, A. (2007). Ibid.

to the ultimate sustainability of the work we are doing in nurturing strong community leaders.

While these new strategies can be applied to supporting change with individuals, organizations, and entire communities, *adding an element of fun* can be a magical ingredient.

I recently learned about a website called *The Fun Theory*.[40] An initiative of Volkswagen, the site is dedicated to the idea that something as simple as fun just might be the easiest way to change people's behaviour for the better. It might be about a change for you, for the environment, or for something entirely different. The point is that it's change for the better.

The top video on the site, Piano Stairs, has been viewed by over fifteen million viewers on YouTube.

Piano Stairs is an experiment that asked, "Does turning a set of subway stairs into a real-life piano encourage people to use them? The answer is yes, 66% more. Another experiment asks whether making a trash can sound like a forty foot-deep well will make people pick up their garbage. Another turned a bottle recycling centre into an arcade game.

Of course, this raised profile showing the connection between fun and changing isn't new to anyone in the field of recreation. From my first days working at the Niagara Falls Boys and Girls Club I knew that creating fun-based opportunities grounded in some kind of learning was a fundamental part of my job.

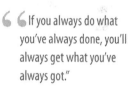

" If you always do what you've always done, you'll always get what you've always got."

— Henry Ford

While to others it may have seemed we were simply playing games or hanging out with the kids, we were in fact helping children learn about learning and consolidate previous learning through curiosity, invention, and persistence. We also helped children use play to learn to work with others and grow their problem solving ability to ultimately help them achieve. We organized group activities that provided children with enjoyment, accomplishment, and a sense of belonging. We nurtured the development of interpersonal skills, such as empathy, trust, and the ability to express ideas, and we used pretend play and arts activities to further

---

40   Retrieved September, 2010 http://thefuntheory.com.

develop the divergent skills and thinking necessary for creativity and innovation.

This same emphasis on fun can be a key to community change efforts.

While supporting the process of change after years of habits, routines, and thought patterns will be a challenge, community leaders need to stay postive and know that it ultimately is attainable.

Community Change Strategies

Just as individuals respond differently to change so too do communities.

According to the late economist, Mancur Olson, cities can reflect different responses to change. As he puts it, when places grow up and prosper in one era, they find it challenging and sometimes even impossible to adopt new organizational and cultural patterns, even though the benefits are well known and accepted.[41]

When a city isn't receptive to change, innovation and growth shifts to the places that *are* able to adapt to and build on the shifts. Olson contends this phenomenon is how England got trapped and also explains why the United States became a great world economic power. It is also an underlying reason for the abundant economic activity that is taking places in such tolerant, diverse, and creative cities as San Francisco, Austin, San Diego, Boston, and Seattle. On the other hand, cities like Buffalo, New Orleans, and Louisville are stalled because they have remained stuck in old paradigms of economic development trying to become the next Silicon Valley and working to attract large industries.

To support positive change in a community there other strategies to keep in mind.

1) If you want change—begin with the early adopters then go wide.

Every community (or organization or business) has these early adopters although it may be that they're not always in the most senior leadership position. They are instead those often described as being "on the leading edge", "colouring outside the lines" or in some cases

41   Olson, M. (1982). *The rise and decline of nations: Economic growth, stagflation, and social rigidities*. New Haven: Yale University Press.

a pain in the you-know-what because they're likely to be challenging the status quo.

Typically though, these early adopters are also system or big picture thinkers. Even though these macro thinkers aren't as common as the micro thinkers, more of them will need to be involved until the vision forward has begun to take shape. The challenge will be knowing when to go wider to include the micro thinkers. As, Ian Hill, once said, the best time to go wide is when the cement (or vision) is dry enough that it has some shape but is still wet enough that everyone can write their own name in it.

2) Ignite change with a significant event.

Growing a community needs to be initiated by something that signifies things are going to change. Unfortunately change is too often ignited by a crisis. Don't wait for that to happen. Find another way to bring people together perhaps through an event or rally that focuses on what is already being done well. It's often best done by bringing in an outsider who can hold up a mirror to the community. Generally that mirror tends to reflect the assets of a community and what they are doing well (the eighty percent) but also the twenty percent that needs to be addressed and changed.

3) Count on rolling out two parallel initiatives—one short term, one long term.

Communities need a short term project or initiative to show what's possible when everyone comes together for the betterment of the community—some might call it the low hanging fruit.

Secondly, a long term, multi sector, and community-driven, community-wide, strategic plan needs to be put into place to ensure collective impact.

Not everyone will want or need to be involved in both, but it does accommodate (a) those who are action oriented and just want to get busy doing something, as well as (b) those who are intuitively wired to be system-thinkers and want to address the community more holistically.

The first focus is a project or initiative(s) that will surface as the result of working together to determine what the community sees as a priority. It might be a playground build, a proposal to develop a trail, a festival or special event, conference, community garden etc. Quite honestly it doesn't matter what it is, as long as everyone sees it as being meaningful and relevant. This will demonstrate to the community the synergy that results when they work side by side and put their shoulders to the wheel. It is essential for building trusted relationships, a sense of community and spirit, and a belief that they can be responsible for the change they want to see.

The second focus needs to be placed on the development of a longer term, multisectoral community-driven strategic plan that places an emphasis on quality of life. This lack of a collective vision for the kind of community they want to be is often what contributes to silo-based thinking and planning, and a lack of the coordinated efforts and collaboration necessary to address the entire community and its overall quality of life.

Each of us will likely be drawn by either the project or the longer term solution-based plan so it's important to be cognizant of that pull and accept that both are important.

4) Diversity equals creativity.

The more diverse the stakeholders, the more innovative and responsive the solutions will be. Different lenses lead to different and more creative and responsive solutions. Any discussion about change within a community needs to involve elected officials, businesses, volunteers, social profits, artists. government staff, citizens of all ages and backgrounds etc.

5) There are no short cuts.

Community growth and development takes time. It isn't just about money. It's about people. That means it needs to be about investing time in having meaningful conversations, determining community values and priorities, and ultimately building the trusted relationships needed for change and growth.

It won't be easy, but it will be the most important work we ever do if we're serious about wanting postive change and growth for our communities.

Applying Strategies for Building Trust

A while back I hit the wall and had something best described as a mini meltdown.

The initiative I'm directing, while incredibly exciting and meaningful, is huge. Even though I'm blessed with a stellar team as well as a decent personal capacity for chaos and big picture thinking, the reality of a project that is attempting to impact the quality of life in communities across an entire province and beyond, is one big hairy beast.

I found myself identifying with those guys on the Ed Sullivan show who spun plates on the tops of sticks and then ran back and forth to make sure they were all spinning at the same time. While they made it look easy, some of my plates were definitely crashing and I knew I wasn't using my time and energy as effectively as I could. I also knew that if I didn't find solutions soon, I would risk putting the initiative, my health, and my colleagues into a detrimental state.

Intellectually, I know that no one person has all the answers. I also have the advantage of experience that has taught me the richness and innovation that results from collaborative decision-making. Yet, even then, I hesitated to ask for help. After all, wasn't I supposed to be in charge? Wasn't I supposed to know what I was doing?

So why was it so hard for me to ask for help from my colleagues? Was it, as the Chinese proverb stated, "Easier to go up into the mountains to catch tigers than to ask others for help?"

Truth is that asking for help makes us vulnerable. After all, what if people change their perception of us? What if they refuse to help or think of us as being incompetent? What if at some point, they use what we share against us in some way?

When I thought about it, those simply weren't realistic concerns in my current situation. I trusted my team and knew I could ask them for help. I knew that with them I would be safe and my vulnerability would be respected and honoured. I was also reminded of a quote from someone who once said, "If you can't ask for help, you can't be trusted." The

> ❝ Asking for help does not mean that we are weak or incompetent. It usually indicates an advanced level of honesty and intelligence."
>
> — Anne Wilson Schaef

bottom line was that I needed other perspectives to solve complex issues. I had to trust and ask for help.

Every one of us has times where we feel overwhelmed by our particular situation and the demands and responsibilities of life, work, family, and friends. It impacts our feelings of competency and our sense of control and balance. When we encounter this in ourselves it is really important to be able to reach out and ask for help. If we don't, the chances are our challenges will continue to grow and we risk spiraling into even greater chaos.

However, in order to reach out and ask for help we need to trust. In order to trust, we need to know our vulnerability will be respected and honoured, and that we are safe. While it may seem risky, I learned that the benefit of being vulnerable is that it also increases levels of trust.

When I did reach out to two of my colleagues for help, their response was far better than anything I might have imagined. First of all they validated my feelings of being overwhelmed by recognizing the responsibilities I was carrying. That in itself made me feel better.

I was also surprised to learn that they were quite willing to carry more responsibility themselves.

Best of all, several of them sat down, without me even being present, and strategized solutions for what they could take off my plate. Most importantly, they've carried through with their commitments, gently and kindly reminding me on several occasions, to back off what was now their responsibility.

When work and life are intense, it is critically important to be able to ask for what you need and to know you are supported. When we fall, we need to be confident there are others there to catch us. This in turns leads to the grounding that results in more clarity, innovation, and growth.

I recently heard that the driving vision for one successful CEO was to have a company where all the employees would be his friends. While it may be somewhat utopian of an ideal, having a community of colleagues who are friends we trust is a worthy goal. Not only does it make a significant difference to the quality of the work, I can personally attest to the fact that it also makes for a rich, fun, and rewarding environment.

Understanding Political Governance

Regardless of the community, there are common themes when it comes to community leadership. Too often this theme is the ineffectiveness of the political leadership—sometimes perceived, sometimes actual.

It seems there is a bit of a time warp in that elected officials have often failed to keep pace with the changes that are demanding a new kind of leadership. Whereas most seem to believe they have been elected to use their judgment and make decisions on behalf of their constituents, the reality is that too often the decisions they make reflect a growing disconnect between the path they are carving and the values and priorities of the average citizen.

On the other hand, if we don't want politicians to make decisions on their own, what is it we do want to see in our elected officials? Here's the start of my wish list.

I want more politicians who understand they don't have all the answers. I want them to stop thinking of our community as something only they can fix. I want them to instead view people in their communities as untapped experts who, when you ask them, will tell you what's good about their community (or province, territory, or country), what's not so good, and of utmost importance, how it can be fixed. I guess that means they need to be good listeners. If nothing else, they need to keep asking the question, "What will success look like"?

If all elected officials were to view people in their communities as untapped resources, we could all work together in a collaborative rather than an adversarial manner. Of course, that means we would also need politicians who know how to engage citizens. And, I don't mean consult, I mean engage. To do that we need politicians who aren't afraid to share power and control and know how to organize to make that happen at all levels.

Additionally, we need more elected officials who understand the importance of planning. Our communities and the issues being faced are more and more complicated. We can't afford to simply react. Issues are complex and resources are limited so we need to ensure more leaders who embrace the idea of having a vision for their community (or region, province, territory, or country) and keep planning for how

77

they are going to get there. Ideally, I'd like elected officials to provide monthly updates for their constituents on the vision and plan.

Also, I'd like to see us elect some politicians who have stiff spines and eyesight good enough to see through the antics of the "squeaky wheels". People shouldn't automatically get their way just because they show up at a Council meeting or write a letter to the editor. After all, there is often a much greater majority with an opposing view who are busy doing other important work. Especially at the local level, it seems that Council delegations are taking time away from more critical issues. Council should be governing and are instead too often dealing with issues that could be dealt with at a committee level.

Last but not least, we must elect politicians who represent the diversity of our citizens. We need young blood, more women, and more who represent the rich and varied cultures within our communities, regions, provinces, territories, and country.

Now that I've ranted somewhat, to be fair there are elected officials who do get it.

I recently met one of them, a young woman who lives in a small northern community. Working in the health sector in a community development capacity, she is aware and concerned about growing health issues in her hometown.

Despite much that is good in town, including a strong economy and even a surplus of jobs, a recent survey of residents showed higher than average levels of obesity, addictions, and mental health issues. Even life expectancies are significantly less than the provincial average. And yet, instead of doing more to encourage citizens to get physically and socially active in the community, elected officials actually did the opposite.

Overruling their own by-law, Council allowed a developer to build an entire subdivision without sidewalks thus making it impossible for residents to walk safely in their own neighbourhood. Ironically, they did ensure that residents would have access to a trail for all-terrain vehicles.

For the young woman, it was the proverbial straw that broke the camel's back. Too many community leaders were making too many short-sighted decisions. Despite not having any political experience, she stepped up to the plate and ran for Council during municipal elections.

She is just one of a number of emerging leaders who are ready to do their part to make the world, or at least their community, a better place.

Very few of them have what experts would call *formal* or *legitimate* power in terms of a position and title within their respective organizations. And yet, not having the instant authority that typically comes with a title hasn't stopped them from emerging as leaders within their communities.

Neither do they have what the experts might call *coercive* power, meaning the ability to sanction others for failure to comply, or the *reward* power that would allow them to give something of value for performance. These are two of the five types of power described by social psychologists John R. P. French and Bertram Raven in their now classic study[42].

What these emerging leaders do have are three different kinds of power that have nothing to do with being in a formal position of authority or being able to hand out rewards or punishment.

Without exception, they have *expert, referent,* and *information* power. The emerging leaders I met have *expert* power. For sure they are smart about their community and how it works and people turn to them for advice and guidance. They also have *information* power. Not only do they know a lot, they are willing and eager to share it with others.

But the power they all seem to have in abundance is *referent* power or what others describe as substance. It is one of the most effective styles of power and one we would all like to see in our elected officials. People identify with them, admire what they stand for, and generally feel better when they are around them. They have a storehouse of what some scholars call *social capital*.[43] People trust them to walk their talk and they choose to follow them.

---

42   French, J.R.P. & Raven, B. (1959). The bases of social power, in D. Cartwright (ed.) *Studies in social power*. Ann Arbor, MI: University of Michigan Press.

43   Hanifan, L. J. (1916) The rural school community center. *Annals of the American Academy of Political and Social Science* 67: 130-138.

There were many who thought a young woman from the health sector without any political experience didn't have a chance of being elected, particularly when she built her campaign on a platform of quality of life and active communities.

To the surprise of many, including herself, she was elected. Not only was she elected, she did it in style by topping the polls. She garnered more votes than the mayor and received more votes than any councilor in the history of the town.

Effective Political Leadership

But, what does it take to be an effective political leader?

Upon retiring as a high school teacher, Bill made the decision to throw his hat in the ring and run for Town Council in order to pursue a lifelong interest in politics. On the other hand, Tracey, an avid volunteer, had never even thought about running until someone asked her to consider it. Carrie's decision to run for local election was prompted by frustration with a Council that too often seemed to overlook social issues and quality of life in favour of economic development. As a young woman in her twenties she also felt it was important to broaden the diversity in her community.

All three were part of a panel our team organized for those considering running for municipal election. Their enthusiasm and advice was a wonderful combination of passion and practicality.

When asked what was involved in getting ready to run, they suggested the work begins even before submitting one's nomination. Their advice included attending Council meetings, reading up on meetings from the past year, researching demographics, community history and current issues, reading the local paper and letters-to-the-editor, and talking with people about issues and the direction they wanted to see for their community. The potential impact on one's job, finances, and family is an additional consideration.

After that, the next step is submitting one's nomination. Gathering the required signatures was considered by those on the panel to be part of their campaign and a first step in getting their name out.

Developing a platform was also discussed. Carrie suggested that rather than having a formal platform, she focused on placing a social lens on what was happening in the community. She also advised against making any promises except to listen, evaluate, and make decisions based on the long term vision and plan for the community. Bill focused on downtown redevelopment and economic considerations. Tracey reported she had learned that what she thought were priorities were not necessarily in alignment with those of the community. As a result, she too stressed the need to listen and act, within reason, on what the community wants. She recognized that quality of life, as well as economic drivers, are important.

Their best advice included, "Be clear about your values", "Be sure to act with integrity, "Don't go in with one agenda", Work to enable community groups to do what they want to do", "Tap into the passion in the community and then get out of their way", and "It's about the long term quality of life in the community, not only the potholes".

They also suggested that campaign door knocking may not necessarily be for everyone as it depends on style and comfort zone. What works for you has to be genuine and authentic. Stepping out of your comfort zone is good though, as is attending community events.

As one panelist put it, "Being an elected official is a huge learning curve, but it is amazing as it brings a different perspective to community. It is something I wish everyone could experience."

It's safe to say that if you're even considering running for election, these panelists would say "Go for it"!

Nurturing Positive Relationships with Elected Officials and Community and Corporate Leaders

Community leaders are more effective as agents of change when they are able to develop positive relationships with citizens including elected officials, and other community and corporate leaders.

You will know what positive relationships are when you find them because they are akin to having a good posse.

I learned this firsthand after spending three days immersed with a diverse group in a think-tank that took place as ACE Communities was first rolled out. As one of the group pointed out, it was like running with a pack of horses who took great joy in running fast and hard. Generally, we headed in the same direction but there were also a lot of diversions as the lead often changed, we slowed down

> "By becoming aware that we are communities, not organizations, we will change the very nature of our relationships, making them less material and more spiritual, less mechanical and more divine, less temporary and more infinite, less cursory and more vital. Then our communities will come alive. Our natural longing to form lasting connections will then transform our affairs—and our planet."

— Lance Secretan

to make sure others were running with us, or sometimes we took interesting and sometimes prickly or serendipitous detours.

In the end, the deep, rich discussion and wisdom in the room resulted in clear and often innovative direction. Yet despite the exhilarating ride, some of us also left at the end of three days feeling a bit uneasy.

There is something about being in a room for three days having real conversations with people you trust and care about that contributes to a very different environment. The difference seems to be that there is time to exchange the stories and personal anecdotes that allow you to really get to know one another. These trusted relationships seem to lead to an environment where others—sometimes deliberately, sometimes unintentionally—poke and prod beneath the surface and the front that each of us typically presents to the world. The end result seems to be the authenticity that is an essential for nurturing positive relationships.

Authenticity, the ability to demonstrate honestly and clarity about who one is and what one wants to do, inspires others to do the same. Ultimately this leads to a culture that inspires synergy and collaboration. It is this knowing of ourselves that is essential because if we don't know who we are—meaning what we stand for, or our calling, we won't be able to lead ourselves, never mind others.

Authenticity also contributes to positive relationships because those who are authentic are typically comfortable empowering others in addition to being open to learnings and to the development of a culture that encourages and supports learning and growth.

Authenticity and positive relationships can be nurtured by finding one's own sense of purpose, paying attention to one's self, surroundings and other people, and actively listening to others.

While authenticity is key, the basic tenets of positive relationships have perhaps best been documented by Dale Carnegie in *How to Win*

Friends and Influence People[44] first published in 1936, in a massive bestseller that remains popular to this day.

- Never criticize, condemn or complain—positive reinforcement works better.
- Become genuinely interested in other people.
- Talk in terms of the other person's interests.
- Be a good listener.
- Make the other person feel important.
- Use a person's name whenever possible.
- Smile and greet others with enthusiasm and animation.

> 66 In organizations, real power and energy is generated through relationships. The patterns of relationships and the capacities to form them are more important than tasks, functions, roles, and position."
>
> — Margaret Wheatley

Carnegie's advice remains sound almost eighty years later.

When information and knowledge are integrated with the insight and charge of creativity, the result will be an unstoppable organization or community where anything will be possible.

My most significant learning regarding the importance of positive relationships with elected officials occurred when I was exposed to the impact of Stephen Harper's leadership style shortly after he became Prime Minister when his party won a minority government in the January 2006 federal election.

At the time I was a member of a coalition of voluntary sector capacity building organizations. As such, we had been working with a number of federal bureaucrats to determine how we could collaborate to strengthen the capacity of social-profit organizations. After six months of meetings and conference calls, trusted relationships were emerging and progress was being made. It was an exciting time.

Imagine our surprise when, rather than the typical friendly exchanges, our first post election conference call began with one of the more senior bureaucrats saying, "If you find the tone of our conversations changing and hear us being less transparent and forthcoming

---

44   Carnegie D. (1936). *How to win friends and influence people.* New York: Simon and Schuster.

about what we can and can't do, we want you to know that it's because we have received new direction from the top."

At first, those on the call didn't take the speaker seriously and joked, "Do you mean to say you've been muzzled?"

To this the senior bureaucrat replied dejectedly, "That is exactly what I'm saying."

Needless to say what had begun with such promise as an honest and spirited desire to strengthen community organizations dealing with funding cutbacks and new demands, struggled to exist within this new micromanaged environment, sputtered, and died.

As a community leader, there may be the frustration of dealing with this kind of political posturing. However, taking the time to nurture and build positive relationships with elected officials, and other community and corporate leaders, is an important investment of time and energy because leaders at all levels have recognized that today's challenges, for businesses, organizations, or entire countries, are far too complicated for any one person to solve. Today's real leaders see the value of trusted relationships, partnerships, and collaborations.

My guess is that the majority of Canadians share a growing belief that our elected officials need to stop competing for power and control, and instead work together to share responsibility for one another's success and ultimately that of our country.

If I were to give leaders any advice these days—not that I have any assurance they'd even want any—I'd say, grow up. Grow as a leader, play nice, and share with others.

Investing in relationships reflects an understanding that one person doesn't have all the answers, and that others are experts in their own right—a unique and important source of knowledge and wisdom that we need to tap. If we want great countries and great communities, "me" needs to become "we".

Effective Media Strategies

I admit that I am an information junkie. I don't collect thimbles like my aunt or souvenir spoons like my sister-in-law. Instead, I collect information. This is good, right? Information is a wonderful thing, isn't it?

Well, the truth of the matter is nowadays I'm not so sure. There are times when collecting wine corks is beginning to look mighty attractive.

Unfortunately, in an age where the experts estimate the amount of digital information in the world is doubling every eleven hours,[45] my pastime is becoming an increasingly stressful one. Like many others, I often find myself overwhelmed and not quite able to deal with the amount of information I receive on a daily basis.

As a result of needing to overcome the data smog that has resulted from this overload, during a recent vacation I deliberately shut down several of my normal communication channels. For instance, I did not turn on my computer, check my email, or read a newspaper.

While I especially missed the ritual of reading the newspaper each day, I found I didn't miss its focus on violence and negativity. It did however get me wondering why the media appears so much better at capturing *breakdowns* rather than *breakthroughs*. Additionally it does appear that good news stories of creativity and success are considered less newsworthy.

All around us, there is a sense that the old way of doing things is no longer working. So, even though we might not be sure what's going to replace the old way, there are indicators that something new and different is being born. Yet, today those responsible for pushing out media too often seem more fixated on the fact that something is dying.

Perhaps this means we need more from our media than the traditional journalism that presents facts and occurrences.

In an era where people are bombarded and overwhelmed by data and information, we need writers who can filter, explain, and share. And, that doesn't happen unless writers can get a person's attention and motivate them to read more.

In my experience what makes many people want to learn more are stories that relate to them, their families, and their communities. The stories are especially effective when tied to factual data that makes

---

45   Retrieved http://news.cnet.com/2100-7345_3-6159025.html?part=rss&tag=2547-1_3-0-20&subj=news.

people think and act about things that matter. Additionally, because our new way of doing things is not yet clear, we need to tap the creative talent of artists to inspire, illuminate, and tell our new stories. Ultimately this means we need to shift the role of the media from static, one-way information dissemination to the conversations and dialogues that will grow the trusted relationships that will encourage reader involvement beyond the smattering of written letters and occasionally phoned in tips.

Generally it appears that people are using the Internet for three main purposes—to search for information, to access news, and for sharing. That means traditional media, like local newspapers, will only be able to counteract a declining and aging readership and the growth in competing media if they focus on these same three purposes—particularly local news and sharing.

What do we need to share? We need to share our thoughts and strategies for how we can develop innovative new strategies to respond to a global, highly competitive, fast changing, knowledge-based economy. We need to learn how we can work together to build a culture of innovation and how we can practice more systems-thinking in our communities. We should figure out how to facilitate access to learning, nurture the aspirations of our youth, and strengthen our cultural well-being. Let's use the media to figure out how to address the rising costs of physical inactivity, obesity and chronic disease, increase waning volunteerism, protect our environment, strengthen the capacity of the social-profit sector, and increase civic engagement and spirit.

Communities are facing these and other challenging issues in complex environments that are continually impacted by forces from the local, regional, provincial, national, and global fronts. The media can be a powerful catalyst for bringing together the diverse thinking and resources that will be necessary for creating strong, healthy, and vibrant communities.

Triggering Media Interest

Recently enroute to a business meeting with a colleague, a rather peppy song played on the car radio prompting us to sing along. As the song faded my colleague told me that while her young daughter used to love that song, she now cringes when she hears it and begs her to change the station.

Apparently her daughter recently spent time with an aunt and had accompanied her to a fitness class. While the class of women did their aerobic dancing to that same song, she sat at the back of the room and watched. Turns out, it might have been a bit of a mistake because now whenever her daughter hears that song all she can picture in her mind are rows of middle-aged, jiggly bums.

Those working in marketing would describe her response to that song as the reaction to a "trigger". Triggers are another idea that marketers are working on as one more way of driving messages into our heads. It is something we've likely all tried at some point in our lives, so while not a new technique, it can be an important media strategy for community leaders to understand.

My grandmother used to put her watch on the wrong hand to trigger something she needed to remember. My mother still puts her ring on a different finger or an elastic band on her wrist to jog her memory. Marketers suggest it is a much more reliable way of remembering because the environmental trigger will do the remembering for you.

Growing up, jingles often served as a trigger. To this day, the Cracker Jacks song remains embedded in my brain as does the Kool-Aid jingle. However, jingles and slogans aren't as effective because only the advertisement or seeing the product itself "triggers" the message. It would be far more effective if the trigger were something one sees or hears more often in their daily environment.

While you will likely see more marketing that uses the trigger technique in the near future to sell more products, I can't help but think that it also has endless possibilities for making the world a better place. If we think about an idea we want to convey and then hook it to something that already exists in the environment we can make that idea travel in a very significant way.

For instance, I recently read about an anti-nuclear testing group that placed signs around the walk buttons on street corners. As a pedestrian points their finger toward the push button, they see a sign that reads "the world could end this easily". The intent is of course to make people flinch and then hopefully think about nuclear testing as they cross the street as well as every time they reach to change a light in the future.

Community leaders will need to ensure media strategies that find and use the right triggers to keep people thinking about active, creative, and engaged communities.

Utilizing the Power of Storytelling

Regardless of the actual media used, community leaders will need to place an emphasis on stories. I was recently reminded about the power of stories as I sat in on a conference session entitled "Community Development in Action". In the one hour and fifteen minute session, local leaders were sharing their respective stories about how they were working to become more active, creative, and engaged. Despite the five-minute time limitation for each presenter, the group managed to deliver compelling stories that had the audience laughing, crying, ooh'ing, ah'ing, and applauding enthusiastically.

Hardly the reaction to a typical conference session, it clearly demonstrated the important and often lost art of storytelling. It was also a reminder that those living in communities are an incredible source of knowledge about the issues they face, as well as the solutions for how they can be addressed.

Two women from a community of four hundred talked about how they served as the catalyst in their small town for a community event that raised $120,000, involved one hundred and fifty adult volunteers, and resulted in a one day event that produced a brand new playground and skateboard park, as well as flower planting and a cleanup of the entire park, arena, and main street.

Another community decided to focus on the development of an organic community garden and greenhouse. They've managed to get their Town Council and the Crown to approve the use of the land for their endeavour as well as to get two greenhouses donated.

One small town generated numerous family-oriented events throughout the year including movie nights at their local hall made possible by the purchase of a projector. Another talked about their planning efforts and the resulting conclusion that a recreation director was needed in their small but rapidly growing town. In one case, three towns close in proximity but insular in how they worked are now collaborating on a regular basis and have raised a million dollars toward a recreation centre.

No two stories were told in quite the same way. One was told as a fairy tale, another with a montage of photographs set to stirring music, and yet another as a video of a skit that involved the town's local mascot and his assorted animal friends.

In telling their stories they somehow managed to build a bridge between the facts of their projects and what it actually meant to put them into action. Their stories opened up those in the room to seeing how things could be different in their own communities and how they themselves could be the catalysts for that change. By sharing the value they placed on the quality of life in their communities, they were able to convey hope that change was possible. Unlike anything else that could have been done in the session, the stories helped participants see their own potential role in shaping the future of their communities.

Prior to the session, it is unlikely the participants would have been able to explain how to be a catalyst for change in one's community. The stories, however, seemed to clarify what might otherwise have been difficult to convey. For example, the stories made it clear that no two communities were alike as well as to illustrate that change was organic and somewhat messy. Almost every story referenced their initial confusion and not knowing where to begin but also conveyed that things eventually got clearer.

While it would be difficult to describe a winning formula for telling a good story, the most effective were those that came from the heart. As always, the best stories are the ones that ring with authenticity and reveal emotion, passion, and values. It is through stories that capture our imagination, take root and grow, that we are able to impart an understanding of what really matters.

Apply Appropriate Social Media Strategies

What's the connection between social media and sex?

Avinash Kaushik, Google's web analytics guru, once wrote, "Social media is like teen sex, everyone wants to do it. No one actually knows how. When finally done, there is surprise it's not better."[46]

But while teens might be misinformed about sex, most of them definitely have at least a grasp on social media. But what exactly is social media?

I'll spare you the convoluted definition posted on Wikipedia, as well as an explanation of the plethora of opportunities provided by tools such as Facebook, Twitter, MySpace, YouTube, Linked-in etc. etc. Instead, I'd like to suggest that social media is the media generated by tools and services that use the Internet to facilitate conversations. And yes, while some of those conversations might be rather trite, social media has also resulted in the democratization of information.

Unlike the more traditional media of newspapers, television, and film that pushes out information or messages at people to read and hopefully absorb, social media has meant most everyone now has the capacity, should they choose to accept it, to have their own voices heard as *publishers*. This availability of social media, on a many-to-many basis, much of it free and surprisingly easy to use, has flattened hierarchies as it provides everyone with the opportunity to share conversations, stories, learnings, and resources; create shared meanings; and serve as a catalyst for action and change. All at lightning speed.

Not surprisingly, businesses have been the first to see the potential of social media and have used it to reach a larger number of consumers (or in some cases a smaller niche target audience) to market their brand and reputation, gain customer input, ensure more relevant products, increase loyalty, and ultimately increase their profit. Organizations and governments, who are often more focused on social rather than financial profit, haven't necessarily been as quick off the mark.

So, if you are a community leader who hasn't maximized the potential of social media, where on earth do you begin? While I could be totally off the mark, here's what I've absorbed as the result of working with an amazing team.

---

46   Retrieved http://news.cnet.com/8301-13577_3-10185477-36.html.

Given privacy issues, new and up and coming social media products, and the fact that you can't always control the content on sites such as Facebook and MySpace, your efforts might best be focused on ensuring you have a website that creates your own opportunities for the engagement of your stakeholders. There is no credibility without a web presence and you are after all, what Google says you are. Try doing a search on your company or organization name and see what surfaces. The advantage of focusing efforts on your website is that you are able to control its content. Also, since your website is your most vital marketing tool, make sure it is a website that you and your team (not just one webmaster) can access and update on a moment's notice.

For those interested in social profit, developing a platform that encourages input from your stakeholders is generally a sound option. In our particular case, we've learned a lot about the power of stories and as a result have placed a priority on blogs written by a variety of our stakeholders that are then pulled into our website.

When you do venture into using specific social media tools, be clear about where you want to go first. Know the target audience you're trying to reach as well as your outcomes. Only then can you select the most appropriate tools. For example, the general public—especially teens—are comfortable with Facebook, whereas Twitter is popular among twenty to forty year olds. In our case, we've made a decision to use Twitter because it fits our demographic and works as a means for driving traffic to our website.

And don't forget as well that many of the free social media tools can also help you operate more efficiently and effectively. For example we store our videos on viddler.com, and operate our team intranet on Google apps (it gives us web-based email for each team member and shared file storage, calendars, and contact information). You can share your photos on flickr.com and PowerPoints on slideshare.com. We've also used ustream.com for live webcasting.

But, keep in mind there are a lot of other options as well. The choices you make will be easier once you're clear on where you want to go.

Is social media complicated? For sure it is. After all, we're talking about a culture shift and totally new approaches to generating business and social profit. But that's where social media differs from teen sex. For teenagers, sex is an option. Today, none of us really have a choice about whether or not we should be using social media if we're looking to generate business or social profit. So, even if we're comfortable in our horse and buggy, it's important for community leaders to drive, or at least test, the new vehicles on the road.

Enabling Groups and Organizations to Collaborate and Achieve Synergy

Growing up in a family of seven there wasn't always a lot of money to go around. By today's standards I'm sure we'd be considered deprived, but the reality is that we had food on the table, clothes on our backs, and more importantly, we just didn't know any better. Having said that, it's also true that we weren't immune to peer pressure because we oh-so-wanted to fit in.

My mother was always muttering about our need to be sheep and asked us on more than one occasion if we'd jump into the canal just because everyone else did. To her credit though, she managed to remain sensitive to our need to fit in with our friends especially when it came to school. I clearly recall her painstakingly removing the orange Levi tab from the back pocket of one of my older brother's outgrown jeans and then carefully sewing it on to a new no-name pair. I also know she saved the "baby bonus" cheques carefully so she was able to ensure we all had new school supplies each September. For her it was simply about making life easier for her kids.

Today, the challenges in our community are often too complicated for one mother, or for that matter, any one organization, business, or level of government to solve on their own. More often than not, solutions need a broader collaboration for synergistic results.

One example of positive synergy recently happened in Niagara when the United Way of St. Catharines and District put together an award-winning collaboration when it was identified that far too many children were beginning each school year at a disadvantage. These kids, from families who were barely able to provide food and shelter, often had little money left to purchase clothing and school supplies. Rather than coming to school confident and ready to learn, these kids, many of whom were already struggling with low self esteem as the result of their family's financial situation, came empty handed and ill-prepared. Being ill-prepared for learning meant they were at-risk for being further distanced from their peers.

> 66 No organization can long survive if it is only concerned with its own perpetuation. It needs a larger vision— a higher purpose to survive the storms of change."
>
> — Paul T.P. Wong

The project that evolved to address this need is called *Backpacks for Kids*. As one of their volunteers put it, "Every child deserves the best environment in which to learn. *Backpacks for Kids* levels the playing field and affords each student the opportunity to be successful."

United Way of St. Catharines and District acts as the umbrella organization for this "equalizing" partnership. As a result, the *Backpacks for Kids* program is helping thousands of kids get the same start to the school year as those who are financially and socially better off. One backpack at a time, the program is making a difference.

When it was first initiated more than five hundred elementary-school backpacks were assembled from hundreds of thousands of dollars worth of in-kind gifts. Since then it has evolved to the point that more than two thousand backpacks are distributed for students entering grades one through twelve.

Items packed in the backpacks typically include lunch bags, pencil crayons, scissors, fine tip markers, rulers, ball point pens, math sets, dividers, binders, three ring paper, dictionaries, and calculators.

In addition to providing in-kind and cash sponsorships, businesses and corporations donate hundreds of hours of staff time to pack the school supplies into these "bags of hope and compassion that open a world of possibilities".

And what's in it for them? In addition to building energy and team spirit, the businesses involved also have the satisfaction of demonstrating sound corporate social responsibility. Taking care of the community in which their employees work, live, and play is part of that responsibility.

The program brought together volunteers as well as more than twenty-five organizations and businesses from across Niagara. Everyone involved had at least one thing in common. They believed, "the only load a child should carry to school on their shoulders is a backpack."

The job and responsibility of a community leader is to encourage, model, and promote more initiatives that reflect this kind of collaboration and synergy.

Applying Diverse Facilitation Models, Skills, and Techniques

I'm writing this during an event billed as a 'Think-Tank'. While I know the intentions were good, the truth is that I'm bored out of my gourd.

If I see one more PowerPoint presentation that is both pointless and powerless, I might just have to override my disease-to-please and overly developed conscience, and leave the building.

I was invited as one of some one hundred individuals representing a variety of organizations, governments, and businesses to participate in a discussion and reflection targeted at renewing public health. I was warned ahead of time that the meeting would likely be more of the same old, same old but I am by nature an optimistic person and carved the time out of a busy schedule to attend.

Unfortunately, as soon as I walked into the room I knew my optimism was misplaced. The fact that the room was set up with a podium, head table, LCD projector, with round tables scattered around the room told me all I needed to know.

The room set up conveyed a hierarchy and a message that those at the front of the room were the experts and the ones in charge. The only redeeming factor is that it would have been worse if the room had been set up with rows.

Consequently, despite participants having been invited to share their thoughts and ideas, we spent the entire morning being talked at by a variety of talking heads. The speakers, mostly government bureaucrats or consultants, also warned us ahead of time that although our ideas would be considered, they might not necessarily be acted upon. As you might imagine, that didn't do much to motivate and engage participants.

Anyway, as my attention wandered throughout the morning, and I shifted to get comfortable from my twisted viewing position, I looked around the room and saw I wasn't alone. Many others were distracted, bored, and disengaged.

Contrast that scenario with another event I recently attended that was focused on developing community leaders.

Upon entering the room, participants found one large circle of chairs. That was it. No head table, no podium, no audio visual equipment. While initially it may have intimidated some of the participants, it conveyed a very different message.

The message was that we were all in it together, we were all equal, and that there was no hierarchy. Additionally, it suggested that our intent was to do things differently and that this meeting would be about change and growth. As circles have always done, particularly among indigenous populations, the message conveyed was that we were in for some real and meaningful conversations.

As participants, we also learned the circle meant there was nowhere to hide as there were no tables or a back of the room to protect us. As participants, we were fully engaged from the very beginning.

When the learning became more intense, tables were introduced into the room on the second day. However by then the group had bonded and the tables did not present a barrier especially since they were positioned so that everyone could still see one another.

As far as the 'Think-Tank' was concerned, organizers did eventually encourage about an hour and a half of small group discussion in the afternoon. While some innovative strategies were discussed and submitted, when we reconvened to the larger room hoping to hear the ideas from the group, we were confronted by yet another panel. I confess, my patience was maxed out and I did leave early.

The moral of the story? Understanding good facilitation is a critical component of a being an effective community leader.

What is facilitation?

Facilitation is generally considered a process in which a neutral person helps a group work together more effectively in a collaborative, consensus-building process. It is guided by three core values: valid information, free and informed choice, and internal commitment to those choices.[47]

---

47   Schwartz, R. *The skilled facilitator: Practical wisdom for developing effective groups.* San Francisco: Jossey-Bass, 1994, 8.

When people have valid information and are empowered to make informed decisions, they become more committed to them. And, when people are committed to a decision, they are more likely to ensure it is implemented effectively.[48]

In order to ensure the design of effective and inclusive community meetings, a community leader either needs to be a good facilitator or make sure they work with someone who is. Facilitators design and implement a process that will advance a group's ability to stay on task and be more creative, efficient, and productive, and to help group members improve communications, examine and resolve problems, and/or make decisions. Facilitators have no decision-making authority themselves as the ultimate decisions are up to the participants, but they do know what questions to ask, when to ask them, and how questions should be structured to get good answers. Of key importance is that they maintain respect for all participants and an interest in what each individual has to offer.

Valuing Both Fact-based and Intuitive Knowing

While my intention is never to annoy others, I know that I sometimes do.

When I was younger, I'd go to meetings and say something that would inevitably draw puzzled looks from the others. It was almost as if I was saying something in a foreign language. After shaking their heads, the other participants would continue their previous stream of conversation—typically one that involved a lot of detail. After being ignored for the rest of the meeting I'd beat myself up thinking, "Why on earth couldn't I just learn to keep my mouth shut?"

Maybe it's because I'm getting older, but the truth is today I speak up far more during meetings and put far less emphasis on whether or not people get what it is I'm trying to say.

Although I'm not as concerned about what people think about me anymore, sadly there still doesn't seem to be much patience with people who see the whole *forest* but don't always excel when it comes to getting the facts right about the *trees*.

---

48   Alberta Recreation and Parks Association (2009). *A toolkit for community leaders.* ARPA: Edmonton. AB.

Trust me, I very much get that I'm not as good as others with the details but why is it that those abilities are the ones that are more apt to be valued? Surely it must be clear that if we only discuss and debate the *trees* that we'll lose sight of the *forest*? After all, there are many times when we had all the facts and details but still didn't have a good grip on the full picture because we didn't pay attention to intuition. I've learned there are some who just happen to be better at seeing systems, patterns, and paths in the forest long before they're visible to others. And, while our language has many words for describing detail and the information we gain from our five senses, we don't have a lot of words to describe this six sense intuition.

Instead, we're more likely to respect and value the people who are good at reporting facts and what research can prove. It's not an unexpected bias given that many suggest between two-thirds and three-quarters of the general population prefer factual data over intuitive data.

This bias means we're not as likely to value intuition and are instead more apt to attribute it to a lucky guess or brush it off as "women's intuition". We're much more comfortable with what we can prove by what we can see, hear, touch, or measure.

However, it is increasingly evident that in today's complex environment, we need both types of knowing—*fact-based* and *intuitive*.

Intuitive knowing comes far easier to me than that which is fact-based. And yet, I've spent an inordinate amount of time honing my fact-based knowing in order to pass muster as a manager. It seems to me, that just as I have spent a lot of time developing my fact-based knowing, so too should all those who are expert in fact-based knowing need to spend time developing their intuition. Those rooted in the concrete of details perhaps need to do more to accept a playful attitude to explore what is possible in order to develop their intuitive side.

> " Intuition will tell the thinking mind where to look next."
>
> — Jonas Salk

Today intuition is far more important largely because we're operating in an unpredictable environment. Applying rational methods in an irrational world just doesn't work. If we attempt to hang onto rationality as the basis for our decision-making, we may lose the window of opportunity for action.

Everywhere I go these days, there seems to be a growing recognition that the old ways and the old rules just don't work anymore. So why on earth would we think that traditional fact-based decision-making is the answer?

> "Intuition is a combination of historical (empirical) data, deep and heightened observation and an ability to cut through the thickness of surface reality. Intuition is like a slow motion machine that captures data instantaneously and hits you like a ton of bricks. Intuition is a knowing, a sensing that is beyond the conscious understanding—a gut feeling. Intuition is not pseudo-science."
>
> — Abella Arthur

Intuitive leadership is less about facts and more about knowledge, character, experience, and wisdom. It is much more about asking the question, "Is this the right thing to do?" and then trusting our gut reaction to the answer.

Unfortunately, the reality is that we too often ignore our own instincts. It recently happened to me on a family vacation.

We were three hours away from home when our van sputtered, stuttered, and eventually lost all power. One tow, five hours, and four hundred and fifty dollars later we were back on the road breathing a sigh of relief. Not for long however, as forty-five minutes later we were once again stranded at the side of a busy highway speaking to our friendly CAA dispatcher arranging another tow. Being a long weekend, the second Canadian Tire didn't have a mechanic on duty, thus the tow to a third Canadian Tire in yet another town. By then they were closed and we were left scrambling to find a hotel room.

The entire incident left me kicking myself somewhat because the day before we left, a little voice in my head had been telling me that we should have taken my car. Knowing that wasn't an especially logical conclusion given my husband's van was newer and more reliable, I quashed that niggling little voice.

Intuition is something we've been talking a lot in terms of leadership these days and yet I'm not sure we really know what it is. We often say we should "trust our gut" or "trust our hunches" and yet that too often competes with our bias in favour of logic and common sense.

It's not unlike how I dismissed my hunch about the van thinking to myself, "That isn't logical, that doesn't make sense, I'm being silly." But perhaps we simply need to be more open to our intuitive impressions. After all, our intuition is just another way of gathering and sensing what we need to answer questions and make sound decisions in all aspects of our lives. In fact, Albert Einstein once said, "The intuitive mind is a sacred gift and the rational mind is a faithful servant. We have created a society that honours the servant and has forgotten the gift."

It's also likely that we all have the ability to tap this intuition or sixth sense. However, we first need to embrace the idea that intuition is a non linear way of gathering information. In other words, it's not logical. When we use reason, we take time to gather and analyze. With intuition we know and know instantly even when we get the information in bits and pieces. Additionally, it is not just the same kind of information we gather with our five senses. Instead intuition is more than raw data because it's often been interpreted for us. Our job is simply to pay attention.

Modeling Optimism and Hope

We didn't have a lot of money growing up but my mother gave me something priceless—the incredible gift of optimism.

It may also be that this gene is hereditary as it seems I've passed it on in a particularly large dose to our youngest son.

Like many others his age, he's struggled with the confusion of overwhelming career choices slammed up against the reality of too few opportunities. Recently he's cobbled together three part time jobs and even then often struggles to pay the rent. Several months ago sensing his growing frustration, I had a lengthy talk with him to help him focus his energies. I asked him to remove all potential barriers and think about his ideal job. If he could do anything, what would he want to do? What does he love to do so much he would do it for free?

He thought about it overnight and as we continued the conversation the next day, he shared that he was passionate about pursuing a career in the music industry. My heart sank because while I want all of our kids to pursue their dreams, even I just couldn't see that one happening—until yesterday.

Yesterday, I met a woman at a meeting who just happened to mention she was having a tough time finding someone to fill an intern position with an entertainment management company. Funded in part by a federal program intended to help young people get on-the-ground experience, it was a twelve week program providing support and, if all went well, a job at the end of the placement. After I picked my jaw up off the ground, I immediately called my son with the information.

While I'm not yet sure how the story ends, the point is that it reinforced for me the power and importance of remaining optimistic, hopeful, and believing that good things will happen.

So optimism isn't necessarily a denial of reality but rather more about viewing life as a glass half full instead of half empty.

While people may poke fun at my Pollyanna-ish approach to life, recent research shows that there are benefits. In fact, optimists live longer and healthier lives.

According to recent research at the University of Pittsburg, the women in the study who expected good rather than bad things to happen were fourteen percent less likely to die from heart disease, and less likely to have high blood pressure, diabetes, or smoke cigarettes. A group of women they referred to as "cynically hostile" were twenty three percent more likely to die from cancer compared to the women who were the least cynically hostile.[49]

But what if you're not as optimistic as my son in believing that good things will happen, is it possible to become more optimistic?

The experts suggest it is possible but it needs to begin with letting go of the idea that you've been singled out to be unlucky or miserable. It is an erroneous assumption that really has no basis in reason or in science.

There's no law that says you have to be a victim or a product of your circumstances. If you're not happy with your life or your community the way it is now, set a new direction and goals—just as my son did, and move on. Quite honestly, I think half the battle is knowing what you want and putting it out to the universe.

---

49 Kindle, H. (Aug, 2009). Optimism, cynical hostility, and incident coronary heart disease and mortality in the women's health initiative. *Circulation*. American Heart Association. http://circ.ahajournals.org/cgi/content/short/120/8/656.

It is also about being grateful for what you have. Things may be tough but everyone has, and should make a list of, the good things that have happened to them. Every time you start to feel pessimistic, pull out that list and read it through.

It is also important to accept that just because you've experienced disappointment in your life doesn't mean you always will. The past doesn't equal the future. While there may have been things in the past that you couldn't control, you can control many aspects of your life—the most important of which is your attitude.

That positive attitude and sense of optimism is the most powerful tool we have for meeting and surpassing the challenges we face today. In our individual lives, organizations, businesses, and communities this seems to be something that US President Barack Obama understands and conveys as a leader.

In conveying hope and optimism, Obama is reflecting an important leadership quality that doesn't always get a lot of attention.

Optimism manifests itself in positive expectations for the future, a hopeful mood, and our belief that outcomes will be good.

It's not so much that we want a leader to deny reality, it's just that when times are tough, we do want a leader who presents a positive view. Obama certainly doesn't sugarcoat the truth. In his inaugural speech, he acknowledged that the United States was a "nation at war, against a far-reaching network of violence and hatred", their economy was badly weakened, homes had been lost, their schools failed many, health care was too costly, and energy strategies were threatening their planet.

And, although clear about the challenges being serious and many, and that they would not be easily met, especially in a short span of time, he also said, "But know this, America—they will be met."[50]

Historically, hope has proven to be an effective strategy. It works and makes others believe that valuable change can and does happen.

Continuing to embrace that same spirit of hope will allow Obama to do his job as a leader. While many would be overwhelmed by the sheer magnitude of the change that will be required, it seems so much more possible when viewed through the a lens of hope.

---

50   http://www.cnn.com/2009/POLITICS/01/20/obama.politics/.

And, while the odds are that none of us will ever have to tackle a job on a scale like the one Obama is facing, we can learn from his example. We all can, and need, to embrace hope in order to live our best lives.

In the end it means we can choose negativity or we can choose hope. I for one, choose hope.

The Importance of Philanthropy

We can also facilitate hope by promoting the importance of philanthropy.

I clearly remember a Christmas when, instead of providing the more typical small gift of chocolates or bubble bath for my teacher, my parents made a donation on the teacher's behalf to UNICEF. I distinctly remember thinking my teacher was not going to be impressed. Being ten years old at the time, I really did think Christmas was a lot about the gifts.

I was, therefore, caught off guard when it was my gift that resulted in a beaming smile and heartfelt thanks from the teacher. She explained that it was truly an honour to know that a donation in her name was going to help children in need. It was a powerful lesson for me and one that nurtured my first understanding of the importance of philanthropy.

I was reminded of this experience again this week when two new events got me thinking about philanthropy and giving. One was positive, the other not so much.

The first story was relayed to me via Ian Hill as he was spearheading a volunteer-driven initiative, sponsored by Kool-Aid, which is helping to build playgrounds and skateboard and fitness parks in communities across the country.

Ian told me about a little girl, who, upon hearing that they were going to build a new playground at her school, called all those who had been invited to her upcoming birthday party. She suggested to each of them that if they were considering a present, she would really like it if they instead donated the amount they would have spent to the playground. The organizers reported receiving $435.00 in donations due to her thoughtful and generous act.

In contrast, my sister recently told me another story with a slightly different ending about a situation at the school where she works.

In the class that she teaches there are two children who were among many left homeless after a fire in a not-so-upscale apartment complex. One family recently immigrated to Canada, the other was headed by a single mother who had recently left an abusive relationship. Barely making ends meet, neither family had insurance on the contents of their respective apartments. As a result, they lost everything except the clothes on their backs. Left homeless, they were eventually given two weeks of temporary shelter in a hotel nowhere near their home and left on their own to figure out how to pay for restaurant meals, get their kids to school, and find and furnish a new place to live.

My sister, who has a heart of gold, made it her mission to rally support at her school and passed an envelope among her colleagues. The total collection mustered was a disappointing $120.00.

The two disparate stories made me wonder about the differences and what we can do to nurture more compassion and philanthropy in today's society. After all, to feel compassion for one another is what makes us human. And yet, in an era of mass media, we see so many horrific images that as violence and bad news escalates, it seems we are in danger of becoming desensitized, turning a less than sympathetic eye to the pain and suffering of others.

This seems to result in a culture that too often reflects more callousness and less kindness and philanthropy.

Why do we need to teach kindness and compassion to our children as well as keep our own compassion alive?

Compassion is necessary for us to survive as a species and for our individual spiritual growth. After all, how can we grow as human beings if we don't experience deep compassion for others?

It may be something that each of us needs to work at constantly in order to make sure we keep compassion and philanthropy alive and strong in our hearts.

Vijai Sharma says that, "Whenever we see or hear, directly or indirectly, about people facing hardship or impacted by a tragedy, we need to make sure we don't let it pass without at least giving some thought to what they and their loved ones may be experiencing."[51] If

---

51 http://mindpub.com/art302.htm. Accessed November 2011.

we are someone who prays, we should include them in our prayers. If we have children, we can express our feelings and thoughts about it to them. If they ask questions, we can answer them to the best of our ability and be grateful that they are expressing interest in their fellow beings. Those in community leadership positions can ensure that compassion, as well as dollars, are factors in prioritizing and decision-making.

My sister hasn't given up on her colleagues and is working to keep her compassion and philanthropy front and centre by brainstorming fundraising ideas that will involve her students. She's also making connections to social service agencies to find those who can help. Moved by her compassion, members of our own family have made donations.

As for the little girl who gave up birthday presents so kids in her community could have a new playground, two anonymous donors heard about her generosity and have since presented her with a $1000 education scholarship.

 **Chapter 8**

Competency 2: Commitment to Continuous Improvement

Practices ongoing personal and professional growth and development

COMPETENCY AREA	INDICATORS TO HELP YOU UNDERSTAND WHAT ENCOMPASSES THIS COMPETENCY	1 = I AM NOT AT ALL LIKE THAT	10 = I AM 100% LIKE THAT
2 Commitment to Continuous Improvement	2.1 I actively seek feedback from others regarding my performance.	1 2 3 4 5 6 7 8 9 10	
	2.2 I participate in new opportunities to improve and grow.	1 2 3 4 5 6 7 8 9 10	
	2.3 I place a priority on scanning for trends, issues, and promising practices.	1 2 3 4 5 6 7 8 9 10	
	2.4 I actively seek information, resources, and opportunities that will enhance my knowledge and broaden my perspective.	1 2 3 4 5 6 7 8 9 10	
	2.5 I initiate and maintain networks with other practitioners, service providers, and community leaders.	1 2 3 4 5 6 7 8 9 10	
	2.6 I am able to present myself using a format which best identifies my brand e.g. skills, knowledge, attributes, and experience.	1 2 3 4 5 6 7 8 9 10	
	2.7 I am able to articulate my personal values.	1 2 3 4 5 6 7 8 9 10	
	2.8 I model integrity and ethical behavior.	1 2 3 4 5 6 7 8 9 10	
	2.9 I understand that my heritage and life experiences can provide me with learning.	1 2 3 4 5 6 7 8 9 10	
	2.10 I promote the value of learning for myself and others.	1 2 3 4 5 6 7 8 9 10	
	2.11 I have life and career goals and a plan for attaining them.	1 2 3 4 5 6 7 8 9 10	
	2.12 I have a professional development plan for learning that will enhance the effectiveness of my leadership.	1 2 3 4 5 6 7 8 9 10	
	2.13 I participate in opportunities for mentoring.	1 2 3 4 5 6 7 8 9 10	
	2.14 I have a healthy life balance and practice self-care.	1 2 3 4 5 6 7 8 9 10	
	2.15 I actively participate in professional associations and the acquisition of relevant professional certification.	1 2 3 4 5 6 7 8 9 10	
	2.16 I adhere to organizational codes of conduct, core values and professional codes of ethics.	1 2 3 4 5 6 7 8 9 10	

Seek Feedback from Others Regarding Performance

Although I try really hard to avoid it, too often these days I find myself doing a little too much just-in-time, management-by-the-seat-of-my-pants. While often challenging, it only works because our team is pretty much a just-in-time workforce.

And, while it means we're nimble and entrepreneurial, it in turn is driving a need for just-in-time-feedback. The feedback we need in our day-to-day work, as well as in our individual performances, can't always wait until the next meeting or the next performance review. Recently it became apparent that feedback sometimes even needs to happen on the fly.

We were on an Aboriginal reserve delivering a community building workshop. Those in attendance were hungry for learning and ready to capitalize on their strengths as well to address the challenges within their community. Knowing the change they desired requires thinking about community leadership in a different way, I asked participants to share examples of the skills, knowledge, and attitudes they wanted to see in their leaders.

Normally, that question prompts all kinds of immediate answers. However in this instance, it seemed to be a tough question. Sensing a stumbling block, the woman responsible for hosting the workshop put up her hand and provided some valuable feedback. She said that perhaps we should answer that question not just by thinking about leaders as being members of the Band Council. She instead suggested to participants that they think of leaders as being those they turn to when they need help or when something needs to get done.

We also asked participants to think about the qualities they personally could bring that would be important to leadership. Well, that certainly unleashed a lot of answers they hadn't been able to generate when they were only thinking about those who held the formal positions of leadership. It was truly valuable feedback as it made the exercise relevant and helped participants think about real leaders in their community.

At the end of the day, when our team debriefed the workshop, we talked about the importance of welcoming and being receptive to constructive feedback. While few of us enjoy hearing about what might amount to our shortcomings, our powers of self-perception only go so far. Others around us notice things that we might not, and we can learn from their input. In fact, the more we actively seek feedback, the more we grow.

In addition to welcoming and being receptive to feedback, we've also learned it just doesn't work to tell a person why their feedback is wrong, or to argue, deny, or justify.

On the other hand, while feedback can be a gift allowing you to grow and develop, some feedback is best ignored. For instance, we asked all workshop participants to complete a feedback form at the end of the day. Typically they are quite positive or provide constructive suggestions for how the workshop could be improved. However, there are usually one or two suggestions that simply don't resonate. While I used to obsess about the negative feedback, I've had to keep it in perspective, learn to let it go, and resist making changes just to appease one individual who might just have been having a bad day.

In addition to receiving feedback, we've all had to learn how to give it. We refuse to be the kind of team who ignores issues that need to be discussed. As a result we're all getting better at selecting the right time and place to provide feedback. We've also learned that you can provide tough and honest feedback in a kind way.

As a team we have also discovered a number of simple but valuable questions that are guaranteed to gather or give valuable feedback in almost any setting including individual performance reviews. These include asking, "What am I doing right that I should continue?", "What should I stop doing?", and "What could I do better?"

Providing meeting feedback typically includes questions such as: "What did we *do*?", "Overall, how do we *feel*?", "What did we *learn*?", "What does it *mean*?" and "How will what we learned *impact* what we do?"

As we did on the reserve, we just need to continue to stop and ask ourselves, and one another, questions that are deliberately designed to seek feedback. Doing that will keep reminding us why feedback is the shortest word in the English language that contains the letters: abcdef. No surprise then that it is such an essential component of community leadership.

Participate in New Opportunities to Improve and Grow

Although I no longer work there, I am delighted that Niagara College has on multiple occasions won the distinction of being number one in overall student satisfaction among all colleges in Ontario. Additionally, it's clear that employers are satisfied with their graduates.

Shortly after hearing of their most recent win, I happened to end up on a long and solitary drive, and had time to reflect on my own education and its role in general. I realized that while my own college and university education has been an important foundation, most of the skills and knowledge I use to earn my living today are those I've learned outside of formal education.

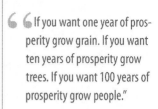

> If you want one year of prosperity grow grain. If you want ten years of prosperity grow trees. If you want 100 years of prosperity grow people."
>
> — Chinese Proverb

Among others these include information technology, relationship building, systems-thinking, analyzing and synthesizing data, community leadership, planning, story-telling, personal productivity, team-building, and even teaching.

This is not about tooting my own horn or taking shots at colleges and universities because if you stop to think about it, a lot of what everyone knows is picked up on their own. Rarely, however, do we think about what it takes to become self-taught.

It is perhaps a question we all need to be thinking about.

I do know that when I was teaching at Niagara College, a commitment to ongoing learning was something some of us tried to instill in students. Unfortunately, our efforts were sometimes met with mixed reactions as most students seemed convinced that it was the degree or diploma that would be their ticket to success. Too often it seemed there were students more comfortable with an education system that measured success and gave them a piece of paper for their ability to memorize and regurgitate specific information.

For me, however, teaching also needed to be about promoting an excitement about learning, analysis, thinking, and innovative solutions. As a result, and to the surprise of some, I often implemented take-home and open book exams. It left many students stumped and scratching their heads. Some, who were used to being honour students but didn't perform well on my assignments and tests, insisted on knowing exactly where the answers were covered in their textbook

On the flip side, there were often results that showed clever and creative thinking. Ironically, some of the best came from students who others had labeled as disruptive underachievers.

So what should we be thinking about including in our curriculums if we are to encourage self-directed, life-long learning? How can we encourage everyone to seek opportunities to grow?

> " You cannot discover new oceans unless you have the courage to lose sight of the shore."
>
> — Lord Chesterfield

If we can graduate students who have a learning attitude in place, their lifelong learning will be a matter of knowing how to research (with Google as a search engine and http://www.wikipedia.com this has become so much easier), listening well in order to "know what we don't know", and staying in touch with experts through reading, networking, and technology.

Once new knowledge is acquired we need to teach how to put it into practice in order to better understand now, and remember more later. For me, writing a weekly newspaper column and blog is a way of applying what I learn each week. For others, the practice strategies will be different.

We also need to ensure graduates who understand the importance and how-to's of developing networks and professional relationships. One of the most powerful sources of knowledge and understanding in my life has been my network of colleagues. They are crucial to challenging my thinking, identifying trends and issues, extending my knowledge, and for referring me to contacts in areas where I need to learn more.

It is essential as well to convey the importance of scheduling time for learning. Having the books on the shelf, websites bookmarked, and a strong network won't help if there isn't a commitment to giving oneself the time to focus on reading, digesting, and implementing knowledge.

As we transition from an industrial-based economy to one where know-how, expertise and intellectual property are more critical, life-long learning will be essential for everyone especially community leaders. As the Wikipedia experts say, lifelong learning is the concept that "It's never too soon or too late for learning".[52]

Passion Fuels Improvement and Growth

Our commitment to improve and grow is much higher when our individual passions and interests align with our job. While our individual and family security is important, it is equally as important to have job opportunities that challenge us to learn and grow. Sometimes those opportunities may involve tough decisions.

Several years ago my husband and I made the difficult decision to leave Welland. We not only left the building, we left the region, and the province. We pulled up stakes and moved from Ontario to Edmonton, Alberta. Even though we didn't expect it to be a permanent move, it was still a tough call. The reality is that we love Niagara and we especially love Welland.

Not everyone understood—not only because it was Edmonton, but also because it was a job opportunity for me rather than for my husband that was the catalyst for the move. And even though my husband's picture framing and art gallery was doing okay, being self-employed takes its toll, requiring a lot of hard work and a lot of hours. Consequently, he too was ready for a change.

For me, the best part is that anyone who really knows me and how passionate I am about community development and community leadership, immediately understood the decision and provided unconditional support and encouragement.

As a result, although I was doubly blessed with both the support of my wonderful husband and family, and the best wishes of friends and colleagues, there were others who thought there were woodchips in the windmill of my mind.

It has, without a doubt, been a great adventure so far. One of my brothers once said that projects are good for a relationship. I think he's right. Our journey across the country was good for my husband and I. We had a lot of time together that allowed for quality conversations. Additionally we had to work together to make decisions

---

52 http://en.wikipedia.org/wiki/Glossary_of_education-related_terms_(G-L). Accessed September 2010.

and get things accomplished. And, since we've arrived and settled in, there certainly has been no shortage of projects.

The weather during the trip was gorgeous and the scenery was spectacular. My son told me that he believed every Canadian should drive across the country at least once in their life.

My new work is pretty close to perfect. Whereas in Ontario, the concept of community development isn't always well understood, it is accepted here in Alberta. This means that instead of working to convince others that community development and empowering citizens is the way to go, my work here is about supporting community leaders with the training and resources they need to make their communities stronger, healthier, and more creative. It is absolutely the best match with my skills and interests I could ever hope to find. I am happy and relaxed. Life is good.

As business guru Tom Peters wrote in his book *Thriving on Chaos*,[53] it's important for everyone to ask two questions: 1) Have I made a difference in the last two years and 2) Am I having fun yet? If the answer is no, you still have work to do.

One of the most important things I learned as the result of that exercise is that it's never too late to try something new. Adventures aren't exclusively for the young. Leaving a good job and moving across the country does tend to add a little excitement to one's life!

It also taught me that it's okay to follow your heart even it if means leaving a good job and a good place. In fact, it's better than okay as in my case it led to financial rewards greater than I had imagined and meaningful work that is a perfect fit with my interests, skills, and experience.

Taking a leap of faith to move across the country also taught me about the importance of letting go. I think my focus on fixing and finding solutions took up so much room in my life it crowded out any other possibilities. I had to learn to listen to my instincts, let go, and have enough faith and trust in myself that I would be able to figure it out.

---

53   Peters, T. (1987). *Thriving on chaos*. New York: HarperCollins.

Community Leadership Programs

While education and jobs are two ways of finding opportunities to grow, learnings can also be found in less formal settings.

Community leadership programs[54] can be found across North America. My personal experience came with Leadership Niagara—a distinctive program designed as a collaborative effort to address the root causes of Niagara challenges, and to build on their assets by bringing together a cohort of leading-edge, systems-thinking leaders from the public, private, and social-profit sectors.

Despite the diversity of the participants in the community leadership programs, they typically share a lot in common. They have all been identified as leaders within their respective organizational or business environments, are committed to making a difference in their communities, and they are keen to learn and grow—from the content of the program as well as each other.

> "Become at ease with the state of not knowing."
>
> — Eckhart Tolle

As it turns out, this propensity for learning and growing is a trait they share with leaders everywhere. Research confirms that the best leaders are those who continually grow.[55]

Jessica, a bright and articulate social service program manager was one of the participants who has spent a good part of her life stretching and growing. In order to receive a degree she deemed to be meaningful, Jessica customized her course load, ultimately attending six different universities before graduating.

However, as Jessica has discovered and as research has identified, real leadership development also needs to incorporate time for reflection and analysis.[56] Thus the need for community leadership programs that encompass a retreat component.

Like the other participants, Jessica was learning before she even got to the Leadership Niagara retreat as the result of a number of pre-assignments. In addition to a number of readings about leadership,

---

54 For more information see http://www.cclnet.org.

55 Retrieved http://www.expertmagazine.com/artman/publish/article_832.html.

56 Densten, I. & Gray, J. H. (2001). Leadership development and reflection: What is the connection?, *International Journal of Educational Management*, Vol. 15 Issue: 3, pp.119 – 124.

participants were required to do an online assessment that would help them understand their personal learning style.

When Jessica's assessment indicated her preferred learning style did not show a predilection for analysis and reflection, she initiated deliberate attempts to ensure she did. By way of example, while she admits she would normally be one of the first to jump into a discussion, at the opening of the retreat she disciplined herself to sit back and practice reflection. Then throughout the course of the retreat, when a comment from a facilitator or participant pushed her buttons, instead of instantly responding, she would ask herself why the comment rankled and then would analyze her response.

In addition to this deeper understanding of themselves as leaders, participants of this kind of a program graduate with a greater understanding of what it means to be a community leader. Their take-away skills and knowledge include learning more about the trends and issues, how to ensure a more proactive approach to developing collaborative relationships and alliances, an enhanced ability to generate creative solutions and lead change and transition, and a commitment to promoting and strengthening their community.

Informal Learning

I learned of an even more informal approach to growth from a colleague—a warm, kind, and intelligent woman unique in spirit as well as wardrobe, she was often referred to as the "last of the flower children". She is a woman who, by her own admission, would never be described as a "fashionista". She has a tendency to favour shawls, colourful hats, and printed, gauzy, floor length skirts and dresses.

One can imagine our surprise then, when on day two of one of our meetings, Paula arrived without a hat or shawl wearing a rather corporate looking navy blue suit.

Curious, I complimented her on the suit and asked her about her new look. Paula went on to explain that it all started when a friend of hers decided to celebrate her 50th birthday with a list of things she wants to do before she dies. Her friend's list included a lot of things Paula already considers to be part of her life—a winter picnic, getting up early to watch a sunrise, and reading poetry to her children.

Regardless, it got Paula thinking about what would be on her own list—thus the suit.

And, while it's true no one really wants to think about dying, the exercise of thinking about what would be on one's personal list of things to do before you die is a good one.

The incident also got me thinking about my own list as well as the type of things everyone might want to think about including:

Leave a legacy. Plant a tree, write a book, fund a scholarship or a bench in the park. Really think about what you are passionate about, what it is that brings you joy, and then figure out how you can use that to give back to others. If you do, you'll end up being part of an even bigger legacy. Complete your family tree. Be someone's mentor or teach someone to read. Memorize a poem and pass it on. An inspiring actor, our youngest son is teaching me snippets from Shakespeare. Give to a charity. If that doesn't inspire you, think about it this way—give someone the opportunity you missed.

Do something that scares the heck out of you. Two people I know recently jumped out of plane. One of them said it was better than sex, but most of us might want to consider something a little less risky. Go skinny dipping or white water rafting. Ski a black diamond run, ride a roller coaster, sing a song or deliver a speech in front of an audience. Ask someone you've only just met to go on a date. Ask for a raise or ask those who you work with to evaluate you. In others words, climb something you were afraid to climb and see something new.

Learn a new skill. Commit to lifelong learning. Sign up for a computer or history course. Learn yoga, golf, or how to play a musical instrument. If you can believe it, my mother recently told me her that her one regret in life was never learning to tap dance.

Say thank you. Write a fan letter to your all-time favourite hero or heroine. Thank someone who made a difference in your life. Call a teacher or coach who believed in you. Send your mother a dozen roses when it isn't mother's day or her birthday.

Spend a day indulging. Spend an entire day reading a good book. Drink wine, eat junk food, chocolate, or a meal fine enough to be your last. Buy one expensive but absolutely wonderful outfit that makes you feel like a million bucks. Invest in a manicure, pedicure, facial, massage, or all of the above.

Do something goofy. Send a message in a bottle. Sleep under the stars. Learn to juggle with three balls. March in a parade. Play with a yo-yo or a hula hoop. Blow bubbles. Set off fireworks. Drive your car around town with the windows down and the music blaring.

Forgive someone who hurt you. Forgive yourself for everything you wish you'd done differently.

Why choose to do any of these? The point is that leaders should never be afraid to try something new.

Scan for Trends and Issues

One of the most important things a community leader can do is pay attention. It is especially important to pay attention to trends and issues.

Some two hundred and fifty years ago Thomas Gray wrote "Where ignorance is bliss, tis folly to be wise." I'm not buying it. These days ignorance is not bliss. Given the current pace of change, being ignorant is more likely to be a risky business.

By way of example, I recently had a conversation with a senior bureaucrat in a small municipality who had been invited by the Mayor to take a leadership role in facilitating the involvement of residents in a community-wide strategic plan. The employee instead chose to opt-out, explaining that he wasn't comfortable in the role. Whereas, he seemed to believe staying below the radar was a safe choice, had he been paying attention to trends related to citizen engagement, he would have jumped on the opportunity. His ignorance of an important trend meant he neither took on the challenge of responsibility to motivate himself to learn more, nor did he understand the potential promise of the new role.

Today, everyone needs to be a trendwatcher as success and innovation in almost every business, government, or social-profit organization requires identifying trends before they fully emerge. For some it is a no-brainer as their curiosity is part of their genetic makeup. However for others it may require some specific strategies.

So, how does one become a trendwatcher?

It is important to first understand that a trend is a pattern or general direction that one sees from past events and their frequency. It is also essential that once a trend has been identified, its potential impact and influence on your business, organization, or community must be analyzed. If you can identify a trend three to five years in advance, the dividends could be significant.

Begin by becoming comfortable with macro trends or those occurring on a larger scale. Pay attention to demographic information, changes in the economy, differences in the political landscape, new technologies, and mainstream media and culture.

Technology has made it much simpler to watch and scan for trends. Subscribe to relevant newsletters or listservs or explore websites that track trends on a regular basis. I use Statistics Canada, trendhunter.com, fastcompany.com, and trendwatching.com. I also follow a number of trend watchers on Twitter. Google Alert is also a valuable tool that brings you search results from the web based on your choice of query or topic.

Read or at least scan the daily newspaper. When driving I also typically listen to CBC to learn more about what's making news across Canada. I also pay close attention to best-selling books related to trends. Most significantly, I make a point of hanging out with smart people who are ahead of the curve.

While having a handle on the bigger picture is critical, it is also important to be clear about what you are collecting trends about and then to go deeper within that area. As a business owner my husband looks for information about consumer trends, whereas I track trends related to leadership and community development. It is essential that you know your interest or industry and follow its unique trends via journals, newsletters, and listservs.

It is also important to read about sectors or industries beyond your own. When I taught at Niagara College I used to periodically visit the bookstore and scan the textbooks and resources from other programs.

Good trend watchers also pay attention to the "word on the street". I've often found the most relevant information comes from the grassroots of communities. For instance, I'm sure it was close to fifteen years ago that a local sport store owner told me that we needed to start considering skateboard parks as being as foundational to a community as tennis courts, arenas, and baseball diamonds. He definitely got that right.

You don't have to like every trend and you also need to be careful that you don't dismiss anything too quickly. Instead of dismissing, ask questions and learn more.

Once you are aware of the trends, ask yourself how each of these trends could impact or change your sphere of influence. For instance, we know the birthrate in Canada is slowing except in immigrant and aboriginal families. What could that mean in terms of potential for your business, community, or organization? Think about how it could potentially impact or influence your company, organization, or community's vision and direction. Could it lead to a new concept, product, service, program or initiative, or could it mean changes are needed in those that already exist?

Of course, while it is impossible to predict the future, it is possible to use a combination of analysis and logic to better understand what's happening today in order to exploit trends as possibilities. As business guru Peter Drucker once said, "I never predict. I just look out the window and see what is visible but not yet seen."

Enhance Your Knowledge and Broaden Your Perspective

That balanced lifestyle I've been trying so hard to achieve has definitely been on the backburner as implementing strategies for ensuring active, creative, and engaged communities has gradually and insidiously taken over big chunks of my life.

While it's been fun, its complexity has been taxing. Sometimes I really do miss the days when work was more straightforward. Like a lot of things these days, it has become complicated as the result of accelerating change and information overload. Just as our initiative requires a team able to demonstrate out-of the box and non-linear thinking to solve increasingly complex challenges, so too does our world in general.

Additionally, our work is making it even clearer that the knowledge and tools from any one discipline aren't enough for understanding and solving real world problems. In our case, we've highlighted the need for interdisciplinary expertise and teams from recreation, culture, parks, health, education, social services, government, and business to work together on common goals and collective impact.

The nature of our work is also a reminder that just as our communities need to respond to change, so too will educators. We will need educators willing to reevaluate the goals of education and the type of minds that need to be cultivated in order to widen our perspective.

Harvard professor, Howard Gardner, famous for his theories of multiple intelligences, tackled this same subject in his book entitled *Five Minds for the Future.*[57] In it he describes five kinds of minds, or ways of thinking and acting. They are not personality types, but ways of thinking available to anyone willing to invest the time and effort in cultivating them. Three of the five minds are related to intellect— the *disciplined mind, the synthesizing mind,* and *the creative mind.* The other two are more about character—the *respectful mind,* and the *ethical mind.*

Gardner, in speaking of the *disciplined mind,* is referring to our need to understand history, math, science, and art. Since it's understood these ways of thinking are challenging to learn and require practice, schools have focused a lot of energy on this kind of thinking.

Even with knowledge of a discipline, there is a need to sort out what is important and what isn't from the massive amount of available information. This is definitely the kind of mind needed by our team as we work to distill the information required for ACE Communities. Gardner refers to this as the *synthesizing mind.* With a synthesizing mind, we are able to make sense of what we have learned, and can convey it to others when needed.

Once we have learned and synthesized knowledge in a discipline, there is a need to think outside the box of that discipline—the *creative mind.* Creativity allows for innovation or meaningful change in how problems are approached. A creative person takes chances but also needs to be prepared for the negative feedback that, if used appropriately, will contribute to progress.

The two additional minds Gardner feels that we too often fail to cultivate in school are the ones that emphasize the human sphere or personal character. The first is the *respectful mind* which, for Gardner,

---

57   Gardner, H. (2005) *Five minds for the future.* Harvard, Mass: Harvard Business School Publishing.

is more than tolerance of differences. It is about cultivating respect as well as emotional and interpersonal intelligence for interacting with one another.

While respect is something even young children can practice in schools, ethics and the *ethical mind* requires more abstract and reflective thinking about one's behaviour. Later in life as we enter the labour force, regardless of the type of work, each person needs to stand back and ask what needs to be done to ensure their work is excellent in quality and ethical in conduct, and then follow through with those responsibilities.

There is a pressing need for all community leaders to do more to cultivate the five minds—particularly the respectful and the responsible minds. Nurturing each of these minds will help ensure that existing and future generations are willing and able to widen their perspective and meet the unknown challenges of the future.

Maintain Networks with Other Practitioners, Service Providers, and Community Leaders

Networks can increase efficiency and impact, spread ideas, generate feedback, strengthen capacity, and mobilize diverse individuals or organizations.

Some time ago, I was one of two Niagara College representatives who met with forty other participants from across the country for two days of meetings hosted by the Association of Canadian Community Colleges (ACCC) and the federal government department now known as Human Resources and Skills Development Canada (HRSDC).

While I was there to represent the social-profit sector, I met an extraordinarily interesting group of college "affinity group" leaders involved in providing training and support as diverse as our country itself. The group also included staff from other colleges who worked in agriculture, apparel, aviation, culture, environment, fisheries, petroleum, law enforcement, renewable energy, tourism, and more.

So what we're they thinking? Why go to the expense of bringing together such a diverse group from across the country?

As with a lot of things these days, it was actually about saving money. Like many top corporations such as IBM, Shell, World Bank, and Xerox, ACCC identified that success and innovation is more likely to occur when employees participate in networks or "communities of practice". Shell has actually been able to document $3 million in savings and $2 million in innovations that were the direct result of networks. Other businesses report that networks have resulted in higher quality decisions, forecasts for new developments, and higher retention rates of professionals.[58]

Probably most importantly, the vast body of knowledge required for any field these days is growing so rapidly it is almost impossible for any single individual to master it. The need for multiple perspectives is a critical contribution that networks can make to any profession. As such, they are a very practical and cost effective way to manage and transfer knowledge.

To further hedge their bets that learning and innovation would take place during the Ottawa meetings, ACCC enriched the pot by ensuring both vertical and horizontal networks participated.

Whereas I was representing a distinct *vertical* network, meaning colleges involved in social-profit sector training and support, some were representing a *horizontal* network of colleges engaged in recognizing the prior workplace learning of individuals. Rather than serving one vertical sector, these groups impacted horizontally across all of them.

While networks certainly can't replace strong institutions, it may be that vertical and horizontal networks provide a better vehicle than traditional hierarchies for learning and growing. The Ottawa networking allowed us to get to know and build bridges to our colleagues from across the country and to exchange ideas and best practices.

Communities of Practice (CoP) are another form of networks. Lave and Wenger first coined the term in their 1991 book entitled *Situated Learning.*[59]

---

58   Wenger, E., McDermott, R., & Snyder, W. (2002). *Cultivating communities of practice.* Boston: Harvard School Press.

59   Lave, J. and Wenger, E. (1991). *Situated learning: Legitimate participation.* Cambridge, England: Cambridge University Press.

They define communities of practice as a group of professionals informally bound together by shared expertise and a passion for a joint enterprise including common challenges and the pursuit of solutions. CoPs generally have a common sense of purpose as a group of colleagues committed to building, solving problems, learning, and inventing together. In my experience, they are more about being a community that learns, rather than learning informally as peers who exchange ideas around a water cooler.

In my experience with ACE Communities, our CoPs reflect mutual respect, between and among us, and a lot of laughter. We take the time to really talk and reflect about what each of us thinks is important. We listen to each other, even if there are differences, knowing we are accepted and not judged by the others in the conversation. We spend a lot of time sharing learning and resources.

It is also clear we are working within a culture where it is okay to make mistakes because learning is valued as much as success. We explore questions that matter and develop a shared meaning that wasn't there when we began. Essentially it is a very powerful yet informal kind of learning that enhances our collective knowledge.

I see it as a very special kind of network that will keep us on the cutting edge by helping us sort out what we pay attention to, what we participate in, and what we stay away from.

It is also interesting to note that research indicates network leadership isn't traditional or hierarchal in nature. Instead it is much more about leadership that is shared or distributed across the network, peer to peer. If the networks showcased by ACCC are any example, this seems to be something that might be more intuitive for women than men.

In fact, the greatest examples of "best practices" came from networks that were predominately female. Regardless, if networks are to be successful, both men and women will need to listen, ensure there is capacity to facilitate processes, and an ability to allow co-creation to happen.

It is also true that not everyone will be attracted to networks. They will appeal most to those like me who are curious by nature, and think it is a waste of time and energy to re-invent the wheel. It is also likely that networking will only be important to those who are committed to improving the quality of learning and the services they provide and see the exchanges as having value for their own organization or community.

Additionally, networks will be challenging for those who like rules, order, and structure. The reality of networks is that they can sometimes be a bit messy and chaotic as well as take time to produce breakthrough results.

In many ways, technology has made networking much more efficient. But even then, we need to ask ourselves whether or not online networking could ever replace the value of face-to-face sharing. Perhaps not. However, for community leaders, networks are incredibly valuable as they reinforce that we aren't alone and teach us that together really is better.

Presenting Yourself and Your Brand

As you now know, I am an information junkie. On the bright side, this commitment to lifelong learning is quite compatible with working as a consultant as I've learned that if I'm willing to do training for others, I typically get access to other conferences and workshops that are often beyond the scope of my training budget. As a result, in exchange for delivering a session, I recently found myself at a provincial conference listening to a dynamic speaker named Mitch Joel who is president of Twist Image, a Montreal-based marketing agency.

I wasn't quite sure what to expect but was definitely intrigued by the description of Mitch Joel as being a marketing and communications visionary, an interactive expert, community leader, freelance journalist, blogger, podcaster, and believer in the impossible.

His keynote was entitled "Building a Legacy" and his opening statement was actually a question.

Joel asked the audience if they had a personal brand? Most seemed somewhat stumped by the question until he showed us a picture of a young man who was wearing a nametag that said: "Hello my name is Scott". Not in itself all that unusual, but Joel went on to explain that Scott Ginsberg is featured in Ripley's Believe It or Not.

As Joel told it, Ginsberg found wearing a nametag to be a simple way to connect with people. Consequently he has been wearing a nametag 24/7 since November 2, 2000. Rumour has it that he also has "Hello my name is Scott" tattooed on his chest. Scott's resulting personal brand as an expert on approachability and networking has translated into a lucrative career as a speaker and author of six books.

Joel suggests that developing one's personal brand as successfully as Scott has done, requires the elements of three types of conversations coming together—personal, one-to-one, and one-to-many.

The first conversation is an internal one. Each of us needs to think about our own values, beliefs, and goals or, in other words, answer the question, "What's your story?" He suggests writing down your story and sharing it with others. If they don't get the real you after reading that story, you need to ask yourself what it is that you aren't communicating clearly.

Underlying this exercise is the idea that each of us is unique and we need to be able to communicate that uniqueness as clearly and concisely as possible. If we don't know what makes us unique, we need to figure it out.

To emphasize this point, he shared a quote by Barry, a member of a rock band named Three Days Grace who sports a Mohawk and a collection of piercings and tattoos. Barry said, "You look at me and laugh because I'm different. I look at you and laugh because you're all the same."

Once you have a handle on your story—what you do and how you provide value, you need to be able to communicate it clearly and concisely to others in one-to-one conversations. He refers to this as your "elevator pitch" meaning it needs to be both short and memorable so you can deliver it within the time of a typical elevator ride. As Joel puts it, if it's not memorable, it is invisible.

He also advises, contrary to what we all heard from our parents, we should talk to strangers, recommending we spend 80 percent of our time with people we don't know.

As for having conversations with many, not surprisingly Joel is a huge advocate of technology claiming each of us are only six pixels of separation away from anyone we want to meet. He is a believer in social networking and the power of online communities.

While facebook.com and myspace.com have been huge attractors for young people today, he also recommends every adult register at linkedin.com.

Mitch Joel definitely made me think about branding in a different way. I now know that branding isn't just for big companies like Coke and Tim Horton's. We are all brands and each of us needs to learn how to make our brand shine. While resumes will always be important, we'll also need to think about presenting ourselves in ways that set us apart as unique and valuable individuals.

Know and Live Your Values

My husband and I are very different. He's pretty reserved, quiet, analytical, and task oriented. I, on the other hand, am more outgoing, impulsive, systems-thinking, and action oriented. Despite these and other differences, we are good together. Somehow we've managed over the past twenty years to raise a complicated blended family, run a number of businesses, support each other's careers, and remain best friends. In hindsight, what appears to make it work are the values we share.

In our case, we value family. While sometimes detrimental to a career path, it has always meant family comes first. When I first met my husband, he was a single parent responsible for two young sons. Working for an engineering firm, he had previously turned down an opportunity to move to Toronto because it would take the kids away from their extended family. Some people wouldn't understand that decision, but I do.

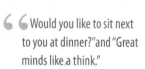

Would you like to sit next to you at dinner?" and "Great minds like a think."

— Ads promoting the weekly magazine, the Economist

We also share similar values about the importance of treating others with kindness and respect, the need for honest and authentic communication, and having a responsibility to give back to our communities in the form of volunteer service. We are like-minded about spending money—we're both pretty conservative and have no desire to "live large". A key value for us is that we also share a belief in the importance of hard work.

Just as individuals subscribe to values, so too do organizations, businesses, and communities. And, if recent signs are to be believed, values are going to become increasingly important in our workplaces. Anecdotal evidence suggests that today employees are looking for an organization or business that fits who they are and what they stand for. Additionally, as workplace and community issues become more complex, it will be the *values* that are essential for making the tough decisions required to deal with today's increasing complexities.

Developing, adopting, and implementing values has been identified as perhaps the single key in the success of many social-profit organizations as well as high growth, high profit companies.

Implementing values energizes everything concerned with it. On an individual basis, articulating and applying values can boost and attract success, achievement, and well-being. Likewise, when companies, organizations, or communities adopt values, their people, products, services, and stakeholders become invigorated.

Essentially, values communicate beliefs, expectations, and a basis for action—definitely a values-added proposition.

For me, values and principles are the filters that help us make important decisions. It is much easier to make decisions when you know your values. Even this week, as I begin work with new team members, I suggested integrating introductory activities that would lead to a discussion about our respective personal and business values.

Not everyone agrees it's a good place to start, suggesting those are rather personal questions. There's no doubt they are personal. But leadership is personal and I've learned the hard way that working with individuals or even within an organization with values that don't align can be extraordinarily painful for everyone. It seems far simpler to be up front about one's own values as well as to know what other people value.

So what exactly are values? Generally a value is a belief you are proud of and willing to affirm. It is also something that is more than talk because it is also about regularly taking action on that belief.

Ultimately it's what you stand for. Those who read what I write will know that professionally I value community leadership, community building, lifelong learning, and empowering others.

I also need to align my personal values by working with people and for organizations that demonstrate respect for people, responsiveness, kindness, honesty, transparency, shared leadership, teamwork, personal accountability, and hard work.

How does one find one's own values?

It won't be something you can google or find in a book. Instead it involves deep thinking about who you are and what is important to you. Chances are you'll find your values in your own mind, in your heart, and in your soul.

Model Integrity and Ethical Behaviour

Billionaire Warren Buffet says he looks for three things in hiring people. The first is personal integrity, the second is intelligence, and the third is a high energy level. "But", he went on to say, "If you don't have the first, the other two will kill you".[60]

During recent years, a number of political sexual scandals have proven him right. While many caught up in these scandals have had a lot going on for themselves in terms of intelligence and energy, In the end it was a lack of personal integrity that brought them down.

The price for these indiscretions is often the loss of their jobs, and sometimes even their families. There are some who believe this price is too steep, suggesting that many other men have been outed for using call girls without being publicly humiliated and losing their jobs.

While there may be some truth to that thinking, the reality is that being elected to a high profile position requires a lot of trust. When a leader violates that trust, they often lose the position. Not because they can't do the job and obtain results, but because they've done something that most people consider to be lacking in integrity, or is unethical or immoral.

When we think about integrity we often use the term interchangeably with honesty. While it definitely is about honesty, it is also about walking your talk. It is an alignment of one's personal values and beliefs with what we say and do. Your reputation is built on this foundation of integrity and you don't want it to be a shaky one.

---

60 Buffet, W. Retrieved August 2010 http://www.intelligentinvestorclub.com/downloads/ Warren-Buffett-Florida-Speech.pdf.

6 6 Integrity is one of several paths, it distinguishes itself from the others because it is the right path, and the only one upon which you will never get lost."

— M.H. McKee

It is this lack of integrity that should be the focus of the media coverage and discussion but typically isn't.

Community leaders will need to talk about values, integrity, and ethics. If they don't, young people especially will be at risk for remaining in a state of perpetual confusion about what is or isn't the right thing to do.

Know Your Heritage and the Learning it Provides

American novelist, James Arthur Baldwin once said, "Know from whence you came. If you know whence you came, there are absolutely no limitations to where you can go."

Leading others in your community requires a confident and authentic leader who has a solid understanding of who they are and what they stand for as well as how they have been shaped by their own heritage and upbringing.

I thought more about this during a recent pajama party with my colleagues from work. Although it has been many years since my last one, our all-female team (we're working hard to change that) needed some intense planning time. As a result, one of our staff offered up their family cottage for our staff retreat. At virtually no cost, it allowed us two days of uninterrupted work as well as some fun bonding time.

Although it seemed like a good idea at the time, I learned I'm much too old for sleepovers. It took me another two days to fully recover from the aftereffects of too little sleep and too much good food. And, in the interest of full disclosure, probably just a little too much wine. Regardless, it was an atmosphere that facilitated deep productivity as well as deep reflection.

In the wee hours of the morning, as several of us shared more details of our lives, we learned that despite very different personalities, there was a common denominator in our backgrounds. In our respective childhoods each of us recounted stories that reflected us as being energetic, confident, and ready to take on the world.

In my case, I told them how it was me who would organize all the kids on our block to produce plays and carnivals. I recounted how we would hike, bike, build rafts, race, and play together. I kept up with the boys as we climbed trees and dove from the high diving board at the local swimming pool. I was fearless.

And yet, as we talked about our exploits we also realized that as we hit adolescence, we lost our feisty true selves along the way. I still grieve that loss. While I can't speak for the others I can tell you that it feels that I am only now beginning to reconnect with that wild and wacky ten year old who was ready to change the world.

In hindsight, much of it was simply the result of the distorted thinking of female adolescence—thinking that everyone else was watching, being categorized by my peers (in my case landing in the uncool category), egocentric thought, feeling vulnerable, and being much too focused on the present.

Perhaps, though, of greater influence was being part of a dysfunctional family. But, even that would have been less serious if we hadn't also moved when I was eleven. That meant that in addition to losing my cadre of friends, I lost my community. I did manage, however, to find my way back to myself by discovering something that I was good at. In my case this key element was sport.

Understanding our own journey is important for equipping us to encourage others to find something they love, to connect with them, and to be purveyors of hope. It is also important to understand our own pain and how it impacts our individual leadership drive, priorities, vulnerabilities, and ultimate behaviours.

One thing I have realized is that a difficult relationship with my father has resulted in me having an overdeveloped conscience, an unhealthy drive and work ethic, challenging relationships with men who tell me what to do, and an overly sensitive response to men who yell or criticize.

While it doesn't seem anyone ever gets over the impact of unhealthy relationships, being aware of both the positive and negative impacts of one's heritage is essential.

Promote the Value of Learning

A while ago I bumped into my ex-husband's wife and their two beautiful daughters. While I'm long over the sadness of the break-up, I was still surprised at the impact the encounter had on me.

Looking back, my divorce was both the worst and the best thing that ever happened to me. The best part of course was that my now husband and our blended family have resulted in me being far happier than I ever could have envisioned.

What did catch me somewhat off guard was that the encounter brought back a wave of memories. I remembered how hard it was to suddenly find myself, then age thirty, as a single parent responsible for raising my son. Working part-time and having only one year of college under my belt at the time, I knew I would have to find myself a better job and a more reliable source of income. The only pathway I knew for making that happen was education.

While I initially approached school with trepidation, in hindsight it was one of the smartest things I've ever done. In addition to making me much more employable, it gave me a new found confidence in my skills and abilities.

I powered through my degree in two and a half years and graduated at the top of my class. And, although I accumulated a debt of over $20,000, almost immediately upon graduating, I walked into a well-paying job with the City of Niagara Falls that would never have happened without the education.

Today, the need for education remains a priority and it is often profiled as being a cure for much of what ails us. Education is a solution to many of the challenges being created by an aging population, fast-paced technological change, and the globalization which has brought new competition to our doorstep. These challenges will have a profound impact on our economy and standard of living.

A workforce, without improved productivity, will hurt our ability to ensure the hallmarks of the quality of Canadian life—healthcare, education, and the environment.

Canada needs more people with a higher level of hard and soft skills. We need to improve industry-specific technical skills but, perhaps more important, are literacy, numeracy, interpersonal skills, customer service, flexibility, and attitude.

One of my former employers reinforced this for me when he hired me at the Boys and Girls Club. Although I lacked many of the key credentials, he said, "I can teach you the basic skills you need for this job in a heartbeat. I'm hiring you because you have the right attitude."

Our training and education systems will also need to be much more flexible and responsive. The need for students to be able to move seamlessly from one educational institution to another is essential. Credits between educational institutions need to be more easily transferred and previous accreditation or experience must be acknowledged.

We're also going to need to step up our efforts to ensure that everyone who can participate does so. Many, such as aboriginal youth, adults with disabilities, and immigrants are facing training and employment challenges. Canada welcomes thousands of immigrants annually and we are paying a high price when we fail to recognize their credentials and qualifications.

Too often there is a lack of long term planning and coordination on the part of government, employers, and educators. Working together to gather labour market data and responding to it just makes a lot of sense.

It is also clear that government, business, and education need to invest financial, human learning, and physical resources in order to provide quality education to an increased number of participants.

Ongoing Learning

Being a better leader also means your learning should never stop. Unfortunately for many of us, school may not always be associated with positive memories. Every year towards the end of August, I feel a compulsion to buy a new pencil case and load up three ring binders with fresh paper. Then I pause, give my head a shake, and remember that I'm not going back to school in September. The resulting emotion is both relief and sadness.

The truth is that while I never really liked school, I've always, and still do, love to learn. Although one would think the two would go hand in hand I have yet to translate my passion for learning into completing another post secondary degree even though I know I should.

Instead, I learn every day by reading and researching voraciously and by hanging out with people who are smarter, different, and much more interesting than I. I google when I come across things I don't understand and use Wikipedia to gain insight into unfamiliar concepts. I'm a regular visitor to youtube.edu, slideshare.net and Open Courseware Consortium.

It is a formula that keeps me ahead of the curve especially in comparison to what is being taught in a lot of colleges and universities. Much of what I'm learning hasn't yet found its way into textbooks. According to the guy who coined the term, my approach to learning makes me part of a growing wave of *edupunks.*

The term emerged to describe a trend reflecting a high tech do-it-yourself attitude, the importance of thinking and learning for one's self, and a reaction against what some see as the commercialization of learning.[61]

Given there hasn't been a lot of mainstream change in post-secondary education, we shouldn't be surprised that new experiments and models are emerging from entrepreneurs, students, and teachers.

My favourite approach is one being utilized by the prestigious Massachusetts Institute of Technology best known as MIT. Typically a degree from MIT costs a graduate close to $200,000. However since 2001, they've been putting all coursework online for free. This includes the syllabi, lecture notes, assignments, exercises, tests, and in some cases even video and audio files. In effect, this means everyone has access to the information. Some 100 million have visited the site to take up MIT on the invitation to learn.[62] It is only those who want the actual degree who need to attend classes, complete the assignments, and somehow find the money to pay the tuition.

Of course, education is much more than using technology to share information. In addition to *sharing information*, there are two other components that need to be considered. The first is *how* we deliver the teaching and learning. Although that always used to take place on campus, now it is much easier to move it online.

The third component is the most challenging aspect of education—*assessment and accreditation.* The colleges and universities leading the

---

61   Kuntz, T. (October 17, 2008).The buzz for 'edupunk'. *New York Times.*

62   http://ocw.mit.edu/about/our-history/. Retrieved August 2010.

way are those that begin the learning journey with the end in mind. This means they have articulated the outcomes or competencies the learner must be able to demonstrate upon graduation. If these competencies are in place as the ultimate destination, it becomes clear there are many ways, rather than one way, to get there.

This in turn allows student-centred learning, with the teacher as the facilitator of learning, rather than being the content expert. It is an approach that ensures students are active, responsible participants in their own learning.

The key to the change necessary for ensuring this shift is that educational institutions separate or uncouple and treat the three components distinctly—the sharing of information, how we deliver the teaching and learning, and the assessment and accreditation.

It is not yet clear what the colleges and universities of the future will look like but for sure they are not that far away. It is also probably fair to say colleges and universities will need to move much faster to get there and to think beyond bricks and mortar if they are to remain relevant and meaningful in today's changing world.

Learning in the Workplace

In addition to post secondary education, workplace learning must also be given a priority.

The issue of employer investment in workplace learning has been the subject of discussion at the national and local levels. It has also been the focus of a number of studies spearheaded by the Canadian Council on Learning[63] and the sadly now defunct Canadian Policy Research Network.[64] The goal of recent research was to identify practical steps to ensure that the quantity and quality of workplace learning in Canada matches the needs of the economy, and maximizes the potential of Canadian workers.

---

63   Canadian Council on Learning (September, 2009). *Securing prosperity through Canada's human infrastructure: The state of adult learning and workplace training in Canada.* Retrieved October 2010 http://www.ccl-cca.ca/ccl.

64   Saunders, R. (April 2009). *Fostering employer investment in workplace learning.* Retrieved October 2010 http://www.cprn.com/ (Note: While Canadian Policy Research Network is now defunct, the report remains accessible).

There are a number of reasons why an investment in developing the skills and knowledge of Canadian workers is something that needs our attention.

The first is simple demographics. One factor to note is that the aging of the baby boom cohorts will bring about a slowing of labour force growth. Another is the lack of younger people entering the workforce. In the past, the ongoing influx of youth into the workforce meant we were also getting new skills. Today, that's something we can't rely on as most of the people who will be in the workforce in 2015 are in already in it today. As a result, we need to make the best use of the workers we have now.

Another reason for the growing importance of workplace learning is the rapid pace of change in technology in combination with the demands of the global knowledge economy. This has resulted in higher and frequently changing skill requirements on the job. Additionally, changes in the labour market also point to the increased importance of workplace learning. On the one hand, skill shortages are being experienced in some sectors or regions while other sectors or regions experience layoffs and/or sustained high levels of unemployment.

Canada's performance in workplace learning has been mediocre. Less than thirty percent of adult workers in Canada participate in job-related education and training, compared to almost thirty-five percent in the United Kingdom, and nearly forty-five percent in the United States.[65]

While there are barriers to making workplace learning more of a priority instead of it being the first budget line cut, Canadian Council on Learning's report called *Employer Investment in Workplace Learning,*[66] provides a number of promising practices.

These include developing partnerships among firms, workers, unions, governments, and educational institutions; active advocacy by business organizations to encourage a training culture; a tool box with a wide variety of supports and initiatives and the flexibility to tailor their application to specific needs and circumstances; aware-

---

65   Goldenberg, M. (2008) Retrieved August 2010. http://www.ccl-cca.ca/NR/rdonlyres/4F86830F-D201-4CAF-BA12-333B51CEB988/0/EmployerInvestmentWorkplace-LearningCCLCPRN.pdf.

66   Goldenberg, M. Ibid.

ness campaigns and the collection of evidence to convince employ-ers about the benefits and returns of investing in workplace learn-ing; and enhanced government financial incentives to firms and/or individuals.

Albert Einstein once said, "No problem can be solved by the same consciousness that created it. We need to see the world anew." Work-place learning is a key strategy for helping each of us to see our world anew.

Just as years ago I needed to ensure my future by investing in edu-cation as a lifelong learning process, so too do community leaders.

Life and Career Goals and Plans

As mentioned, my husband and I have worked through some signifi-cant life and career changes. Most of the changes were driven by us giving serious thought to what it is we want to do with the rest of our lives. Like many other boomers, we've sought work that will "feed our souls".

In the midst of one especially difficult struggle to sort out my next steps, an email arrived from a colleague telling me, among other things, that I had brought innovation and genius to the social profit sector. Me?! While I was so very flattered by the compliment, I defi-nitely know I'm no genius. However, I do think her compliment is likely because she sees the passion and enthusiasm I bring to any work that involves community building and community leadership.

According to author David McNally in his book, *The Eagle's Secret: Success Strategies for Thriving at Work and in Life,*[67] finding what you are passionate about is essential for everyone.

In order to determine what sets apart individuals who thrive, from those who merely survive, McNally surveyed hundreds of public and private-sector workers—from CEOs to frontline supervisors, educa-tors, and entrepreneurs. As a result, he is able to suggest a number of practical strategies that anyone can use to cultivate their genius.

If like me, you aren't certain you have an inner genius, McNally suggests you begin by looking for patterns in your life. Although many

---

67 McNally, D. (1998). *The eagle's secret: Success strategies for thriving at work and in life.* New York: Dell Publishing.

of us have a tendency to overlook or devalue what we do best—likely because it has come so easy—we need to take the time to review the events in our lives. The threads of continuity are likely to be more obvious if we ask ourselves, "What is it we have been praised for? What is it we have consistently enjoyed? Additionally, ask yourself which of your accomplishments makes you most proud?

The answers to those questions will help put you on the right path to your inner genius.

McNally also suggests when you are feeling relaxed and spontaneous, you will be most "yourself" and your natural gifts and talents will be most visible. He suggests we give ourselves the opportunity to let go and to play more in order to discover new creativity and passions.

He also suggests we break out of our established patterns by trying something new. Are there things you assumed you are not good at but would love to try? Why not do at least one new thing every month? Think of something you've always wanted to do and do it. If you fail, make a mistake, get laughed at, feel embarrassed, who cares? Fear is what keeps people mired in mediocrity.

Being honest about what you love is part of the process. What do you feel passionate about? What do you have fun doing? Finding what you love is finding what you were made to do, and what you were made to do, is what you have an aptitude to do. He suggests it will take courage to admit what you love but once you do, your genius will surface.

A Plan for Learning

It took more energy than I had anticipated and when it was over all I wanted to do was lay down and take a nap. No, it wasn't the workout at the gym that I should have been doing. Instead it was delivering a guest lecture for a class of first year university students studying leadership.

While they have been there physically, they didn't exude much energy or excitement about learning. I found myself practically tap dancing to keep them focused, resorting to sharing more stories than theory, and asking questions to engage them.

It was sad really but likely not their fault. Somehow we seem to have created a culture where too many view education as a necessary evil instead of a key to continued growth and success. I'm not sure if they've grasped that a formal education is only the beginning, particularly in a knowledge economy fueled by rapid change. Acquiring new skills and knowledge is a must for everyone so a commitment to ongoing, self-directed learning is rather essential.

However, if kids aren't excited about learning for learning's sake, perhaps we could motivate them, as well as ourselves, to embrace and plan more for learning by providing information about why it is so important. After all, there are a lot of solid, practical reasons why learning can, and needs to be, part of our daily lives.

> "Organizations can keep searching for new ties that bind us to them—new incentives, rewards, and punishments. But organizations could accomplish so much more if they relied on the passion evoked when we connect to others, purpose to purpose. So many of us want to be more. So many of us hunger to discover who we might become together."
>
> — Margaret Wheatley

A commitment to learning will help you find yourself. We all have innate yet sometimes undiscovered talents. In addition to identifying our natural talents, learning can help us find what we're passionate about. While many may think it is money and material rewards that will make us happy, latching on to one's talents and passion is ultimately what leads to a rewarding and fulfilling life.

Learning will also make you a much more interesting person. While quoting sport statistics or being knowledgeable about celebrities might make you popular within your immediate circle, a wider range of knowledge will allow you to draw on a variety of perspectives and engage with others at a deeper and richer level.

Knowing more will increase your potential for the innovation that is so critical in today's world. The broader your knowledge base, the better the odds that your thinking will be creative and original.

Learning will also help you be a more confident person. I wasn't exactly a stellar student in high school but going back to university and finding success as a mature student made me realize I had something to offer. It also helped me adapt more quickly to new situations.

Ultimately though, learning is essential because we are learning creatures and practicing lifelong learning is what makes us human, and our lives worthwhile.

So how does one incorporate learning for learning's sake into one's life? Can you plan for learning beyond being involved in purely academic, formal instruction? Of course you can. History is full of examples of people who have succeeded as the result of being self-taught. Additionally, we are blessed to live in an era where knowledge is at our fingertips as the result of the power of the Internet and the media.

Begin by developing a deep understanding of what matters to you most. It might be related to your job, a hobby, special interest, or an issue in your community. Then work to develop a broader understanding of the world in general.

Challenge your curiosity by acknowledging gaps in your understanding of the world. Heighten your awareness of what you don't know and receive it as a challenge to learn more to fill that gap.

Practice patience. Learning something new can take time especially if you are out of practice. It may be frustrating to learn new terms, models, and information that at first may seem irrelevant. However, if you are patient, you will find yourself moving from basic knowledge to more advanced concepts.

Connect the dots. This is probably the hardest part about lifelong learning. Take time to learn how a new body of knowledge can relate to what you already know. The more you seek and see the connections between different learnings, the easier it will be for you to connect to new concepts.

In the end though, it is those students I keep thinking about. My hope is that they figure out that learning is fundamental to life and that by embracing and planning for lifelong learning they will find their surest path to a future filled with the utmost of adventures, growth, meaning, and joy.

Seeking Opportunities for Mentors and Mentoring

While I've often thought I'd like to have a mentor, the truth is I never thought much about being one until we had a very young guy join our team.

Most people in this young man's community knew him as a Junior B Hockey player. However Stacey Green, one of his instructors in the Recreation and Leisure Services Program at Niagara College, identified him as an emerging leader.

Upon graduating from college, he took a risk and moved to Edmonton from Niagara at his own expense to join our ACE Communities team as a Youth Engagement Coordinator. Although it was also a risk for our team, something just seemed to click from the first phone interview.

Cameron is a band member of the New Credit First Nation and was born and raised on Six Nations Reserve in Ontario. He had firsthand experience dealing with change at an early age, having to move off-reserve to attend high school and to play junior hockey in the Niagara region. He believes those experiences helped him identify with the changes many youth are dealing with these days.

Additionally, he has learned, and shares, how sport and recreation can serve as a catalyst for leadership, community development, and overall well-being.

Although still quite young, he has a fair bit of experience in both paid and volunteer positions, developing, implementing, and evaluating programs for children and youth that include day camps, after school programs, and youth drop-ins. He has also worked and volunteered as a youth hockey instructor, special needs and education assistant, and as an Aboriginal mentor assistant.

As his new employer, I figured it was my job to create an environment that would help him learn more from those with more experience in his chosen profession as a recreation practitioner, manage his career, and ultimately be successful. The reality is that it took me a while to figure out exactly what that entailed.

From this experience, I now know that being a mentor first means getting to know one another and to build trust. It helped that Cameron billeted with my husband and I for the first two weeks after he arrived. It didn't take long to learn that he was polite, appreciative, and eager to learn.

Part of being a good mentor, I learned, meant opening doors to new experiences. As a result, when we met with providers to discuss a multi-media campaign, Cameron came along to observe. When we toured a number of small communities, we put him on the spot to do the introductions. There was no one prouder than I to learn he is a gifted and natural speaker in front of an audience.

I found that being a mentor may also involve serving as a confidant, sounding-board, and advisor on both work and personal matters. It also meant keeping an eye out for potential threats to one's mentee allowing them to adjust before they become significant problems. Although in Cameron's case there weren't any serious issues, we provided feedback about different strategies for staying organized.

There were also many "teachable moments" where all members of our team demonstrated generosity in transferring knowledge, sharing their experiences, and recommending assignments. Having a mentee among us kept all of us on our toes as we knew we were modeling ethics, values, beliefs, attitudes, strategies, and procedures. We also had to be keenly aware of our own behaviour and what it said about our organization.

As for Cameron himself, he modeled the behaviours one would hope to see in a mentee. He was honest and open, receptive to feedback and insight, proactive about seeking information and feedback, and willing to follow through on advice and direction. But, we would be the first to say it wasn't all one-sided. There was definitely some reverse mentoring going on as he taught us a great deal about aboriginal cultures, how to deal with youth, and the importance of sport.

As a result, mentoring is a win-win situation for everyone involved.

Healthy Life Balance

It is so sweet that my mother still worries about me. Specifically, she worries that I work too hard.

During my last visit, I tried to explain that there was a blurry line between my work and my leisure because I enjoy what I do so much.

Not sure that I had dispelled her concerns, I finally blurted out, "Work just makes me happy!"

I went on to explain that I don't expect everyone to enjoy working as much as I do, but I am simply a much happier person when I produce. I'm not a workaholic as I don't feel driven to work; it is instead something I consciously choose to do because it brings me deep joy and fulfillment.

On the other hand, I'm not so good at taking care of myself. Musing out loud as to why I too often choose work instead of working out, my husband insightfully suggested, "Because your work is more fun for you?"

He is a wise man and exactly right.

Both conversations got me thinking. First of all, I was reminded of how blessed I am to have work that I enjoy so much. Secondly, and especially because my career roots are in recreation leadership, it made me think about the importance of leisure education in our lives.

By that I mean helping people develop an appreciation, as well as the skills and opportunities, to use their leisure time in a way that is personally rewarding. For sure, how we choose to spend our free time contributes to our individual quality of life.

A common denominator for ensuring both work and leisure that is joyful is being able to zero in on what brings out the best in one's self. While I think I lucked into much of what I do today, author and consultant Jim Collins has refined a simple and profound set of three questions that he calls the "Hedgehog Concept"[68] for those who need help.

The essence of the Hedgehog Concept is to attain clarity about how to produce the best long-term results in your life. It is based on Isaiah Berlin's famous essay, "The Hedgehog and the Fox" where, based on an ancient Greek fable, he divided the world into hedgehogs and foxes.

The message is that the fox knows many things and views the world through the lens of a single defining idea, whereas hedgehogs

---

68   Collins, J. Retrieved August 2010. http://www.jimcollins.com/media_topics/hedgehog-concept.html#audio=79.

draw on a wide variety of experiences and therefore could never boil the world down to a single idea.

In addition to being a tool for helping to determine how to live one's best life, Collins also recommends the hedgehog concept for those wanting to build great organizations, businesses, and communities.

The concept is brilliant in its simplicity in that it is about you answering three questions. He suggests you use one sheet of paper for each question and initially address the three independently.

The first question is, *"What am I deeply passionate about?"* Think about what it is you love to do.

The second is *"What am I genetically wired to do?"* In other words, what are you good at? What fits your psychological makeup and capabilities? It is also what you think you may have been put on this earth to do.

The third question is, *"What are the possibilities for making a living?"* Of course, this one will be much easier if finances are not an issue for you.

Once you have answered the three questions, the idea is to find or create a practical intersection of the three circles to determine what you can be the best at doing.

It may be that you won't be able to come up with that intersection on your own. If so, give copies to others who know you well to get their perspective on where the three circles intersect. Once you sort out the intersect it can become a filter or compass for navigating your life and keeping you on track.

As a starting point, make an inventory of your activities today and determine the percentage of your time that falls outside the three circles. Collins suggests that if it is more that fifty percent then it might also be about creating a stop-doing list rather than a to-do list as well as exercising relentless discipline to say, "No thank you" to opportunities that fail the hedgehog test.

Just as a great piece of art is as much about what is in the final piece as well as what is not, finding joy and life balance is often about having the courage to discard what doesn't fit. It may mean cutting out parts of your life that have already cost days or even years of effort. In the end, just as it is that choice that sets the truly exceptional artist and beautiful art apart from others, so too will it delineate a mundane life from one that is truly joyful.

Learning to Take Care of Yourself

Having a healthy life balance—mind, body, and spirit—means taking care of yourself.

There is no doubt, especially during tough times, that business, organizational and community demands impact everyone at all levels. And, when we are stressed and worn out, the consequences are felt at a personal level.

Stress affects us physically, generating a range of problems that could potentially include flu-like symptoms, colds, backaches, allergies, stiff neck, tight shoulders, headaches, memory problems, difficulty concentrating, depression, fatigue, reduced or increased appetites, or challenges in sleeping.

This is compounded by the fact that when we're exhausted and stressed, most of us don't treat ourselves well. Too often we end up self-medicating with coffee, tea, caffeine-loaded soft drinks, or alcohol. We overeat, don't eat, or eat the wrong things. Exercise doesn't even make it on to our to-do lists.

So what can we do to better manage our stress?

Know that exercise helps. When we get active it reduces the physical tension in our bodies thereby inducing relaxation. Personally it somehow makes me feel as if I'm more in control of my life even when I'm not.

Taking mental or physical breaks is also an important strategy for dealing with workplace stress. For example, get up from your desk on a regular basis and walk around or get out for some fresh air. Do some deep breathing, stretches, or just close your eyes for a minute.

Finding effective ways to set boundaries is also an important exercise. It might be deciding not to check email from home, listening to music on your drive to and from work, or carving out specific time for fun hobbies and family activities. It is important to ensure you have a life away from work.

Also if you feel stress from workplace demands, it sometimes helps to rethink the work. Look for ways to streamline what you do. Planning, organizing, and prioritizing are effective stress managers.

Sometimes for me that simply translates to cleaning off my desk and generating a to-do list. Other tactics include defining roles, clarifying expectations, setting up reasonable timelines, and completing tasks ahead of deadline. By gaining focus, you can reduce the stress you feel during a task and head off the stress that may occur when new tasks land on your desk.

Also know that we're all more effective if we allow time for recovery. We need to build time into our routines to recharge just as professional athletes build time into their training routines to revitalize. Relaxing is critical for clear and innovative thinking, solid relationships, and optimum health. If you truly leave the job behind at the end of the day, the time and energy you spend away from work will ultimately enhance your productivity as well as your capacity for dealing with workplace stress.

We all need to be reminded that pushing one's self at maximum capacity one hundred percent of the time results in little or no long-term performance gains. Time to relax and recharge is critical for innovation, clear thinking, good health, and meaningful relationships.

In challenging times, it's easy to get sucked into the vortex of negativity. Reduce your stress by keeping focused on the vision you want for your future, as well as all that *is* well and good in your life. Count your blessings.

Laughter Can Be the Best Medicine

Laughter and fun are also amazing anecdotes to stress.

At a staff meeting a number of years ago I remember discussing the pending relocation of our offices. On the plus side, the upcoming change would mean that all the staff in my unit would be housed in one location instead of being spread across two. However, it also meant some staff would have to share office space.

Post meeting, one of the staff launched into an absolutely hilarious routine in order to demonstrate how little space she would need at the new office. Straight faced, she sat herself in an empty cardboard box (no mean feat given the box was about the size of a small laundry basket). Then, she propped a recycling basket in front of her to use as a table, and with her knees drawn up to her chin, perched her laptop somewhat precariously and began to type. She really got us roaring when she flipped up her laptop to show how she could even store her lunch underneath in the recycle bin. We all laughed so hard, we were gasping for air. It sure was fun.

Thinking about it afterward I realized laughing that hard not only made me feel better, it reminded me of how much we need laughter and fun in today's busy and often stressful workplaces.

The experts agree. Dozens of studies have documented the importance of on-the-job laughter. Laughter can enhance productivity, problem-solving ability, creativity, imagination, and risk-taking. In addition to serving as a bonding agent for building strong teams, it can help prevent stress and illness.

Why do we laugh? Some believe the first human laughter began as shared relief when danger passed. Others believe the purpose of laughter is related to making and strengthening human connections because it typically happens when people are comfortable with one another and can be open and free. Laughing is also important because the more laughter there is, the more bonding occurs within the group.

Given that, one would think we'd be encouraging people to laugh all the time. Instead, it seems life has the opposite effect. Research shows that children laugh on average 150 times a day whereas adults laugh on average of only six times a day. During an average day, an adult will smile less than fifteen times but a child will smile 400.[69]

No one knows exactly why we laugh or why something funny causes us to make such a peculiar noise. But, for some reason when something strikes us as being funny, our diaphragm flutters up and down and we laugh.

Research also shows that when we laugh, naturally produced morphine-like endorphins are released by the brain. The result is that we feel a sense of euphoria and well-being. There is also evidence to indicate that laughter can have a positive impact on our immune system.[70]

Although many still believe using humour in work or community settings makes one appear less professional, the opposite may be true.

---

69   Holden, R. (1994). *Living wonderfully.* New York: Harper Collins.

70   Lefcourt, H. M., Davidson-Katz, K., & Kueneman,K. (March,1990). Humor and immune-system functioning. *International Journal of Humor Research,* 3:3, 305-322.

Most employers see a sense of humour as an asset and employees who can evoke chuckles during a tense meeting or prompt others to snicker during hectic times are seen as commendable.

So, does this mean we should brush up on our jokes? Probably not. Humour has little to do with jokes, particularly those that insult or offend. It has more to do with enjoying life and being able to take yourself lightly.

> " If you lose the power to laugh, you lose the power to think."
>
> — Clarence Darrow

Anyone can develop a sense of humour. Simply remind yourself of your right to "make a joyful noise" and, ensure that you add new non-work interests into your life.

Community leaders can assist by creating an awareness of the importance of laughter and by making it acceptable to laugh and, occasionally, be silly. Laughter is no joke. It can contribute to healthy, productive staff and volunteers who have a sense of "joie de vivre". After all, as the saying goes, "She who laughs lasts".

Taking Care of Our Body and Our Spirit

I recently tried a new approach to dealing with stress. It was a first for me. And, while I knew it would likely be a good experience, I didn't anticipate that it would be quite so emotional.

The occasion was my first ever therapeutic massage.

A badly broken and dislocated ankle a number of years ago has managed somewhat insidiously to impact my hip and my gait, eventually throwing the right side of my body off kilter. Over the past few years I've flirted with physiotherapy, orthotics, and acupuncture all of which provided some, but not a lot of relief.

Although not a good thing, I realized that exercise ramped up the pain. Consequently, I gradually became less active distracted by exciting work and the challenge of putting roots down in a new community. Ultimately things got worse, and with warm weather prompting a desire for outdoor activities, I knew I had to be proactive about getting healthier.

My search led me to a wonderful chiropractor who is working to adjust what turns out to be a one inch difference on one side of my body. It is a painful and slow process but there is progress. The same chiropractor also recommended therapeutic massage.

While I know some people swear by it, I've never really felt the pull. Although a part of it might just be the idea of getting naked and being touched by a stranger, I think I did see it as an indulgence I could do without. Instead, influenced by my strong Ukrainian peasant roots, I chose to soldier on.

However, I reached the point where I felt I needed to exercise all options for getting stronger. As a result, I decided to expand my comfort zone and put myself at the mercy of a massage therapist.

The force was with me as I was referred to a woman who has truly been gifted with healing hands. As she moved her hands along my body, I could feel tension being released. I could also feel hot sensitive points in my neck, spine, and hips that were extraordinarily uncomfortable. Initially tensing as she hit the hot spots, I learned to relax into the pain and even scoop under it so the pain could be released and pulled away. She finished the one and a half hour session with gentle soothing motions that brought tears to my eyes and raw emotion to the surface. It was moving and somewhat surreal.

Caught totally off guard by my reaction, I realized that there were much deeper lessons playing out for me.

It taught me how much actual pain, as well as memory of pain, we hold in our bodies. It also reminded me that as much as I like to think I'm growing and evolving, I'm never going to get there until I learn to nurture and take care of myself. Like many others, especially women, who put themselves last on the list, we need to get better at making ourselves a priority if we are to be strong, healthy, and vibrant.

Easy enough to say, but how does one actually do that?

Well, I'm learning that it means airing your feelings rather than keeping them bottled up inside. Using "I" words to share good things as well as anger and disappointment with someone you trust is essential. Partners, as well as good friends who listen, support, and can "be there" for you are invaluable.

We also need to take time to play, knowing that we deserve to do things just because they make us feel good. I'm trying not to forget to laugh, especially at myself. I'm way too serious sometimes and will work at occasionally just being silly.

I'm also working at embracing the idea that it's okay just to relax. It is relaxing that will help my body heal as well as sharpen my mind.

Getting comfortable with saying no is okay. One of my techniques now is to respond to requests that I'm not sure I can handle by saying, "Can I think about that and get back to you?"

I'm going to work especially hard at stretching my muscles and breaking into a sweat. I will walk and work out regularly, ride my bike more, park further from the door, and take the stairs. On the other hand, I'm also going to have more manicures, pedicures, and candlelit bubble baths knowing that pampering pays good dividends.

Probably though, the message that the massage reinforced most strongly is that we need to make sure we pay more attention to our spiritual lives. Even if our lives are rich and meaningful, we need to slow down, practice sitting quietly, listen to our inner voices, and spend time thinking about the things that will bring peace and serenity.

What's most important about taking care of ourselves and dealing with stress is to simply pay attention. Be aware of how your body is responding to stress. If you feel your head throbbing, jaw clenching, shoulders tightening, or heart racing, recognize that it is your body's response to stress, and it is time to do something about it.

 **Chapter 9**

Competency 3: Big Picture Thinking

Utilizes a proactive system-thinking/ holistic approach

COMPETENCY AREA		INDICATORS TO HELP YOU UNDERSTAND WHAT ENCOMPASSES THIS COMPETENCY	1 = I AM NOT AT ALL LIKE THAT	10 = I AM 100% LIKE THAT
3 Big Picture Thinking	3.1	I understand the people are interdependent and are involved in symbiotic relationships.	1 2 3 4 5 6 7 8 9 10	
	3.2	I can apply strategies for learning about a community, its key stakeholders, and its resources.	1 2 3 4 5 6 7 8 9 10	
	3.3	I demonstrate knowledge of the roles and responsibilities of the business, government, and social-profit sectors.	1 2 3 4 5 6 7 8 9 10	
	3.4	I demonstrate knowledge of social capital and organizational and community assets e.g. physical, human, financial, environmental.	1 2 3 4 5 6 7 8 9 10	
	3.5	I can apply techniques that will generate creative and innovative thinking.	1 2 3 4 5 6 7 8 9 10	
	3.6	I nurture social innovation and creative environments.	1 2 3 4 5 6 7 8 9 10	
	3.7	I am aware of legislation and policy which could have an impact on my community.	1 2 3 4 5 6 7 8 9 10	
	3.8	I understand the importance of a community's culture, personality, and brand.	1 2 3 4 5 6 7 8 9 10	
	3.9	I facilitate the development of teams and coalitions to work proactively to address common goals.	1 2 3 4 5 6 7 8 9 10	
	3.10	I work proactively to develop diverse teams.	1 2 3 4 5 6 7 8 9 10	
	3.11	I support collaboration.	1 2 3 4 5 6 7 8 9 10	
	3.12	I recognize complexity and help facilitate appropriate processes and systems.	1 2 3 4 5 6 7 8 9 10	
	3.13	I practice reflection.	1 2 3 4 5 6 7 8 9 10	

Acknowledge Symbiotic Relationships

Small town living and the movie Avatar might just have something in common.

Recently a colleague and I delivered a community building workshop in a very small village—population 190. A surprising forty five people from a variety of backgrounds attended including business owners, elected officials, volunteers, and social profit and government staff.

As we were setting up for the workshop, Mayor Bob mentioned they had just graduated a bumper crop of high school graduates in the same hall the previous week. Curious as to what "bumper crop" would translate to in a town of less than two hundred, I asked, "So how many students graduated?" The mayor advised there were six. While that made me smile, what was astounding is that he went on to report that six hundred people attended the graduation ceremonies.

That graduation explained more than anything about what it is that people love about living in small communities. It manifests the belief that we are all interconnected at some level and therefore are interdependent and reliant on one another. In that small community, everyone cared and watched out for one another. And, when six of their own achieved a significant milestone, they celebrated the success together.

The lesson of the importance of this interconnectedness was emphasized in Avatar. The movie promoted an understanding that people are not different races, but rather interconnected beings inhabiting the same planet.

On some level, we all seem to have a vague sense of understanding that the ecosystem of planet Earth is delicate as it too is intimately interconnected and interdependent. However, we have sometimes chosen to conveniently ignore that all species will be at risk for extinction if we mess with the delicate balance and relationships of the ecosystem.

As Avatar stressed, relationships are inevitable for any living being whether it is a plant, an animal, or a human being. In nature we see the importance of symbiotic relationships where two organisms of different species live and work together, each one of them benefiting from mutual cooperation. In these symbiotic relationships the two entities need each other to survive and prosper. A good example is that of the bee and the flower. Bees get nectar from flowers but pollination also takes place when the bee flies from one flower to another.

> " ... abundance is a communal act, the joint creation of an incredibly complex ecology in which each part functions on behalf of the whole and, in return, is sustained by the whole. Community doesn't just create abundance— community is abundance. If we could learn that equation from the world of nature, the human world might be transformed."
>
> — Parker J. Palmer

151

Avatar got me thinking that these same kind of symbiotic relationships are also essential within communities. When we don't bond with one another enough to understand, respect, and ultimately care about the life around us, we too are at risk.

Many are sensing the erosion of this bonding and connections in communities particularly as they grow larger. The decline is especially evident in communities that have made economic development their main priority. For example, while there is no doubt the oil and gas industry is essential here in Alberta, the successful communities are those that have balanced its removal against the care and concern of people and the ecosystem.

At the end of the day, the messages from the small village and from Avatar are that we all need to keep our focus and priority on what is best for people and the planet. That means it needs to be about investing time in meaningful conversations, determining community values and priorities, and building the trusted relationships needed for change and growth. It won't be easy but it will be the most vital and significant work we ever do as community leaders.

Strategies for Learning About Your Community

I recently talked to a friend who is seriously considering a move west in her search for new opportunities for both herself and her family. While I was genuine in my support and encouragement, I thought afterward about how responsible I would feel if they did actually pack up and move. While a move from Welland to Edmonton worked out well for us, it is definitely a challenge getting to know a new community.

In our case, I was fortunate to have worked in Edmonton on a consulting basis before we moved so I had an opportunity to get to know both the city and a number of colleagues. In making the difficult decision to relocate, we spent a lot of time searching online in order to learn more about the community.

I also bought a large map of the city and a good friend shaded in the neighbourhoods where she thought we'd be happy living. That kind of locally grown expertise is important to find and tap.

Another good friend of ours, who was originally from the west, gave us the gift of two tourist guide books. In addition to being fun to read, the books helped us learn more about the history and hotspots in our new community and gave us tips on where to eat, what to do, and where to go.

When you first move to a new community, the focus is by necessity placed on unpacking and getting settled. However, we also made getting Internet access a priority as it made locating the nearest Canadian Tire, grocery store and Walmart easier. Those early errand runs took longer than usual but they did help us get our bearings.

We did find, however, that walking and bike riding were the best ways to get a feel for our new neighbourhood. We located a great website at www.walkscore.com that promotes walkable neighbourhoods by showing what's within walking distance of your specific address.

Subscribing to the local paper was also one of the first things we did as it was key to providing information about our new community including local events and advertising for stores and restaurants. We also looked for free magazines and flyers on local bulletin boards to learn more. The library and Cable TV also provided relevant information.

Additionally, there were a lot of other practical things to do that we hadn't anticipated. Simple but complicated things like finding a new doctor, dentist, chiropractor, hairdresser, and favourite restaurant. Most ended up being the result of asking our new colleagues but sometimes it was just a guess that either worked or didn't.

We also learned that one of the best ways to meet new people and get connected was through our leisure activities. For my husband, that meant finding a new curling club almost as soon as we got here. He also connected with others at a kite festival. For me it was joining a local gym. Others I know have joined service clubs, volunteered, taken classes that interested them, or joined a sport league. For some, the best way to meet friends is through their faith community.

While sometimes it may mean you have to stretch yourself and take the first step in inviting someone for coffee or over for dinner, in the end a new community can be whatever you decide you want it to be. For my husband and I it was, and continues to be, a great adventure that requires us to work and explore together.

That's not to say it has been all sunshine and rainbows because the truth is we always miss our family and friends in Niagara. As John Ed Pearce once said, "Home is a place you grow up wanting to leave, and grow old wanting to get back to."[71]

Understanding the Business, Government, and Social Profit Sectors

Too often leaders lack an understanding that their communities consist of three broad sectors: the Government or Public Sector, the Business/Private Sector, and the "Third" or Voluntary, Non-profit, or Social-Profit Sector.

I grew up in a household supported by the business or private sector and my Dad's GM paycheque. While there were lean times, particularly during labour strikes, we generally did pretty well, even in a family of seven with one wage earner. Thanks to GM, my Dad also has the benefit of a comfortable retirement and a generous health care plan.

GM recently made headlines as they announced negotiations had resulted in cuts to benefits and wages that would save $22 per hour.[72] The union was especially excited about having saved the pensions. One union negotiator said something to the effect that when someone from GM retired after thirty years of work, they wanted to be damn sure they would be treated with the respect they deserved. As a result of these concessions, GM was eligible for millions of dollars in government support.

While I'm happy for GM and I fully appreciate their contribution to our economy, I can't help but think of all the people I know doing extraordinarily meaningful work that don't even make $22 an hour to begin with. Additionally, 63% of them will retire without any employer sponsored pensions at all.

---

71   http://thinkexist.com/quotation/home_is_a_place_you_grow_up_wanting__to_leave-and/193341.html. Accessed February 2011.

72   Globe and Mail. Retrieved August 2010. http://www.theglobeandmail.com/globe-investor/taxpayers-fork-out-billions-for-gm-pension-aid/article1148545.

I'm talking about the 1.3 million Canadians who are employed by 69,000 community organizations.[73] To put it into perspective, it is important to understand this sector of social-profit organizations (think daycare, recreation centres, sport, social services, health services etc) is eleven times larger than the entire automotive sector, and provides 6.8 percent of Canada's gross domestic product (GDP). It is a large and complex sector—26 percent of its employees work in social services, 17 percent in health, 16 percent in development and housing, and 11 percent in sport and recreation. The majority of the employers are small organizations—75 percent have fewer than ten employees.

It is a predominantly female (74 percent) and aging workforce—39 percent of the sector's employees are over the age of 45. They are very well-educated with more than 60 percent having post-secondary education and 30 percent working in professional occupations.[74]

We also know that Canada has one of the largest and most vibrant community social-profit sectors in the world.

Measuring 7.8 percent of the gross domestic product (GDP), one can't help but see the energy and commitment behind the annual $9 billion in donations; two billion hours of volunteer time; 22.2 million donors; 11.8 million volunteers; over two million fulltime equivalent workers; 750,000 unincorporated community organizations; 81,000 non-profit corporations; and 80,000 registered charities.[75]

This depth and breadth is a rich tapestry developed in response to the issues that Canadians care about most.

The community social-profit sector builds strong neighbourhoods, helps maintain safe communities, provides victim support, emergency shelter, and re-integration of criminal offenders into communities. They support multiculturalism, economic, environmental and natural disaster relief, immigrant settlement, aboriginal employment, and international development. They promote our official languages, contribute to Canada's arts and culture, and contribute to our health

73 Statistics Canada. (June 2005). *Cornerstones of community:Highlights of the national survey of nonprofit and voluntary organizations.* Cornerstones of Community. Statistics Canada: Ottawa.

74 Statistics Canada. Ibid.

75 Imagine Canada. (2006). *National survey of nonprofit and voluntary organizations* (NSNVO). Retrieved August 2010. http://www.imaginecanada.ca/node/32.

and community capacity by organizing a multitude of events and programs.

Canada's social-profit organizations are a catalyst for engaged and active communities. They are what anchors many communities—the YMCA, Big Brothers, faith organizations, hostels, women's shelters, and sport leagues. They are key community partners in building the quality of life for which Canada is respected around the world.

These organizations are essential in maintaining and strengthening our democratic systems and are a common measure of a nation's commitment to civil society. In the National Survey on the Quality of Life in Canadian Communities, "Three-quarters of residents say they have a great deal (27 percent) or some (50 percent) confidence in leaders of charities and other community-based organizations" and place the greatest confidence in the leaders of local social-profit organizations in making a positive contribution to improving their community.[76]

So no, these people are not making cars, they are instead working within a sector known for its resourcefulness, resilience, and determination to make sure the hungry are fed, children and families have a roof over their heads, and seniors and those with special needs are safe and healthy. These employees work shoulder to shoulder alongside volunteers in every single community in Canada to serve, train, advocate, mentor, protect, care, strengthen, develop, support, build, create, and entertain.

They're doing it within many areas of activity—social services, health, education and research, environment, development and housing, arts and culture, sport and recreation, advocacy and policy, international, religion, philanthropy and volunteerism.

They support us in our time of need, lobby for our rights, learn and teach new skills, build and maintain community halls and parks, look after our natural environment, plant gardens and trees, provide music, dance and put on shows, help us worship in prayer, offer advice and assistance, and facilitate our play and our festivals.

They provide prenatal and palliative care and everything in between, enrich our lives with recreation and sport activities, teach us

---

76   Community Foundations of Canada (2009). Retrieved August 2010. http://www.vitalsignscanada.ca/nr-2009-public-opinion-survey-e.html.

about health issues or illness and how to fight it, run recycling and environmental programs, organize community festivals and celebrations, deliver services for children and seniors, guide our lives spiritually, keep us healthy by supporting research to find cures for disease, and give Canada a respected place in the world through work in international development.

The contribution of the social-profit sector in Canada began before the country was even official, transforming colonies of explorers and traders into communities. Today social-profit organizations continue their work in supporting, caring, and responding with compassion to meet individual, social, and environmental needs. In short, through social profit activity, Canadians care for each other in virtually every aspect of life.

Yes, cars are important, but those within the social-profit sector are responsible for work that improves our quality of life through shared interactions, events, and celebrations, enables people from diverse backgrounds to join in, provides opportunities for people to share responsibility, and ensures responsive and relevant services.

Today the sector responsible for this work is often struggling with staff turnover that is the result of falling wages, as well as a sometimes growing gap in working conditions between the social-profit sector and the private and government sectors. These challenges are compounded by the unstable employment that is the result of less long term secure funding from government and foundations and more one-off project and contract funding. We're already seeing a serious, negative impact on the capacity of these organizations to serve our communities.

The stories of these challenges don't typically make headlines so it's not a story many fully understand. However, community leaders need to pay attention nonetheless as we are potentially heading toward conditions that could have grave consequences for our communities.

For sure we need the kind of jobs that employers like GM provide. On the other hand, without the jobs and services provided by the social-profit sector, we may not have the kind of communities where we want to live. Ultimately, like many things in life, it is a lot about balance. There are many who aren't sure the general public either understands, or fully appreciates, the Third, Voluntary, Social-Profit, or Community Nonprofit Sector.

Even when the general public typically understands the critical contribution made by the one in four Canadian adults who volunteer, they don't always understand there are also a lot of paid staff who work within the sector. When you dig a little deeper, it's clear this perception is likely more about a lack of value and appreciation for the sector in general. Both staff and volunteers play essential roles but it is volunteers that make the sector unique. At the very least every social-profit organization has a volunteer board of directors. It is this choice to become involved as volunteers that sets the sector apart from the government and the private sectors.

The social-profit sector does more than provide services. Veteran Canadian politician Ed Broadbent has often talked eloquently about how central the sector has been to making democracy work.[77] Social-profit organizations bring their expertise in working with communities and individuals to public policy debates and identify social priorities to governments—even if it means being critical. He also believes the sector is the most important means of engaging citizens with each other and with governments.

Through voluntary action, we learn to cooperate and to give of ourselves—a process that builds trust and a sense of community. Through participation we acquire the basic skills of democratic life—how to find a voice, and to use it for the common good.

The Benefits of Working in a Social-Profit

While it's true some social-profits are powered largely by volunteers or under-paid workers fueled by their passion and dedication to a specific cause, many organizations simply don't fit that description. And, even when salaries are lower, the benefits may be better.

For sure the social-profit sector is a place to grow and learn. Working for a social-profit organization typically means more flexibility in one's job description and in the opportunities to stretch. They are also fabulous learning environments for young employees or those seeking a career change as it's typical to wear many hats and become

---

77   Retrieved August 2010. ttp://www.thephilanthropist.ca/index.php/phil/article/view/120/1h20.

involved in a variety of activities. As well, there is the opportunity to make great contacts and develop strong community networks.

Social-profits also generally provide a positive work environment as they tend to look out for individuals and families more than the average business or government organization. While wages are not always competitive, they are often offset by generous vacation time, sick days, and flexible schedules.

Working for a social-profit means you get to work for a good cause, feel passionate about what they are doing and make the world, or at least some part of it, a better place.

Together, social-profit organizations provide opportunities for citizens to join hands in the effort to make their world a better place. They are essential—social, environmental, and economic challenges cannot and will not be met by business or government alone.

Social Capital and Asset-based Approaches

While many might not understand its significance, it was by far the most meaningful speaker's gift I have ever been given.

I was presented with a beautiful eagle's feather after delivering a workshop at an Aboriginal community capacity building conference. The eagle plays an important spiritual role in aboriginal culture as it is the eagle that is identified as the messenger of the Creator and the creature who flies the highest and sees the furthest. I was told that when one receives an eagle feather, that person is being acknowledged with gratitude and respect.

It was another reminder for me of how much there is to be gained from better understanding Aboriginal culture. Recently I've learned more about the powerful lessons of the medicine wheel as well as the seven sacred teachings honouring the basic virtues that are intrinsic to a full and healthy life—love, respect, courage, honesty, wisdom, humility, and truth.

I see the wisdom in the powerful message of each generation being responsible for ensuring the survival of the seven generations to come, and the reminder that the decisions we make today will affect many others tomorrow. Grounded in centuries of history, these, like many other Aboriginal traditions, remain wise and relevant to this day.

And yet, despite these wise traditions, there are still far too many who see Aboriginal communities as something needing to be fixed. Just as with other communities and cultures, the reality is that we instead need to shift from a *needs-based view* to one that is more *capacity focused*. In other words, shift our thinking to understand that every individual and every community has strengths or assets. Instead of focusing on deficiencies, problems, or needs from a top-down or outside-in approach, we need to recognize the skills, talents, and gifts that each individual and community already possess.

If we are truly committed to strengthening individual capacity, we must build from our respective strengths. And, if we want social and economic revitalization, we need to start with what is already present within a community—not only the capacities of the residents as individuals, but also the existing businesses, social profit, and government organizations.

This asset-based approach to community development, promoted by John McKnight[78] from Northwestern University, typically begins with asking a community, "What has been successful in your community that you could share with others?"

Citizens, informal associations and social-profit organizations, land (and everything on it), formal institutions, and the economy (things that are shared, purchased, traded or exchanged) are the types of assets that need to be mapped or recorded as part of an inventory.

And, as it is ultimately the people who are the answer, McKnight suggests it is critical to focus on finding who has what assets in a community and how they can be connected and used to address challenges. The advantage of this asset-based approach to community building is that it also reinforces the idea that citizens and local community stakeholders can be active change agents rather than passive beneficiaries or clients.

It is this focus on local strengths and the connections between them that will strengthen the social capital within our communities

---

78   Kretzmann, J. and McKnight, J. (1993). *Building communities from the inside out: A path toward finding and mobilizing a community's assets.* Evanston, IL: Institute for Policy Research, Northwestern University.

and the degree to which a community trusts, networks, coordinates, cooperates, and collaborates for mutual benefit.

The individual capacities of residents are the basic building blocks of any community. Everyone has strengths and assets and everyone and every community is a glass of water half full, not half empty.

Of course being clear about our assets isn't the answer in and of itself. The assets will also need to be applied to broad based community capacity building. This became clearer to me at a recent meeting where I listened as participants took turns providing updates on their work as it related to community capacity building. One government employee reported that a clear direction was being communicated at a number of different levels. The direction she and others were hearing? Action! Enough research and planning already!

Elected officials and senior staff were conveying that they wanted to see new or improved programs and initiatives delivering relevant and meaningful outcomes related to individual, social, economic, and environmental well-being. Apparently, their current focus on research and conducting

> " Do not follow where the path may lead... go instead where there is no path and leave a trail."
>
> — Ralph Waldo Emerson

needs assessment, while seen as an asset, was too often resulting in *analysis paralysis* and a lack of progress or any real change. While research and planning is an important part of the solution, it needed to be balanced with more application. Like many others, they were struggling with the how-to of applying their assets to a change process.

There's no doubt we live in challenging times as we move from a manufacturing to a knowledge economy. Unfortunately in too many cases, we've tried to apply old planning approaches to new times, as well as to new and complex problems. Today it seems people are more likely to be looking for a road map and, especially in times of change, one that provides clear direction, expectations, process, and action steps.

I'm not saying community leaders should be telling us what to do. I think instead they need to design and support a *process* for action. Today the challenges are complex, and one person—regardless of how smart they might be—is never going to be able to solve them on their own. That means the leader's job is not to dictate direction or solve problems but rather to ensure a *process* that engages a broad range of stakeholders in working together. Involving more stakeholders from the beginning of the process, will also ensure they are committed to implementing the identified direction and change as it evolves.

Our work has also taught us that this process for action is far more successful when an assets-approach is utilized. That simply means identifying both individual and community strengths or successes and then levering them. This is generally a far more effective approach then using a "needs assessment" that tries to fix challenges that might be overwhelming and therefore contributing to analysis paralysis.

In their recent book, *Switch: How to Change When Change is Hard,* authors Chip Heath and Dan Heath[79] suggest these assets or "bright spots", as they call them, provide the road map. And as we've learned, they are also suggesting we need to switch from *traditional problem solving* to *scaling successes* and *bright spot evangelizing.*

> ❝ ❝ The lightning spark of thought generated in the solitary mind awakens its likeness in another mind."
>
> — Thomas Carlyle

In community settings this means identifying what's working and then figuring out how to do more of it or to explore how it could be ramped up. This approach can be applied to individuals, businesses, organizations, or to an entire community.

To find their bright spots, communities need to look for unique or authentic restaurants, landmarks, festivals, retail outlets, businesses, talents, or historical landmarks. Once they've found their unique bright spot, they need to do more to capitalize or scale the success. In that way, one bright spot can become a magnet and multiplier for growth as well as a brand for the community that eventually leads to a tipping point for success.

The end result is that leading with, and scaling successes, is a surefire way of reducing analysis paralysis and increasing traction and action.

---

79   Heath, C, and Heath, D. (2010). *Switch: How to change when change is hard.* New York: Random House.

Generate Creative Thinking and Innovation

I'm very proud of the years I spent teaching at Niagara College. It was a good fit for someone like me who was born practical. I used to joke that while universities were definitely about the *wings* meaning theories and philosphies, colleges were much more about the *landing gear*. While one needs both wings and landing gear to fly, I am without a doubt a landing gear kind of woman.

So, while I'm always intrigued by new concepts, ideas, and solutions for building communities, my real test for innovation is whether or not something really makes a difference for people. As a result, innovation needs to be about challenging the status quo as well as believing that we can, and ought to, do better.

The challenge, of course, is how to foster a culture of innovation that accelerates improvements to quality of life in our communities. It seems to be a delicate balance between order and chaos especially since we know that new ideas are rarely hatched in rigidly structured environments.

Like many others, I used to think that innovation was a blinding flash of brilliance from a lone inventor. Some quirky, genius-level individual who looks for insights to develop into ideas and then shapes into value-adding innovations. He or she then makes sure it works and does their due diligence before eventually getting it ready for market.

CBC's television show, Dragon's Den, reinforces this thinking as do the stories passed down about inventors—think Thomas Edison and Henry Ford. However, I'm learning that innovation might be about something more than a brilliant idea from one person. Instead, in our community building work, I'm seeing that innovation is more likely to be about the relationships or networks that bring together already existing ideas or resources to apply them in different ways.

> " A leader these days needs to be a host—one who convenes diversity; who convenes all viewpoints in creative processes where our mutual intelligence can come forth."
>
> — Margaret Wheatley

History supports this same observation. A painter who became a secretary, Betty Nesmith Graham, used her knowledge of how artists painted over their mistakes to invent "Liquid Paper". Henry Ford's

163

best known invention of the assembly line was the result of taking existing learnings from Singer sewing machines, meat packing, and Campbell soup, and combining them in a totally new way to build cars efficiently. Although Nikola Tesla invented the alternating current, it was Thomas Edison who got the credit. His team and extensive networks resulted in electricity being a breakthrough or mainstream innovation.

It also explains how US President Obama got elected. He used existing Facebook technology in a new way at the grassroots level that allowed him to harness supporters and donations.

Today in the health field, *translational research* is bridging the gap between academics and practitioners to make sure what's being researched has a practical use as well as to show how existing ideas can be applied in new ways. The new networks being set up to take research from academic to clinical settings and then to mainstream adaptation often result in creative re-combinations or applications rather than one flash of brilliance.

It would seem these innovations are as much about the social side as they are about the technical. *Real innovation might just be the result of relationships, trust, and networks.* Not just any relationships but instead extensive and diverse networks. In fact, the more diversity within the network, the better the fix is likely to be.

> "Your future is whatever you make it, so make it a good one."
>
> — Doc, Back to the Future III

Ultimately this means that we are all an important part of creating the culture of innovation that is essential for enhancing and improving our lives. You don't have to fit the image of a mad scientist but you do have to be curious, willing to embrace experimentation, risk taking, exploratory thinking, and idea generation. Of critical importance will be an acceptance that it will also be necessary to hang out with others who may not typically be part of your network.

So what can community leaders do to help create a culture of innovation?

A culture of innovation is an environment or a vibe that is conducive to leading edge or breakthrough thinking, collaboration, and the nimble implementation of new ideas.

It is also important to think about what it isn't. Anyone who has worked in an organization that isn't innovative can give you an idea of how to recognize the lack of it.

If you work in a place where people are bemused by your ideas or you often hear the phrase, "You can't do that because we've always done it this way", chances are there isn't a lot of innovation going on. Likewise if you can't remember the last time anything happened that was really cool—as in the kind of happening that you'd want to share with your family and friends over dinner, then chances are your workplace isn't embracing innovation.

If your organization tends to spend most of their time focused on process rather than success, or, if there is a heavy emphasis on budget cuts and the dollars for training and development continue to be reduced, you're also at-risk for a lack of innovation. Other indicators of a lack of innovation just might be an excess of baby boomers, extensive policies and procedures (as in red tape), little diversity, and few people under the age of thirty.

But perhaps most indicative of a lack of innovation will be the management style. Innovative organizations and businesses are not bureaucracies run by managers. Instead they have leaders who work with both their internal and external stakeholders, including a genuinely involved workforce, to develop a compelling vision for their future, clear values and priorities, and a pretty flat hierarchy to make it happen.

Innovative organizations and companies act differently. In these organizations ideas flow freely, both success and failure are championed, and innovation is encouraged and supported throughout the organization. This will also result in innovations being celebrated on a regular basis and the word "innovation" being reflected in planning initiatives, policies, and position descriptions. Employees never seem to be bored and often suggest that if you are, you should just wait five minutes.

You will also know you're part of an innovative organization or company by the sheer number of innovators. How will you recognize an innovator?

The innovators will be those who aren't afraid to challenge the status quo if they don't like what currently exists. They will be those who understand the importance of vision and dreams, and who will expand their own comfort zones and take risks to inspire new thinking. Innovators will be okay with appearing foolish, the risk of not looking good in the eyes of others, and living with uncertainty and chaos. Innovators will, without exception, be committed to hard work, ongoing communication, lifelong learning, and will practice a combination of intuition, research, and analysis.

These innovators will be people thriving within an environment that places an emphasis on thinking constantly about how to do things better and differently. New ideas will be seen as a critical investment and rather than saying, "It can't be done," people will be asking, "How can we make this happen?"

During difficult times, maintaining the status quo is in itself an achievement but ensuring innovation will be even more so. It is even more important to keep that innovation manifesto and the leadership it requires front and centre when we're bogged down in the administrivia of our day-to-day reality. It will be essential to demonstrate innovative leadership.

A key component of that leadership is ensuring vision, as nothing happens without a vision. It is that vision, together with the outcomes that it entails, that will keep us everyone motivated and focused on the possibilities.

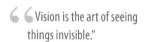
6 6 Vision is the art of seeing things invisible."

— Jonathan Swift

However, even once that vision is in place, creativity has to be married with the discipline of management if innovation is to occur. It is also important to learn to work in an environment that is constantly changing and to accept uncertainty, take measured risks, and sometimes fail, but always dissect, discuss, and learn from what went wrong. We will also need to be much more courageous about admitting when we're doing something that isn't working, even if it means backing up and starting again.

It is, as a wise person once said, "We all want progress, but if you're on the wrong road, progress means doing an about-turn and walking back to the right road; in that case, the one who turns back soonest is the most progressive."[80]

---

80 Lewis, C. S. (1942). Retrieved August 2010 http://www.rhube.com/category/politics/.

A commitment to innovation also means embracing the idea that many of the answers being sought may already exist. Instead of inventing something new, sometimes it is better just to be more proactive about finding promising practices, sharing them, and sometimes applying them in a different way.

Honesty, originality, and authenticity are other traits that seem to be essential for innovative organizations. Teams that can be honest and truthful with one another always seem to get to something new and to real breakthroughs without even trying. There's something unmistakably original and truthful about innovative leadership.

I've also worked in organizations where I learned that being vocal about a problem wasn't always well-received and that even when there was consensus about a problem, the innovation required to solve it was seen as being the domain of management rather than that of the collective. Too often there seemed to be far more interest in policies, procedures, and maintaining the status quo than there was in taking advantage of trends and issues.

Innovative organizations are those where thinking about how to do things differently is embedded within their culture. For example, Apple Computers embraced innovation with their 1997 advertising slogan "Think Different" and maintains it to this day.

The text that accompanied that campaign has become something of a mantra for innovators around the world.

"Here's to the crazy ones. The misfits. The rebels. The troublemakers. The round pegs in the square holes. The ones who see things differently. They're not fond of rules. And they have no respect for the status quo. You can quote them, disagree with them, glorify or vilify them. About the only thing you can't do is ignore them. Because they change things. They push the human race forward. And while some may see them as the crazy ones, we see genius. Because the people who are crazy enough to think they can change the world are the ones who do." [81]

The most effective community leaders will be those who understand and are able to nurture this same receptiveness toward innovation.

---

81   Retrieved September 2010. http://en.wikipedia.org/wiki/Think_Different.

Nurture Social Innovation and Creative Environments

Nurturing Innovators

Recently while shopping for a gift, I came across a poster with a picture of a rock climber reaching upward along a sheer face of mountain. The caption below read, "You gotta stretch to touch the future."

It struck me that most of my energy these days is focused on that kind of stretching. Those I'm working with are working hard to find new ways of working with community leaders to build active, creative, and engaged communities.

In our case, the blessing and the curse is that the leaders are sprinkled across the province as are the staff and contractors providing community development coaching. As a result we're relying more on technology to support the interactions and resource sharing between, and among, those involved.

Sounds simple but the reality is that out-of-the-box technology to support community development doesn't really exist. This means we're working to develop that technology with a smart and innovative woman named Dianne Renton Clark from Trendspire Canada Inc.

As one might imagine, it's not without its challenges. Users have difficulty seeing possibilities beyond what they are used to seeing in a typical organizational website. Few are able to see our vision of something that is more like a drop-in centre combined with a coffee shop and library. In other words, they are only able to see what is currently available rather than what has yet to be invented.

> " Opportunity always involves some risk. You can't steal second base and keep your foot on first."
>
> — Frederick B. Wilcox

Those involved in overseeing the entire initiative have built the trusting relationships that allow open, honest, and very direct feedback. As a result, in the course of a discussion about the challenges of trying to ensure an ongoing investment of time and resources in something that has yet to be invented, one of the team members bluntly referred to herself as a techno-midget and said she just simply did not like technology. Although she went on to say she knew it was important and essential for the initiative, she also admitted she would find it difficult to be the one charging up the hill waving the technology flag.

That honest and courageous admittance of her inability to be an early adopter of technology helped everyone involved rethink and refocus plans for moving forward.

The learning is that not everyone is cut out to be an early adopter. Even fewer are cut out to be innovators like Dianne.

A number of years ago, the late Everett Rogers, achieved academic prominence for his *Diffusion of Innovations*[82] theory that addressed this same issue.

Rogers proposed that adopters of any new innovation or idea could be categorized as innovators (2.5%), early adopters (13.5%), early majority (34%), late majority (34%) and laggards (16%).

This means that typically there is a very small percentage of those who actually innovate, and a small majority of those who pick up quickly on ideas, don't mind taking risks, and enjoy the experimentation and adventure. Some only adopt or change when the innovations have been debugged and evidence demonstrates their soundness and effectiveness. The majority are reluctant, often lag behind, and will need to be urged and pressed to change.

These categories provide a common language for innovation researchers. Each adopter's willingness and ability to adopt an innovation would depend on their awareness, interest, evaluation, trial, and adoption. Additionally, people fall into different categories depending upon the innovation.

> "Genius, in truth, means little more than the faculty of perceiving in an unhabitual way."
>
> — William James

So while my colleague and good friend Dianne is indeed an innovative techno-queen, the other is a techno-reluctant late adopter of technology. However that same colleague without a doubt is an innovator when it comes to building and sustaining the new partnerships and relationships that are essential to our initiative.

So should we be worried about this apparent lack of commitment to innovation and change? And, if we don't want to change and we're not very good at it, do we need to keep banging the drum about it?

If one's business, department, organization, or community has a positive reputation, a strong profile, credibility and healthy finances, it may not be as much of an issue.

---

82   Rogers, E. M. (1962). *Diffusion of innovations*. New York: Free Press.

On the other hand, if there's room for improvement, you just might need some innovating and stretching in order to make sure you can "touch the future".

Social Innovation

Truth be told, I have been known to irritate those in charge, albeit not intentionally. This week, as we worked to expand the team putting legs under our initiative, I did it again.

I realized afterward that it was largely the result of my assuming that everyone understood the nuances as well as the values brought by individuals who are best described as social innovators.

And yet, when it became clear that others didn't necessarily understand their value, I floundered somewhat, finding it difficult to describe their characteristics and why they are so important.

It also became clear that our need for social innovators means that even our approach to recruitment is different. While most begin with a job description and then recruit, our approach has been to seek talent and values first.

We also learned that we may need a new lexicon to help us understand the different way of working that social innovators reflect. Not only do we need to understand the importance of what they do, we need to figure out how they fit or don't fit with the jobs typically seen on an organization chart. And, while we're at it, let's just admit that the traditional org chart gets in the way of social innovators who work best in a very flat hierarchy.

I do know that the social innovators we are looking for don't tend to respond to typical job advertisements or want to work in a traditional nine to five environment. And, although money is important, it's not their key driver. They're passionate about making a difference and as a result too often settle for less money and more hours. They think and strategize on their own time, and because they get excited when they've simplified something really complicated, they often give away their knowledge to others who may not value the learning curve it took to get there.

But what exactly is a social innovator and why are they important?

Successful innovators tend to understand that the *how* is far less important than the *who*. Those I'm working with now always put the emphasis on people and relationships. This ability to nurture and strengthen relationships is a critical talent as it allows them to learn as well as spread and adapt ideas at all levels. These relationships, as they deepen over time, are what will ultimately sustain new approaches, and make success travel.

As they build relationships, social innovators work across silos to forge alliances with the public, private and social-profit sectors, harnessing the power of both established institutions as well as those at the grassroots level. Along the way, they find unexpected allies, identify areas for working together, and develop formal and informal networks, coalitions, and collaborations. In this way, step by step, and yet not without some pain along the way, barriers to change are eliminated.

Despite the fact that social innovators are often very diverse, they do seem to share some common characteristics.

They're usually persistent (some might call it stubborn), collaborative, good communicators, comfortable with chaos, creative, and entrepreneurial.

Adept social innovators also typically bring a talent for being able to balance thinking and acting. As they work within complex, often chaotic settings, they seem to have this ability to stand still and identify a theme, pattern, or system. Then they move quickly to take advantage of the opportunity.

One of my colleagues did that just this week, when she connected some rather obscure dots that led to a brilliant business model for the work we're doing in communities that has the potential to sustain our work beyond the parameters of the project funding. Another one of our team members prompted a technology company to develop a system of credits that would allow social entrepreneurs like her to exchange her ideas and solutions for technical support.

Social innovators seem to be able to bring people together to learn and solve problems creating a synergy that moves vague, nebulous aspirations toward a clear vision and effective action.

So why are social innovators important to us?

If we're going to make our communities better places to live, work, and play, we need social innovators who generate ideas, adjust, adapt, rework, and, in due course, create.

171

Creative Environments

A while ago, I spent two days in a marathon planning session and was left rattled by a rather unexpected revelation. Could it be that planning is fun?

If you'd asked me for adjectives to describe a closeted two-day weekend with both board and committee members, as well as staff, fun probably wouldn't have made the top ten list of adjectives. However, the reality was that it was quite enjoyable. There was spirited discussion, disagreements, and ultimately some breakthrough thinking and productive results.

For me, and perhaps others, it was due in part to what author Jerry Hirshberg calls *creative abrasion*. In his book, *The Creative Priority: Putting Innovation to Work in Your Business,* Hirshberg stresses that in many organizations and cultures, conflict is viewed as being negative and counterproductive to team spirit and harmony. He suggests that too often everyone edits their real thoughts in order to reduce conflict and maintain harmony. As a result, there is less likelihood of innovation. He suggests that the bureaucratic need for predictability, structure, and conformity, is in fact more likely to be conducive to killing ideas.[83]

While Hirschberg is not suggesting we make conflict a priority for conflict's sake, he is suggesting it can lead to creative abrasion, original thinking, and innovation. He cautions that it is difficult to implement as it requires a culture that accepts a certain amount of conflict as normal and productive. It also takes courage to manage creative abrasion as one needs to be able to see past the discomfort of conflict to its potential benefits.

While some might find the idea of conflict counterintuitive to a healthy work environment, he also points out that if a workplace is safe for ideas, it's sure to be safe for people.

A culture that nurtures creative abrasion is also one where failure is allowed. If failure is okay, risk-aversive behavior isn't a by-product. For instance, in our planning session, our group felt comfortable taking the risk of discarding the process proposed by the facilitator when it became clear that it simply wasn't working for everyone. Playing

---

83   Hirshberg, J. (1999). *The creative priority: Putting innovation to work in your business.* New York: Harper Collins.

with, and building on each other's ideas, the end result was a totally new approach to organizing the resulting strategic plan. Creative abrasion also occurred because of the different filters and lenses provided by those in the group as well as by combining those who had a deep history of the organization with those who were newbies.

In addition to the right culture, Hirshberg suggests we need divergent leadership. As he puts it, sometimes the right person for the job might just be two people. To ensure creative abrasion, you need to hire people who are different from one another.

I learned this years ago working for the City of Niagara Falls when, as a new manager, I hired a head lifeguard. Instead of seeking someone with skills and thinking different from my own, I hired a young woman who was much like me. Not surprisingly she drove me mad because we were both weak in the same areas. While divergent pairs are still likely to drive each other crazy, if their skills and knowledge are a fit with the job, they will have a better chance of solving the most challenging of problems as well as forming new ideas by combining their different perspectives.

Even divergent leaders though will need to be careful to question previously formed beliefs and known standpoints, or to define the problem without having an already preconceived answer in mind. Hirshberg also stresses the need to step back from the canvas when you are too close to the problem during problem solving sessions. Sometimes not working is the most effective thing you can do to move work forward. Direct contact with information and research also helps to stimulate the imagination.

> " When in doubt, make a fool of yourself. There is a microscopically thin line between being brilliantly creative and acting like the most gigantic idiot on earth. So what the hell… leap."
>
> — Cynthia Heimels

The end result is that creative abrasion is good, and creative abrasion doesn't happen by playing *by* the rules, it happens by playing *with* the rules.

Engineering Creative Environments

A leader can also deliberately engineer an environment to be conducive to creativity. For instance, our office staff used to celebrate "Cheesecake Friday". Although not a celebration generally acknowledged by those outside our walls, it was held about once a month usually on the spur of the moment.

I am sure that others in our office building who saw us taking time in the middle of the afternoon to sit together talking, laughing, joking, and eating cheesecake, must truly have wondered about the quality of the management decisions being made. However, it truly was a wise investment of our time.

The truth of the matter is that our work was complex and multi-pronged. We cared deeply about those we served and worked hard as a nimble and entrepreneurial team to deliver meaningful outcomes. We learned that time-outs were essential for rejuvenation although I must admit that the intense post sugar rush did sometimes trigger an overwhelming desire to nap. However, we also learned that having fun through a variety of experiences does impact a team's communication, engagement, and ultimately the quantity and quality of our program and products.

Recent studies show that creativity and innovation are directly related to how we feel, and, how we feel, is related to our creativity and innovation.[84]

One Harvard study[85] shows that one happy day (perhaps a cheesecake day?) led to more creativity the next day as the result of an overnight incubation of ideas. If there is also a supportive work environment, creativity will be enhanced even further.

When people are happy, they tend to be less tied to the "tried and true" and more likely to either seek new ideas and actions or, pay more attention to, and be more receptive to those happening around them.

Quite honestly, and as we all know, it's not easy in today's fast-paced world to create and sustain a happy and productive work environment. Mere cheesecake isn't going to make that a reality. It will also require a flattened hierarchy, good communication, and respect for one another and the varied strengths each person brings to the workplace.

---

84   Fredrickson, B. L. (2003). The value of positive emotions. *American Scientist*, 91, 330-335.

85   Amabile, T. M. and Kramer, S. J. (October 2003). *The best (and worst) days in creative project teams: Some preliminary results.* Paper presented at the Society for Experimental Social Psychology, Boston.

However, there are other specific activities that can be used to facilitate creativity within a work environment.

Graphics, pictures, or drawings can help to illustrate ideas. I've recently discovered a software program that allows us to illustrate models and ideas. My boss is notorious for his use of whiteboards.

We've also learned to think in opposites and quite often ask the question "what if"?

One of my now former co-workers was our unofficial "Director of Fun". I think every organization should have one. She was very good at planning for recesses and making sure we took time out to laugh. She had a stellar collection of movie and audio clips that always got us going. She was also renowned for playing the theme song from "Malcolm in the Middle" and singing along to "You're not the boss of me now." In fact, music is always good. During a planning session one group of co-workers did a rap to explain the many hats worn by their department. It was laugh out loud funny.

Dressing casually also seems to contribute to creativity as do props. This week our staff took turns wearing a headband that included bobbing shamrocks. We also have a collection of troll dolls that sometimes have the names of real people attached allowing us to vent in a healthy way.

Engineering this same kind of creative environment will be especially important for today's community leaders who are being pressured to address rising health care costs, poverty, struggling social profit organizations, cultural diversity, crime, environmental concerns and more.

In our work we've seen creative environments lead to innovative community solutions. One tiny community decided to combat obesity by organizing their own version of the television show, "The Biggest Loser".

Another town has incorporated a state-of-the-art indoor running track within the seating of a newly built arena. As a sustainability strategy, with a population of only 15,000, they've also managed to include skyboxes that were sold out to corporations before the arena opened. Within the same building, they've added a fitness centre, swimming pool, and co-located with a university in order to provide a kinesiology lab, fitness testing, physiotherapy, and a host of others services in order to truly become a centre for well-being.

Another community struggled with what to do with a perfectly good arena in the wrong location. They knew that accessibility would be increased if a new one could be grouped with all of the other recreation facilities at a different location. The clever solution was to renovate the existing arena to become the new city hall and library. Skylights were added and many of the exposed ducts and struts were painted in colourful hues. The reception area is bright and open with offices added around the perimeter. The resulting ambience is quite wonderful.

So while creativity is essential, it might just be the result of blending the facts of logical and rational thought with intuition and a bit of behaving in a slightly outrageous way. When information and knowledge are integrated with the insight and charge of creativity, the result will be an unstoppable organization or community where anything will be possible.

Awareness of Policy and Legislation Which Could Have an Impact on Your Community

While there are policy junkies among us, I don't happen to be one of them. If it were up to me, policy would be shaped much more by first implementing and piloting programs and practice and then writing the policy. In reality, policy is more often shaped by elected officials and bureaucrats far removed from programs and the impact of their implementation. It is especially frustrating, as our organization has experienced recently, to see government staff totally ignoring feedback from the stakeholders who will be impacted by the policy.

Regardless, to be big picture or system thinkers, community leaders need to be aware of policy and legislation which could potentially impact their communities.

Why is it important to pay attention to policy? For government, policy reflects the basic principles by which their government and decision-making will be guided. Policy lays out the priorities they will seek to achieve on behalf of their constituents. Legislation is the actual making of the law that will implement the policy direction.

As policy and legislation is developed at all levels of government—for Canadians this happens at local, regional, provincial, or territorial as well as at the national level—it may appear at first glance to be an overwhelming task. But, if you aren't a policy junkie, you may simply have to work in a different way to stay in the loop.

First of all, it is essential to stay connected to the daily news with your ears tuned for news related to legislation and policy. Policy could relate to human rights, climate change, crime prevention, housing, transportation, education, land use, environmental issues etc. For some that may mean reading the newspaper, subscribing to listservs, or listening to the radio.

It is also important to stay connected to elected officials. Their constituency newsletters are generally a good way to keep your ear to the ground. Getting to know your local politicians is also a good strategy as a lot can be learned over a cup of coffee or during a quick phone call.

Take time to nurture relationships with staff within ministries or departments related to your work as they are typically involved in gathering feedback and writing actual policy documents. Many member associations also play a key role in staying connected to policy development and advocacy. Join those of particular interest to you e.g. municipal affairs, recreation and parks, government administrators, or, stay connected to their work via their websites.

Once you are made aware of the policy, your decision to get involved will be dependent upon an analysis that considers the type of policy, the importance of the policy at issue, the number of stakeholders affected, the effect of the policy on your community, and the urgency of the issue in question.

Understanding the Importance of a Community's Culture, Personality, and Brand

Whether or not we acknowledge it, a community's culture and its brand is all around us. Although we may take them for granted, we are likely already familiar with the values and traditions of our schools, family, community, and the region where we live. Collectively these values and tradition form a local culture which in turn provides a sense of identity for communities and residents.

This identity facilitates the common understandings, traditions, and values which are a foundation for ensuring and strengthening well-being. Culture contributes to building a sense of local identity and solidarity, and shapes the confidence communities have for coming together to address specific needs and problems. This local commitment among residents, regardless of economic or political conditions, can serve as a valuable tool for shaping the effectiveness of planning, growth, and action, as local residents can encourage development that preserves or promotes their culture. This is particularly important in development efforts that seek to elicit local participation, volunteerism, and community action.

Yet, how does one get beyond the raw economic data or surveys to find the real personality of a community?

It is, in fact, much more about the stories, the chats with residents about the "good old days", community gatherings, local bloggers, the art and music scene, and the local newspaper and cable television programming. It is these informal channels of communication within a neighbourhood, town, city, or region that tells you more about the personality or "brand" of a community.

> "Never tell people how to do things. Tell them what to do and they will surprise you with their ingenuity."
>
> — General George Patton

In many ways, Richard Florida's[86] innovative discussions about the creative class are really about the personality of a community. The personality or brand of a community is really what makes your community unique and distinctive. It is what you brag about and what you miss if you were to move away.

But why is it that some communities are successful in building on the brand and culture of their communities by generating innovative solutions while others get stuck?

According to the late American business guru, Peter F. Drucker, innovation is "change which creates a new dimension of performance".[87] So instead of thinking about innovation as a specific event or prod-

---

86   Florida, R. (2002). *The rise of the creative class: And how it's transforming work, leisure, community and everyday life.* New York: Perseus Book Group.

87   Hesselbein, F. (2002). *Hesselbein on leadership.* San Francisco: Jossey-Bass.

uct, these communities have understood, as Drucker suggested, that innovation is an integrative process that can be used for solving complex problems and enhancing their brand. They've learned that the process of innovation is strengthened through social exchange, and a collaborative, agile, and ongoing community development process that explores assets, challenges, and opportunities—ultimately getting them to the place "where need meets opportunity".

This is important to understand because if a community's personality is conducive to collaboration, it can be the DNA or critical element required for improving innovation and performance.

Developing Teams and Coalitions

Years ago I did some work with a very funny, self-employed motivational speaker. As a one person operation there was a lot involved in getting him promoted, booked, and on the road. As a result he put his daughter to work. At the age of nine, he bestowed upon her the title of Vice-President of Photocopying. She had her own business cards and a paycheque based on an hourly rate—albeit one quite a bit below the legislated minimum wage.

While it made for a humourous anecdote he often used in his speeches, it also spoke to his belief that it is critical to acknowledge the importance and contribution of each and every team member.

I thought about that recently as I was reflecting on the depth and richness of our own stellar team. In one conversation I told Rose, one of our staff, that we should make her vice president of nurturing. She responded by saying that she'd often been referred to as den mother but that she sort of liked the VP title.

The discussion was a reminder that the best teams really are those that have different strengths. Being able to build a dynamic team—a group of individuals capable of pulling smoothly in the same direction—is important for all leaders. As such it requires understanding that people are different and differences are essential. Those who have skills and abilities, approaches, and leadership and communication styles different from your own aren't deliberately trying to annoy you—they are simply different and different is good.

It is, of course, impossible to divide the entire population into four personality styles but many assessment tools are based on findings that do just that. As previously discussed, four styles are often determined by whether an individual is more oriented to *people* or to *tasks* and *goals*, as well as whether a their temperament is more *extroverted* or outwardly public, or *introverted* and private by nature.

There are **Nurturers,** like Rose, who have a high tolerance for almost everything and keep people calm. They pay attention to feelings, are sociable, enjoy the company of others, and are friends with everyone. They are usually good listeners, non-competitive, and willing to take direction. Nurturers respect effective leadership, and are often happy building someone else's design rather than creating their own.

In addition to needing a Nurturer, there are other roles that will be important on every team. These include **Energizers, Researchers,** and **Organizers.**

Energizers are charismatic, buoyant, and full of life. They are open to new ideas and invitational to people. These are people who approach tasks and projects with great enthusiasm and energy. They will demand the freedom to work on their own, or volunteer to lead. Energizers enjoy competition and all out excitement. Because they enjoy being around people they are often the catalysts for moving the team forward.

Every team needs an **Organizer** as they are typically the dynamos who get things done. They are action-oriented, strong-willed people who always seem to get a lot accomplished in a short time. Organizers often have endless ideas, plans, and ambitions. And, they are also capable of keen insights, practical decisions, and sound judgment. Organizers place high regard on traditions, hierarchy, and clearly defined roles and expectations. They are attentive to detail, enjoy routines and systems, and are also usually the first to notice if a protocol or formality has been breached.

Researchers are also important to a team because they are conceptual thinkers who seek knowledge and understanding and like to solve problems or deal with that which is innovative by exploring ideas or developing models. Researchers have exceptional analytical abilities and are able to easily foresee a project or proposal's potential obstacles and hidden dangers.

Nurturers, Energizers, Organizers, and Researchers. Each is important because each brings different strengths to the team. If one begins to study the most effective teams, it becomes clear they will be the ones that have all four roles represented. Identify the role you play on your team as well as who might be missing. And while you might not end up as the vice-president of photocopying, you will have a team that fires on all jets.

Note: For access to a free leadership style assessment that measures the above, see http://acecommunities.ca/downloads/.

What Makes a Valuable Team Member?

Although everyone should always be mindful of the need to be seen as a valuable team member, when efforts are directed toward ensuring more active, creative, and engaged communities, it becomes even more important.

A number of years ago I hired an amazing woman named Alison who distinguished herself during a very competitive interview process. Her answer to one question in particular has stayed with me over the years. The question asked was, "What three words would a previous employer use to describe you?"

Her first two words were ones I had heard before—team player and good communicator, but it was the last one we all loved the most and made us certain she was the one we wanted to hire. Alison had answered, with an impish grin, that we would have to consider her answer as being one hyphenated word even though she knew it was actually two. Her third answer was, "low-maintenance".

It was an extraordinarily accurate word to describe her and one that I definitely was looking for in a team member. It is also a trait that has made her an invaluable resource to the organization where she still works. My guess is that if layoffs were ever to occur, she would likely be one of the last ones standing.

When we worked together I valued Alison's intuitiveness when it came to communicating. She kept me in the loop but never overwhelmed me with information that I didn't really need to have. She's viewed by everyone who knows her as a hardworking woman who gets things done efficiently and effectively and always with a smile on her face. Chances are every employer will value someone like Alison who stays positive and enthusiastic during stressful and busy times.

Rose, the Operations Coordinator on our current team, reflects that same positive spirit. She always manages to convey a calming presence when things get tense. Her first month on the job, entirely on her own initiative, she submitted an update that outlined her accomplishments and posed questions regarding future direction. In the same report, she also showed how her resourcefulness had saved us thousands of dollars.

Rose also demonstrates another quality that would endear her to any employer. She not only communicates her desire to take on more responsibilities, she has backed that up by taking courses on her own time. Now in addition to her expertise in operations and administration, volunteer management, bookkeeping, and event management, she's honing her skills in human resource management. This diversity makes her an even more valuable member of our team.

Her ability to anticipate the needs of our team, and dependably respond to them, has also added to her value. One day I skidded into the office to grab what I needed for a meeting at another location and found she had, without ever having been asked, packed a box for me that included everything I needed, including the copies I was coming in to make as I raced to the meeting. She had even thought to include promotional items as gifts for the volunteers.

While I've sometimes had employees who think it is enough just to be physically present at their desk, Rose understands that you also have to be mentally present in order to identify issues, present solutions, and be responsible for implementing them.

Rose also demonstrates that she is definitely not a backbencher when it comes to volunteering for extra duties. Her willingness to organize our social events, including monthly birthday celebrations with her to-die-for culinary extravaganzas, has also made everyone value and see the importance of the rare time we take to slow down and connect as a team.

Ultimately though, I think what I love the most about Rose is that she thanks us. She's grateful for what she's learning and for the opportunity to grow.

What Makes a Valuable Team Leader?

If you were to judge the man by his office alone, chances are you might not be all that impressed.

It's clear that paper rules in his office. There isn't one inch of surface in his office that isn't covered with stacks of paper. And, describing them as stacks, isn't an exaggeration. When he ducks his head a bit, you can't even tell he's in the office. Meetings in his office are pretty much impossible as the couch, chairs, and coffee table are also buried. A recent visitor laughingly described his system as open concept filing.

Despite the clutter, the reality is the guy is a brilliant CEO. The paper in his office represents hours and hours of research that has provided him with the knowledge and understanding, as well as practical examples, of what his organization must do in order to be well-positioned for the future.

That, in addition to his being receptive to feedback from others, has resulted in growing credibility among movers and shakers as well as the opening of doors to powerful offices that were once closed to the organization. The consequence of his work is that government funding and corporate sponsorships are now much more than a pipedream.

While there's no denying his filing system does need to be tamed somewhat, the reality is his passion for paper is one of the traits that makes him a successful team leader.

Experts agree that being on top of trends and issues is essential for today's leaders as is a willingness to take action on that information and knowledge. Part of what facilitates that action are two other things he's also good at doing—focusing on networking and viewing the world through the perspectives of others. But there are other qualities of a good leader that he also reflects.

One of them is the ability to enjoy ambiguity. Leaders often find themselves in grey zones where there may be no clear-cut answers, so they have to be able to thrive in those situations. While I'm not sure he really likes being in the grey zone, he does it well, somehow embracing the theory of chaos knowing that just when it seems it will never make sense it suddenly does.

While it may take a while to see him as the warm and fuzzy guy he is, it is apparent he has a skill for, and interest in, developing talent and bringing out the best in others. He has built a team reflecting diverse talents and abilities across a spectrum of ages. The combination of young, energetic and keen staff, together with the wisdom and experience of those more mature, is unbeatable.

While very diverse, the team shares a number of core values. The most important of these is a passion for the field, a strong work ethic, and a strongly honed sense of responsibility and accountability for their work. They're all just a wee bit quirky too, making for a fun, and at times, slightly wacky atmosphere.

It's clear that as a hardworking CEO he doesn't suffer fools gladly but he is also extraordinarily good at giving credit where it's due. He doesn't accept personal accolades for work done by his staff. He instead makes sure compliments are directed to those who performed the work.

All in all, it may be that a messy office might be more sensible than meticulous planning and storage for leaders. After all, Sir Alexander Fleming was also untidy and it was his untidiness that resulted in him not cleaning the petri dish that led to the discovery of penicillin.

While I'm not suggesting you want to let fungus grow in your office, perhaps it is as Albert Einstein once said, "If a cluttered desk is a sign of a cluttered mind, of what, then, is an empty desk?"

Developing Diverse Teams

In one of our many reflection meetings, one of our community coaches described the importance of diversity by saying, "The weirder the mix the better the fix."[88] We've learned that everyone in the community needs to be involved. The more diverse the stakeholders, the more innovative and responsive the solutions will be. Different perspectives lead to different and more creative and responsive solutions. It is especially important to ensure the inclusion of diverse populations.

---

88   Driedger, K. (Jan, 2009). ACE Communities Planning Meeting.

Aboriginal Learnings

Like many Canadians I should, but don't, know a lot about Aboriginal communities. My only exposure was the result of having three brothers who played lacrosse against teams from Six Nations. Typically they were outplayed and ultimately trounced. Within my rather white-bread high school of some 800, there were a total of two aboriginal students.

All I really knew is that Aboriginal peoples were the first to live in Canada. They had many different spiritual beliefs and cultural traditions including a very special relationship with nature.

Consequently my understanding came primarily from a media too often focused on the negative rather than on their many strengths and the richness of Aboriginal culture and values. Recently I've had the opportunity to learn more as the result of hosting and participating in a number of meetings involving a variety of Aboriginal communities. What I learned as one of the few white people in the room did not make me proud.

We did work hard to be sensitive to the differences in cultures. For instance, we made sure the room was set up in a circle to convey our belief that we were all equal and wanting to listen and learn from one another. We also began by smudging. While

66 Diversity is the one true thing we all have in common... celebrate it every day."

— Herbert Hoover

I didn't get it right initially, I now know that smoke from burning herbs is used to drive away negative energies and help one achieve a state of balance. It's not unlike washing your hands before eating except that it's an essential preliminary to almost all Native American ceremonies. You draw in the smoke with your hands first above your head and fan it to encircle your head and shoulders. Then to your heart and then down your legs and under your feet to ensure you are cleansed and ready to begin.

We began our two days of meetings rather tentatively knowing we would have to go slow in order to build trust and the longer term relationships that would be required for shared learning and resources.

Along the way I learned more about the historic inequities that have left many First Nations children, youth and families needing, and lacking, essential support and services. Many are still feeling the impact of having lost not only their land but also their cultural traditions, livelihood, and their unique way of life. Children were removed from their families and sent away to residential schools—where many were abused. As was pointed out during one of our meetings, it often resulted in many who never experienced the value and support of families and communities and never learned to be good parents or good citizens. Too often their pain was passed on to the next generation. While it was emphasized that healing is different for each individual and some are much further along in their journey, it is a contributing factor to the pain that often manifests itself in alcoholism, drug use, gambling, and violence.

The good news is that recreation, sport, arts, culture, and heritage activities are increasingly being seen as a solution. For youth it can result in improved fitness levels, personal development, enhanced self esteem, and leadership growth. As we've all learned, keeping kids busy keeps them out of trouble, reduces gang involvement, bullying, and the use of alcohol and drugs. An emphasis on traditional games and arts is also contributing to a greater sense of community, pride, and spirit.

Like other communities there is work ahead if we are to deal with declining volunteerism, lower community and parental involvement, higher participation costs, reduced resources, the increasing impact of technology as a diversion for youth, and the challenge of some-times ineffective political leadership.

What is clear, however, is that Aboriginal individuals, families, and communities are surfacing from shadows that have contributed to years of faulty perceptions and unhealthy relationships. We're seeing an emergence of the traditional holistic values of mind, body, and spirit, and, a greater understanding of the importance of family, community, and stewardship of the land.

While much of the work that needs to be done will have to take place within Aboriginal communities, other Canadians must also be ready and willing to make space for their rich and meaningful presence.

Importance of Immigrants

A number of years ago I landed at a meeting in St. John's, Newfoundland with a number of my colleagues from across the country.

One of the participants was a last-minute meeting replacement for an Executive Director who had recently moved on to another job. While it was clear he was a bit out of his element, it was also evident he was a twenty four year old keen to learn more about Canada's social profit sector. Already having graduated from university, he was clearly intrigued by a sector that was focused on making a difference. For him social capital appeared to be a far more appealing concept than that of contributing to the financial bottom line of a company.

Bright, attractive, polite, and personable, it was easy to include Bassam in the actual meeting as well as the sidebar conversations over lunch and dinner. Curious about the origins of his name, and the hint of an accent, I asked him about his heritage. As it turns out he was Assyrian and had moved to Canada when he was ten years old.

Bassam spent the first eight years of his life living a relatively normal life in a village in Iraq where his father worked in the military. Their life was turned upside down when Saddam Hussein, then President of Iraq, arbitrarily decided that more people needed to live in the cities. He subsequently ordered the demolition of Bassam's village as well as many others. Bulldozers simply reduced the village to rubble and Bassam, his mother, father, and nine siblings were left homeless. At that point, Bassam's father made a decision that he has never regretted despite the hardships that followed. He made the courageous decision to leave his country with his family and begin again to build a future.

Bassam and his family spent the next two years in a refugee camp in Turkey before finally being accepted for immigration to Canada. While many of their acquaintances ended up in Toronto, Bassam's family had very distant relatives in London, Ontario and the decision was made to move there. Once they got to London, Bassam's family immediately began looking for work. Fortunately, like others from Iraq, his father had grown up learning a lot about gardens and growing. He subsequently joined forces with an acquaintance in a maintenance and landscaping business where he continues to work hard and earn a respectable living to this day.

Bassam reports that although his mother misses her family in Iraq, especially now that many of her children have moved away from London, all are doing well. As soon as they were old enough, they got part time jobs. Some went to university and some are married and have children. All work hard.

In many ways they are typical of the hundreds and thousands of new arrivals before them who have come to Canada.

My own grandparents came to Canada from the Ukraine because the land my grandfather had inherited from his father was one seventh of the original plot. The other six portions went to his six siblings. Unfortunately it wasn't enough land to support my grandparents. However, it was just enough money to purchase two boat tickets to Canada. Unlike Bassam's family, my grandparents had no choice as to where they would live. At the time of my grandparents' arrival in Canada, Manitoba needed farmers, so Manitoba it was. They too worked hard, raised a family and contributed to their communities first in Manitoba and then in St. Catharines, Ontario.

Immigrants like Bassam's family and my own grandparents are the foundation of Canada. In addition to contributing to the rich culture of Canada, they typically worked hard and long at jobs other Canadians couldn't, or wouldn't, do.

Every year, hundreds of thousands of newcomers risk everything for the promise and possibility of Canada. They come speaking many languages and with diverse skills and abilities. Today, given Canada's aging baby boomers, they are also playing an increasingly important role in addressing our lack of skilled workers.

But perhaps what is even more important is that newcomers come to Canada with the motivation and the drive to make a better life for themselves and their families. And when they succeed, we all succeed.

> ❝ Leadership is not about being the one who pushes or pulls. 'The essence of leadership is to shift the inner place from which we operate both individually and collectively.'"
>
> — C. Otto Scharmer

Supporting Collaboration

I was recently in London, Ontario exchanging learnings regarding the how-to's of community building. The two days involved working with a stellar municipal team who've done a remarkable job of getting some 140 children, youth, and family-serving organizations to commit to applying an integrated service delivery model.

While integrated, systems-thinking services would seem like a no-brainer given that people don't come in segregated departments, too often we've built systems to serve them as if they do. Worse yet, these segregated systems become entrenched, bigger, and extraordinarily difficult to change.

As if segregated departments within a municipality aren't complicated enough, services could also be delivered by other levels of government, social-profits, or the private sector. As a result, we often seem to have lost sight of being people-centred and holistic-thinking, and are instead bogged down by funding silos, mandates, specialization, and turf protection. The average person in need of services related to social services, housing, recreation, health, education and the like, often gets lost in the complexities of the system.

There is a growing movement to suggest that business or privatization could do a better job of managing the system. At the very least, the thinking is that government and social-profits simply need to adopt a business approach to ensure a more integrated and consumer-focused system.

However, the more I work with communities, the more I am of the opinion that no one sector has the answers. While perhaps businesses could help social-profits increase efficiencies and reduce costs, money isn't the only measuring stick of success. Using business-thinking doesn't always help with complex social issues and challenges that typically require thinking and measures more aligned with fairness and human rights. If business calls the shots it is quite likely that competition, revenue generation, and returns on investment will trump the compassion, cooperation, and collaboration required for social change.

On the other hand, business thinking does nurture innovation, reward entrepreneurs, and generally results in improved products and performance because of the response to market feedback. They draw on the talents of individual employees and often share their economic rewards.

Government doesn't have the answers either as most of their responsibility is focused on ensuring basic security and social order. They protect democracy and the public interest while making decisions in the best interest of society and ensuring a level playing field of opportunity and a common framework of laws and their enforcement. As a result, the "p" services dominate—pipes, pavement, police, parks, planning, property assessment, public health etc.

Social or non-profit organizations celebrate, build, and protect the many values that are essential for healthy and vibrant communities. They work to ensure everyone has access to the support and services they need to develop their full physical, mental, and spiritual potential. They create spaces to celebrate the joy of culture and artistic expression, help to protect the environment, and contribute to economic development.

So while each of the three sectors have their own respective priorities, focus, and modus operandi, all three also have important pieces of what's needed to build healthy and vibrant communities. It is both a blessing and a curse because although there is a need to work together to ensure active, creative, and engaged communities, we don't have a neutral infrastructure from which this can take place.

Some have suggested that what is required is a new hybrid of organizations that incorporates the best of the three traditional sectors— private, government, and social profits—and as such falls within a new fourth sector.

What makes this kind of fourth sector or "For-Benefit" organization unique is that they would be grounded by a foundation of core principles that brings into play the best thinking and practices from within each of the sectors. As has been said before, new times require new thinking. However, it is just as true that new times just might require new infrastructures.

Recognizing and Responding to Complexity

Reverend Eugene Rivers is an American activist and Pentecostal minister based in Boston, Massachusetts. He was brought to Toronto several years ago to assist in curbing the rapid growth of gangs. Rivers is credited with initiating an innovative approach to dealing with youth violence that resulted in Boston's homicides dropping from 150 in 1990 to 31 in 1999.

The Boston approach involved police, youth workers, and black clergy reaching out to gang members, expressing zero-tolerance for violence, and cracking down on flare-ups. Their methods included breaking up street level drug markets, mounting federal prosecutions, and changing the conditions of supervision for parolees.

While there is no doubt some merit in these strategies and I'm sure Reverend Rivers is a great guy, his strategies didn't work in Toronto. They didn't work because they were neither created nor "owned" by the citizens of Toronto. Despite what the authorities may think, one expert, regardless of how good he or she might be, is not going to be able to provide the magic solution for fixing the complex issues that result in youth violence. What Toronto leaders didn't seem to get is that the wisdom and the answers are almost always in their own backyard.

Rather than importing an expert, Toronto should be importing a *process*. To be successful, they need a process that will involve working at the grassroots level to help stakeholders develop their own vision of success as well as the strategies for making that vision a reality. If they use that approach the chances are they'll come up with something far more innovative and resourceful than anything Reverend Rivers could suggest. More importantly, because the solution isn't imposed or dictated, it is far more likely to be implemented than a plan dictated by an outside expert.

This idea of collective vision and this wisdom of groups is explored in much greater detail by James Surowiecki in his book entitled *The Wisdom of Crowds: Why the Many Are Smarter Than the Few and How Collective Wisdom Shapes Business, Economies, Societies, and Nations*.[89]

His deceptively simple idea is that large groups of people are smarter than an elite expert, regardless of how brilliant he or she might be. Groups are much better at solving problems, fostering innovation, making wise decisions, and perhaps even predicting the future. Surowiecki suggests that organizations should open up the decision-making process and aggregate or combine the information

---

89 Surowiecki, J. (2004). *The wisdom of crowds: Why the many are smarter than the few and how collective wisdom shapes business, economies, societies and nations.* New York: Random House.

and intelligence that is usually scattered across its different parts. He also cautions that four conditions must be in place if this wisdom is to be maximized.

First of all, *the more diverse the group, the better*. A group with many different points of view will make better decisions than one where everyone knows the same information.

Independence of members will also be important as it will be this independence that keeps people from being swayed by a single-opinion leader.

He also suggests *decentralization* so people's errors balance each other out. "Power does not fully reside in one central location, and many of the important decisions are made by individuals based on their own local and specific knowledge rather than by an omniscient or farseeing planner."

Lastly, you need some way of *aggregating or combining the individual answers into a group response*. The best way to harness a group for the purpose of designing something would be for the group's opinion to be aggregated by an individual who is skilled at incorporating differing viewpoints into a single shared vision and for everyone in the group to be aware of that process. Aggregation seems to be the trickiest of the four conditions to satisfy because there are so many differing ways to aggregate opinion, not all of which are right for a particular situation.

> " If your actions inspire others to dream more, learn more, do more and become more, you are a leader."
>
> — John Quincy Adams

Regardless, aggregating all opinions effectively guarantees that the results are "smarter" than if a single expert had been in charge. Satisfy the four conditions and many of the errors involved in decision-making are also cancelled out.

Seems to me, more community leaders might want to read Surowiecki's book. If they heed his advice, they will likely find that groups of their own citizens are not only remarkably intelligent, they are often smarter than the smartest people within them.

Velvet Leadership

Several months ago I spent three days with a group of very impressive local community leaders. Despite their tremendous accomplishments, most of them would never think to label themselves a leader.

One of them said she never thought of herself as a leader. "After all", she said, "I'm a nurturer, I take care of people. I see my job as getting everyone to collaborate and work together." Another, when asked if she saw herself as a leader was uncomfortable even answering the question.

And yet, these and other remarkable individuals like them, have raised thousands of dollars and worked shoulder to shoulder with others to find resourceful strategies for bringing needed services and programs to their communities.

Like many others, it seems they've bought into the more commonly accepted view of a leader as a charismatic figure of power and authority, who tells us what to do and how to do it. I'd like to think that's changing. These days it seems a more successful leader is likely to be one you might never notice. They're more likely to apply an approach more akin to velvet leadership—soft yet rich in colour and texture. It seems this velvet leadership is most typically or intuitively, but not always, taken on by women. Sadly, despite its richness, it is too often overlooked and undervalued.

Perhaps due to how they were socialized, or perhaps inherent within their nature, women appear to have a capacity to work with a lot of people at one time to build consensus, collaboration, commitment, and action.

Meg Whitman, the CEO of Hewlett-Packard, suggests female leaders are more likely to reflect a willingness to reinvent the rules, an ability to sell their visions, the determination to turn challenges into opportunities, and a focus on 'high touch' in a high tech business world.[90]

Another study shows that women leaders are more assertive and persuasive, have a stronger need to get things done, and are more willing to take risks than male leaders. "Women leaders are venturesome, less interested in what has been than in what can be. They will

---

90 Furst, S. and Reeves, M. (2008, June). Queens of the hill: Creative destruction and the emergence of executive leadership of women. *The Leadership Quarterly*. pp 372-384.

run the risk of occasionally being wrong in order to get things done. And with their fine abstract reasoning skills, they will learn from any mistakes and carry on."[91]

The experiences of the primarily female ACE Communities team reflects an eclectic team that shares leadership and works collaboratively to gain synergistic results. Their work reflects the encouragement, support, pushing, planning, and leading by example that is essential for times of change.

In our work, we have learned that, velvet leadership isn't about being soft or invisible as much as it is about being visible in a way that invites freedom, expression, engagement, and connection. It is a style of leadership that encourages people to take responsibility for their work and their accomplishments.

Whereas we have observed traditional leaders who find gratification in the spotlight and applause, the velvet leader is more likely to find joy in contributing to an environment that empowers people and their respective communities to learn and grow.

Perhaps the most important aspect of velvet leadership is that it ultimately is one that allows everyone involved to say, "We did it ourselves".

Male Energies

Unlike me, my husband reads and understands instruction manuals.

As a result, he is a bit of a geek when it comes to technology. Over the years, albeit with some cursing along the way, he has taught himself how to assemble computers, operate complicated software programs, and build his own websites. However, something quite extraordinary happened about a month ago after he had wrestled with the increasing complexity of the website for his online kite store.

> "The key to successful leadership today is influence, not authority."
>
> — Kenneth Blanchard

My husband admitted that regardless of how hard he worked or how many manuals he read, he needed help. He subsequently hired some genius working in India for what amounts to about ten dollars

---

91   Caliper Corporation (2005). *The qualities that distinguish women leaders.* Retrieved Sept 2010. http://www.caliperonline.com/brochures/WomenLeaderWhitePaper.pdf.

an hour who made the required upgrades and changes in less than a day.

While it was a tough decision for him to admit he didn't have the answers, I was quite impressed. Although he may think it's less manly to admit he doesn't have the answers, like many women I don't have any such notion as I absolutely know I don't and am quite okay admitting it on a daily basis.

It seems that understanding one doesn't have the answers is critical for any leader operating in today's complex environment. Even if one is brilliant and sitting within the top box of the organization chart, they are still not likely to have all the answers.

For some, the shift to admitting they might not have all the answers, will often need to rely on others, and must work collaboratively in a flattened hierarchy, seems to be particularly difficult. It seems especially challenging for men who have an established formula for success and have progressed within their careers to the point where they are perceived as experts in their field. There is a great deal of pain and ego involved in letting go of their lone ranger mentality, when historically it has worked well, and instead admit that working as a team is essential. As in the case of my husband, it takes a confident and self assured man to be willing to share power and control and adapt to a new way of working.

Understanding one doesn't have the answers is critical for any leader operating in today's complex environment.

However, our observation and discussion with others tells us that for some people working in leadership positions within municipal government or the education, health or social systems, the shift to a less hierarchical way of working is a challenge. Working in partnership with the community, rather than making decisions top-down, requires being comfortable with not having all the answers, relying on others, working collaboratively, and sharing power.

While there is no doubt a need for male energy, spirit, and the unique skills they bring, there is a new and growing appreciation of the traits used to ensure strong families and communities that have more traditionally been identified with females. These include such traits as shared leadership, nurturance, flexibility, empathy, and contributing to the greater good. While these leadership attributes may be more associated with women, they are essential for both males and females who want to make a difference.

Importance of Reflection

A while ago I spent several days immersed with our project team focused on the planning that would ensure the community leadership that will result in active, creative, and engaged communities. The time was productive but I think most of us also walked away having learned something about ourselves we hadn't planned on learning that ultimately has made us grow.

The time together also reinforced that stories, relationships, and the reflections they bring, are tools that can impact our lives in a positive way. Additionally it made me realize how little time we make for both conversations and reflections.

The challenge is that in our fast paced world, people can't or don't make time for stopping to connect and reflect. It seems to me that previous generations did much more connecting and reflecting. Instead of gathering around the television as we too often do today, our parents and grandparents used to gather around the kitchen table or sit on the front porch not only to relax but to tell stories and reflect.

It may also be that we don't reflect because we don't realize its importance, value it, or know how to do it.

But the truth is we sometimes reflect and adjust our golf game more than we do our own relationships and reactions to others. The same way golfers analyze and adjust their swings to get better, so too do we need to stop and think about relationships and how they impact our job and life performance. Whether it's golf or relationships, we need to analyze what we could have done, should have done, or might have done, and then adjust our game to get better.

Our team has learned to formalize this process by simply adding an item to every meeting agenda called "learnings". It forces each of us to think about what we've learned since the last meeting or during the current one.

During our most recent retreat, we added an evening storytelling session complete with a circle of chairs, hot chocolate, and even a rocking chair that each of us moved to as we voluntarily shared our stories. As we listened, we not only got to know one another on a deeper level, we were also forced to reflect on what moved us or triggered a reaction.

More of our team leaders are also making time to blog as it too is a form of reflection not unlike keeping a journal.

Each of us also needs to carve out personal time for reflection. Mine often happens in the shower or while walking. It also tends to happen more when the television is turned off.

It also means we need to get more skilled at asking the right kind of reflective questions. I know that for me writing a weekly newspaper column and blog is a form of reflection each week. Faced with a non-movable deadline, I'm forced to stop and think—What worked this week? What didn't work? What situation triggered emotional responses? What can I learn from that situation? What would I do differently next time?

I'm also learning to look for what that reflection tells me about values, principles, patterns, and systems. Along the way I'm finding that the more I do it, the more I see it as a valuable tool that helps me grow as an individual and in my community leadership work.

 **Chapter 10**

Competency 4: Catalyst for Citizen Responsibility

Places a priority on engaging and cultivating community ownership and responsibility

COMPETENCY AREA		INDICATORS TO HELP YOU UNDERSTAND WHAT ENCOMPASSES THIS COMPETENCY	1 = I AM NOT AT ALL LIKE THAT		10 = I AM 100% LIKE THAT
4 **Catalyst** **for Citizen** **Responsibility**	4.1	I believe I have a responsibility to my community.	1 2 3 4 5	6 7 8 9 10	
	4.2	I believe that citizens are capable of and have the right to make decisions that affect their community.	1 2 3 4 5	6 7 8 9 10	
	4.3	I believe that each person has knowledge, experience, and skills that strengthen a community.	1 2 3 4 5	6 7 8 9 10	
	4.4	I can apply a community development approach to my work within the community.	1 2 3 4 5	6 7 8 9 10	
	4.5	I actively value and seek diverse viewpoints and perspectives.	1 2 3 4 5	6 7 8 9 10	
	4.6	I encourage everyone to contribute to their community.	1 2 3 4 5	6 7 8 9 10	
	4.7	I can apply strategies for generating citizen engagement and buy-in.	1 2 3 4 5	6 7 8 9 10	
	4.8	I understand the importance of articulating community values.	1 2 3 4 5	6 7 8 9 10	
	4.9	I am receptive to alternative solutions and foster receptiveness in others.	1 2 3 4 5	6 7 8 9 10	
	4.10	I develop relevant and beneficial partnerships and collaborations.	1 2 3 4 5	6 7 8 9 10	
	4.11	I implement strategies to facilitate community change.	1 2 3 4 5	6 7 8 9 10	
	4.12	I can facilitate consensus building.	1 2 3 4 5	6 7 8 9 10	
	4.13	I mobilize human and financial resources.	1 2 3 4 5	6 7 8 9 10	
	4.14	I actively support investment in volunteer development.	1 2 3 4 5	6 7 8 9 10	
	4.15	I utilize the power of information technology.	1 2 3 4 5	6 7 8 9 10	

Responsibility to Your Community

It was a perfect example of imperfect leadership. It was also an example of a leader having the courage to stand up and publicly admit a mistake.

This story is the result of a townhall meeting that had been designed to grow the community by engaging a cross section of stakeholders. After a fair bit of discussion during the evening, it became increasingly apparent the town was poised on a precipice.

In many ways a bedroom community for a nearby larger municipality, the town had the advantage of proximity to amenities but lacked a clear understanding of what made them unique and authentic. Because they weren't quite sure what kind of community they wanted to be, over the next few years they will likely face the risk of being absorbed as a suburb of the encroaching city.

Those at the meeting eventually concluded that the most pressing issue for their town was this lack of a vision and identity.

That's where things got a bit sticky. As it turns out, municipal staff had recently led an exercise that had resulted in a vision for the town. Unfortunately, it seemed to be a well-kept secret. Asking for a show of hands for those who were aware of the vision or had been part of the process, not a single hand was raised.

As the townhall meeting drew to a close, the facilitator invited participants to share one thing they were going to do differently the next day. As it turns out, one of the senior staff members who had led the planning exercise that resulted in the vision no one knew about, was in the room.

To her credit, this woman stood up and acknowledged her role. She then went on to say, "We missed the boat. If none of you know about this vision, we got it wrong. A vision is essential for our town, it guides our decision-making every day but if you haven't heard about it, we have a lot of work to do. Tomorrow I start to rectify that mistake and invite each of you to help me out."

Her delivery was real, honest, and heartfelt as was the loud applause that followed.

Rather than seeing her as an ineffective leader, every person in that room was moved by her courage to resist the temptation to deny the situation, blame others, or make up excuses. She demonstrated integrity and courage by owning the responsibility for the mistaken direction and as a result gained the respect and trust of those in the room by acknowledging her responsibility to the community.

While that sounds relatively simple to do, it clearly wasn't. We all saw the emotion on her face and heard it in her voice. It was, though, a wonderful lesson in leadership because ultimately leadership is about learning and change. We all were reminded that successful learning involves analyzing the past and acting differently in the future. And if learning is about change, we all learned that to lead change we all need to accept that we're human and that change rarely comes without us making mistakes along the way.

The situation also reinforced that it is only through mistakes that we learn. We rarely learn through our success. Failure sets us up to learn. In this case, the director will no doubt figure out that a community's vision can't be driven by city hall. Instead, it will need to be citizen driven and owned if it is to be embraced and implemented.

A community leader truly is one who not only demonstrates responsibility to their community but also has the moxie to admit mistakes, learn from them, and then be strong enough to correct them. After all is said and done, we often discover the best way to do things is by learning what doesn't work. And, if we don't make mistakes, chances are we'll never find the innovative solutions we will need to get it right.

A Foundation for Responsibility

It is also essential that community leaders lay a foundation for others to take responsibility for their communities.

> " The opportunity to preserve what is good on earth, to support what feeds the soul or stimulates the intellect, to encourage a talent or save an endangered species or to keep alive the dreams and aspirations of others is not only a privilege but a sacred responsibility."
>
> — Richard Ivey

I recently read a newspaper article that reported a growing trend toward more school children taking the initiative to support charitable causes. In the examples cited in the article, teachers and parents encouraged students to see beyond their own homes and classrooms to support a spirit of giving to others.

This is translating into birthday parties where kids pick a cause to support instead of receiving gifts. Guests are asked for money for a favourite charity or for items the charity can use such as food, cleaning supplies, or office items.

One little guy, a passionate animal lover, asked for donations of pet food that were then donated to a local animal shelter. One local food bank even offers tours for the kids, and a local Humane Society is offering onsite birthday parties.

The article led me to thinking about rights and responsibilities and what a colleague told me a number of years ago about an issue he was seeing.

He told me that while our generation of baby boomers has done a fabulous job of raising a generation who understand they have *rights*, we haven't done as good a job teaching them that with those rights come *responsibilities*.

Responsibility is one of the most important elements of good character. All of us can lay a foundation that will encourage responsibility by reflecting a belief that everyone should contribute to the well-being of all, regardless of their age or level of ability.

We can build a ramp to responsibility by helping our kids gradually take on more.

In the case of the birthday party scenarios, even young children can be empowered by making the decision about the particular cause or charity they want to support. By engaging and empowering children at a young age, we are preparing them for lives as active and responsible citizens. As they get older, we can do more by modeling and encouraging volunteering and giving back to our communities.

Ultimately it may be that the answer to the question "How do we ensure young people grow up to be more responsible?" might not be terribly complex. It might, however, require a change in how we as adults deal with them. While we need to continue to embed young peoples' right to be heard and listened to in matters that affect them, we also need to involve them in opportunities to shape and influence the responsibilities that come with those decisions.

Rights and responsibilities are inextricably linked. Happy and responsible adults need both.

Susan Aglukark, a unique, three time Juno award winning singer, helped me to better understand the complexity of the balance needed if we are to encourage children and youth to take responsibility for the greater good. During our exchange, Susan, a lovely, intelligent, thoughtful woman known for her social activism, shared a bit about the cultural influence of her Inuit background.

She explained that the harsh reality of the Arctic meant she was raised in a culture where thinking about survival had to be a priority. To survive, it was essential to downplay one's own individualism and think instead about the broader community and their collective needs. Putting oneself first could put others at risk.

As she pointed it, while putting community first was valid for Inuits, it wasn't necessarily a great strategy for developing her own career as it meant she just wasn't conditioned to putting herself first. Instead, it was something she had to learn.

That conversation was somewhat at odds with one I had the next day with a senior educator from western Canada who said that enrollment numbers in all of their community and social service programs was dropping off despite the demand and job opportunities for graduates. Anecdotal evidence was suggesting it was because the jobs weren't perceived as being well-compensated. In his opinion, the idea of helping, making a difference, or giving back to the community appeared to be declining as a motivating factor for students.

While the two conversations represent extremes, I'm thinking that somewhere in between there needs to be a healthy balance of caring for both ourselves and for our communities. Without this balance, today's young generation will miss out on the joy of giving. Additionally, there's no doubt our communities will suffer.

So what can we do it about it?

Newfoundland has a long standing program called SWASP— Student Work and Service Program for Secondary or Post-secondary students. It is a simple but brilliant concept. SWASP is designed to assist individuals who plan to attend or return to a post-secondary institution. Employers receive grants to help offset the student's salary for a minimum of five weeks to a maximum of fourteen weeks.

In addition to their salary, students receive a $50.00 per week tuition voucher for every week worked under the program. Students who are undecided about their career paths have the option of completing an 8-week (280 hours) community service placement with a nonprofit organization and receive a $1,400 tuition voucher as well as a $105 weekly stipend (to a maximum of $840).

It's a win-win situation in that often under-resourced social-profit organizations get additional help while students are exposed to careers related to communities and get help paying for university or college. It often means they are able to work at jobs in their own communities.

The Toskan Casale Foundation, founded by the family that created M.A.C. cosmetics, has initiated another innovative program to promote youth involvement in community with a program called YPI (Youth and Philanthropy Initiative).

Motivated by a desire to be impactful with the money they distribute to charities, they introduce young people to the joy of giving by having them go out and research a charity of their choice using a variety of tools provided by their Foundation.

The students then come back to their schools and share what they've learned with their classmates, explaining what the organization does for the community and why they deserve a grant of $5,000. A panel from the school then decides a winning charity from among those presented. The best part is that even if a charity is turned down, the kids who did the research stay engaged with the organization sometimes raising even more than $5,000.

These are both excellent, tried and true programs and, while on some level it seems strange that we should have to teach the joy of giving to one's community, it might just be one of the most important investments we could ever make.

Believing Citizens are Capable

It began, as do many success stories, with a small group of determined individuals sitting around a table.

As someone once told me, when you hit bottom, the best thing to do is stick out your legs and push. And push they did.

When a community is in trouble, the pushing off typically begins with a small group of individuals coming together to talk. These conversations are the beginning of change and ultimately the solutions for an active, creative, and engaged community.

In this case, the conversation was the result of a growing crisis in a small, somewhat isolated rural community. Here there were serious issues within their youth population—drugs, violence, poor health, and now, several deaths.

Sitting around the table, the small group talked about the kind of community they wanted to be, and what it was going to take to get them there. As part of the process, they reviewed work previously done on a community-driven strategic plan. They revisited their vision and values, purpose, and strategic priorities.

To their surprise much of what they had set out to do the previous year had been accomplished. With renewed energy they tackled new specific actions and a plan for moving forward. One of the actions would be a focus on developing young community leaders.

As they were talking, the meeting facilitators noted that one of the participants had been sketching. Curious, she asked him if he would mind sharing his drawing. The young man held up a beautiful rendering of an eagle. Beneath it he had written, "It takes more than one feather on the eagle's wing to soar above the clouds."

It was such a simple yet profound message.

Today, community issues and solutions are complicated and ambiguous. And, as each community is unique in its challenges, resources, and solutions, there isn't a cookie cutter, one-size-fits-all solution. Nor is there a cookie cutter leader. Instead we need leaders who recognize that those who live in the community are knowledgeable and capable. It is the collective that is able to impact the quality of life in their communities, and who are reflective of the feathers on an eagle's wing. It is their wisdom, energy, and resources that we need to be able to tap.

We need to work together and be brave enough to acknowledge that the old ways and the old rules don't work anymore. We need to ask questions, reflect thoughtfully, and be willing to try new approaches that engage and empower citizens.

One of the activities recently put into place in this particular community was a youth leadership conference that involved over one hundred youth. They participated in a variety of learning opportunities, heard from inspiring speakers, created vision boards for their personal futures, and planned recreation and sport activities for the upcoming year.

In the closing activity each participant was handed a basketball which they then shot toward the hoop. As they shot the basketball they were each asked to share a word that described their individual strengths. The words were positive and inspiring. All reflected hope and a much more positive picture of their future.

It was a remarkable achievement. In a few short months, they had moved from despair to hope and a new found belief in the power and possibilities that lay within their community.

Although too often untapped, every community leader needs to understand that this same wisdom and capability exists within every community.

Each Person has Knowledge, Experience, and Skills

My mother at the age of eighty two has completed five weeks of training to qualify her as a palliative care volunteer. While some might question why a woman at her age would make that kind of commitment, she told me she knows her health and happiness is dependent upon meaningful work that involves giving to others. She also told me that as she sat in the training it struck her that she was doing exactly what she was meant to be doing.

Each and every one of us has knowledge, experience, and skills to give. As my mother intuitively understands, living a good life is dependent upon using those capacities and talents. In her case, my mother was also able to recognize that her gifts of kindness and compassion, in combination with her spiritual beliefs, could be used to comfort those facing serious, complex illness.

When we are able to recognize and tap our talents we feel valued, powerful, and connected to those around us. In turn, the community around us is more powerful because of the contribution we are making. Ultimately, that is why strong communities are places where the talents and capacities of local residents are identified, valued, and utilized. Communities that fail to mobilize the skills, capacities, and talents of their residents or members will never be as successful.

McKnight[92] is at the centre of a growing movement that considers local assets as the primary building blocks of sustainable community development. Building on the skills of local residents, the power of local associations, and the supportive functions of local institutions,

---

92 Kretzmann, J. and McKnight, J. (1993).*Building communities from the inside out: A path toward finding and mobilizing a community's assets.* Evanston, IL: Institute for Policy Research, Northwestern University.

asset-based community development draws upon existing community strengths to build stronger, more sustainable communities.

In addition to assets, McKnight also recognizes local residents have needs, problems, and shortcomings. However, he believes it is their capacity that builds powerful communities. As a result, he discounts the importance of typical community building efforts that begin with a needs assessment, instead promoting the concept of mapping or creating an inventory of assets or strengths.

He believes that if we want to create more powerful neighbourhoods and communities, there are three kinds of information we need to collect. We have to discover our neighbours' gifts, seek out local strangers, and find the groups people belong to, and the institutions where they work or have connections. He suggests we can do this by visiting individual neighbors or calling a meeting.

McKnight describes four kinds of gifts. The first three are the gifts of *head* (knowledge), *heart* (what you're passionate about) and *hand* (your skills of any kind). The fourth is what you are willing to *teach*.

After the asset mapping is complete, the next step is to support communities to discover what they care enough about to act. The final step is to determine how citizens can act together to achieve those goals.

As McKnight puts it, "No community has ever been built on the needs and problems of its people. It has always been built on their gifts and capacities and the use of the assets that are there."

It is a significant and important paradigm shift for community leaders to embrace.

Community Gathering Places

While most would agree that each person has the potential to strengthen their community by virtue of their knowledge, experience, and skills, there isn't as common an understanding of the important role played by community gathering places in bringing them together.

By way of example, a while back, thirty somewhat funky looking pianos were placed in public spaces around the city of London, England with "Play Me, I'm Yours" printed on their sides. Despite their reputation for a being a tad starchy, Londoners responded enthusiastically as professionals and amateurs alike stepped up to the piano while others gathered to sing along. The talent seemed to be as diverse as the people who played. One pianist dressed as Chopin, and a musical comedy duo played on twenty four of the pianos within an eight-hour period.

The innovative, interactive art project was designed by artist Luke Jerram and sponsored by a social-profit arts group called *Sing London* in order to "get people talking to one another and to claim ownership and activate the public space." Jerram's point was that he saw London's public spaces as a blank canvas for everyone.

Old, unwanted pianos were collected, painted, and then secured to the ground with metal cables. A piano tuner travelled among them to ensure they all stay in tune and, in the event of rain, they each had plastic covers.

The initiative seems to have brought out the best in people as they politely relinquished their places at the piano to allow others to perform. Additionally, not a single piano was vandalized.

The piano project highlights the importance of what urban sociologist, Ray Oldenburg, refers to as *third places*[93] In contrast to the first and second places of home and work, these third places are neutral public locations where people can gather and interact. He argues that parks, bars, coffee shops, recreation centres, general stores, and other third places are essential to civic engagement and community vitality.

Third places allow people to put aside their concerns and simply enjoy the company and conversation around them. Third places "host the regular, voluntary, informal, and happily anticipated gatherings of individuals beyond the realms of home and work."[94] Additionally, social equality is promoted because the playing field is level as everyone is there as a guest. This also not only pulls us away from our computers and TVs, it provides a setting for grassroots politics, citizen involvement, and opportunities to contribute and support one another.

As those gathered around the piano in London will attest, third places reflect a more playful, light-hearted mood than is typically found in our home and work settings. For those whose lives are caught

---

93   Oldenburg, Ray (1991). *The great good place.* New York: Marlowe & Company.
94   Oldenburg Ibid. p. 16.

up in the daily grind of home to work and back again, the sense of community gained from these third places is even more important.

While we're still likely to find these third places in smaller towns, they don't seem to be as common in larger communities. Oldenburg, however, suggests we can and need to transform public spaces into vibrant community places, whether they're parks, plazas, public squares, streets, sidewalks, or the myriad other outdoor and indoor spaces that have public uses in common.

He suggests the starting point for developing a concept for any public space is to accept that the community is the expert and to work from the beginning to honour and utilize local talents and assets. Tapping the local expertise at the beginning of the process will also help create a sense of ownership in developing a third place that provides the sense of welcome and comfort that is essential.

The redesigning or building of third places isn't always easy but ultimately these places are a key strategy if we are to help find the sense of community and belonging that so many have lost.

Apply a Community Development Approach

You can't always do it yourself. Go ahead and sing it now. Channel your inner Mick Jagger because sometimes you can get what you want if you don't always try to do it yourself.

Maybe it's because we're all so busy these days or, maybe there are simply a lot of people who like to control, but it does seem there are a growing number who think it is just quicker and easier to do it themselves. I keep being reminded that while it may be a tempting quick fix to do it ourselves, it is a rather myopic view that doesn't set us up well for the long haul in our personal lives, workplaces, or the communities where we live.

I first learned about the importance of letting go of power and trusting others while working for the City of Niagara Falls a number of years ago.

New to the field of municipal recreation I had been hired as a community development coordinator to assist the many volunteer-based groups who were responsible for the bulk of the recreation, sport, arts, culture, and heritage activities across the city.

Among my responsibilities was a travelling playground program that provided activities for kids in city parks throughout the summer. It wasn't long before I got tangled in the issues and demands of trying to meet everyone's needs, and bumped up against challenges I wasn't sure how to resolve. Quite certain I was going to be fired, I walked into the next meeting of the volunteer advisory committee crying uncle and asking for help.

To my surprise, the committee immediately got to work brainstorming, sharing ideas, and weighing potential solutions. While it's not necessary to share the details, in essence the group demonstrated collective wisdom in action, and an end result that included a number of brilliant strategies.

Even better, every single member of the volunteer committee stepped up to help implement the recommendations. We ended up having one of the most successful seasons ever experienced by the summer playground program, and a record breaking number of kids who were active and engaged. Ironically, while I had been afraid I was going to lose my job, I was instead commended for doing such a great job of engaging the volunteers and finding innovative solutions.

Who knew it could be as easy as asking for help?

While I might have been able to find and implement interim solutions on my own in less time, for sure they wouldn't have been as effective as what the group was able to do as a collective. Even more importantly, because they designed the solutions, they owned them, and therefore took responsibility for putting them into place

As the solutions evolved in a process that was wasn't always orderly, I must admit there were times when it was tempting to step in and take the reins. However, I'm glad my lack of experience stopped me from doing that because I now know that could have been interpreted in a negative way and communicated a lack of trust.

While loosening my grip and encouraging more collaboration and ownership, albeit accidently, was initially challenging, in the end it made my job easier by having others shoulder the burden. It also helped me learn an important lesson about leadership. It showed me that the job of a community leader is not to make the decisions and solve problems, but rather to implement a process that will help others do it on their own.

Seek Diverse Viewpoints

The shoe is on the other foot now.

In previous work environments I was sometimes asked for my opinion on a specific matter or to provide feedback as part of a larger group. It was frustrating to find that when the final decisions were made, it often appeared my voice hadn't been heard at all. Consequently, I found myself wondering why I had bothered to contribute in the first place and would be tempted to hunker down and just mind my own business.

Nowadays the position is reversed as I'm the one who is often soliciting feedback and opinions from the others on our team. In fact, it's even more than that for me as it's not only about feedback and opinions, it is also about ensuring consensus and collective decision-making—a key principle of our community development approach. With a team as diverse as ours, the end results are always more sound, richer, and innovative.

On paper that sounds great but here's my dilemma. What happens when decisions are time sensitive, opinions vary too widely for consensus, or decisions are better made by those with more technical knowledge and expertise?

There are a lot of times when I feel like I'm caught between a rock and a hard place.

Not only am I left wrestling with how to maximize the contributions of team members, I'm struggling with a new realization. The realization is that sometimes those who bring a business background move too fast because they place less importance on feedback and collaboration. Alternatively, those from the social-profit sector tend to be so much about collaboration and consensus that it can slow them down.

Eventually I've realized that neither the business nor the social-profit viewpoint is right or wrong. Communities, after all, need to make business-oriented, economically sound decisions just as much as they need to engage and involve citizens and community organizations.

So maybe the answer is that we need one another.

Something quite wonderful does happen when individuals with diverse backgrounds, skills, and knowledge are brought into the mix. This allows us to become more aware of what we know and what we don't know.

So here's what I've learned.

When asking for feedback, I need to be clear up front about the level of team engagement being sought. While empowerment is probably the ideal, there are situations where that just may not be practical or feasible. Sometimes we are simply seeking ideas or feedback that will be considered.

For instance, in making decisions about our logo, empowering the team to make the decision just didn't work out. The team came back with many diverse opinions on the matter and, even though I really wanted them to have the final say, the knowledgeable feedback from the graphic designer was just too sound to ignore.

I guess the reality is that it can't always be about real empowerment. Sometimes we can only seek opinions or ask others to be involved in the decision-making and action.

After the logo exercise I had to write an email to explain to the team why the logo they chose wasn't the one used. That is something else I've learned. When you ask for someone's feedback and then seemingly ignore it, at the very least, you owe them an explanation.

Most importantly, I've learned that my job is to be clearer in the first place about whether I'm seeing feedback, empowering the group to make a decision, or something in between.

After all, as another of our wise team members suggested, "In community development there is no one best way. Instead, there is a way."[95] And, together is definitely better in finding the way to active, creative, and engaged communities.

Encouraging Everyone to Contribute

It is just so ironic.

---

95   McFall, S. (May 2009). ACE Communities Planning Meeting.

I'm sitting in a conference session called "Conversations, Consultations, and Community Engagement". The session description talked about the importance of ensuring citizen support, input, and participation. Always keen to learn, especially on a subject near and dear to my heart, I was eagerly anticipating the session.

Unfortunately, I am so bored that instead of listening to the speakers, I'm writing this.

The room set-up should have been my first clue. A panel of four speakers sat at the head table, the first already standing at the podium firing up a PowerPoint presentation.

Participants sat, classroom-style, in rows of chairs lined up behind narrow tables.

While the presenters certainly had good intentions, as well as significant experience, they absolutely failed to engage their audience. Within ten minutes, glazed eyes and yawns were in evidence. I kept thinking, if they failed to engage the participants in the room, how on earth could they engage an entire community, never mind get them to contribute?

> ❝ Community is not about profit. It is about benefit. We confuse them at our peril. When we attempt to monetize all value, we methodically disconnect people and destroy community."
>
> — Dee Hock

So what exactly is community engagement? Well for certain it is about engaging citizens. But it is much more than that. It is the process that results in people working collaboratively for the betterment of their community. It also results in people having the skills and power to identify their issues, make their own decisions, and create their own solutions.

Ideally, community engagement is about working and learning together to create bold and confident visions for the future.

If the community is involved, higher quality solutions will be created, conflicts reduced, and a greater sense of community created. Communities that are truly engaged take greater responsibility for what is happening in their community and create the momentum for addressing the identified issues, not only with vision, but with movement, change, and solutions.

The problem is that community engagement really isn't always clear cut as it exists on a continuum that isn't always understood. At one end of the continuum is engagement that simply informs by

214

communicating information to the public. While it has a time and a place, too often it ends up like this conference session—yawn.

At the other end of the continuum and, what in most cases would be ideal, is the kind of engagement that has local residents and organizations initiating, learning, leading, and contributing—sometimes with external support and coaching—on issues identified as important. The community shares decision-making power and the positive synergy that results.

In between these two extremes are forms of engagement that seek, but don't always heed, community opinions. In some cases, though, attempts are made to engage the community in decision-making and action.

Organizing this conference session isn't all that different from organizing sessions to engage the community.

What could have been done differently to engage participants?

A more inviting room set up would have helped. Perhaps a circle of chairs or at least a u-shape would have better conveyed that presenters wanted interaction with the participants. To make participants more comfortable, introductions would also have been a good thing. A facilitator to clearly articulate the session outcomes and to keep the speakers on track would also be positive. In this session, as is almost always the case, two of the presenters exceeded their time limit.

It would also have been a better session if the presenters understood they weren't the only experts in the room. When we did get to the last ten minutes and participants were finally allowed to provide feedback, it turns out there was a lot of wisdom and experience in the room. For me it was the most valuable part of the session.

The presenters themselves seemed surprised by some of the great ideas. The sad part is that they shouldn't have been. Good ideas usually do result when people are encouraged to participate.

Articulating Community Values

There is wisdom in our communities. That belief was reinforced for me after spending three days in a leadership retreat with a group of amazing local community leaders. A unique mix of staff, volunteers, business owners, and elected officials, they came with very different experiences and skill sets. But, as one participant pointed out, the challenges and solutions within their respective communities may have been unique, but their paths to success were in fact very similar.

While I totally agreed with the statement, it struck me that their paths were likely similar because they shared many of the same core values about community. In addition to being very cool people, it was perhaps those values that made everyone want to hang out together despite the differences.

It also occurred to me that discussing and identifying our personal, as well as the values of our communities, is going to become even more important in the future. After all, strong, healthy, and innovative individuals, organizations, and communities seem to be those who have made a point of identifying and living by their values.

Values are those things that really matter to each of us—the ideas and beliefs we hold as being of special quality, worth, and importance. Values explain what individuals, organizations, businesses, or communities stand for and what will be made a priority as decisions are made. In times of rapid change, values become increasingly important as a filter for prioritizing how we invest our time and resources.

So that got me thinking, what values did the community leaders at that retreat have in common?

Here's the feedback I gathered about their perception of the community values that were essential to being an active, creative, and engaged community.

1) **Citizen Engagement**
   Citizens should be actively engaged in problem solving, decision-making, and policy development. In other words, individuals should be involved in the decisions that affect them.
2) **Collective Responsibility for Community Building**
   Individuals and communities have a collective responsibility to help support the care and well-being of others. This manifests itself in a belief that government can't pay for everything that is deemed to be a priority in a community as they are simply one of many partners. This also demands the sharing and distribution of leadership and power. As one elected

official put it during the retreat, "My job is to unleash the passion and get out of the way".

3) **Integrated Systems**

Trusted networks and strong, sustainable, integrated delivery systems provide a much more efficient and effective range of support and services in a community. Collaboration within, and across, the business, government, and social profit sectors is essential.

4) **Diversity**

Diversity is valued and respected. Differences involving ability, ethnic origin, religion, culture, lifestyle, and beliefs are valued and viewed as contributing to enriched communities.

5) **Creativity**

Creativity is valued and nurtured. At the heart of a strong quality of life is the freedom to innovate and create effective systems that nurture the creativity of individuals and groups.

6) **Sustainability**

Sustainability of our natural and built environment is at the core of a high quality of life. Protection and preservation of natural resources, diverse habitats, and cultural assets demands a consistent culture of stewardship.

7) **Recreation, Heritage, Sport, Arts, and Culture**

Recreation, heritage, sport, arts and culture are recognized as being integral to social, economic, and community well-being and as such are assigned priority in public policy.

8) **A Brand or Personality**

Thriving communities are those that have placed a priority on something that makes their community unique or special. It is that something special that instills community pride, and is what citizens would miss the most if they were to move away.

9) **Strong Communication**

A variety of communication vehicles must be utilized to ensure citizens are engaged and to keep them informed about issues, opportunities, and local decisions.

10) **Status Quo isn't Good Enough**

Accepting a community that is less than it has the potential to be just isn't good enough. As a result there is a commitment to being proactive, building on existing assets, and to ongoing continuous growth and development.

As responsible citizens we all need to be thinking about our community values and how each of us can ensure they are applied. It is especially important to ask politicians about their values and how they plan to apply them if elected. After all, while having values is clearly important, they lack meaning unless they are put into practice. Regardless, whether we live or lead during the best or worst of times, values provide perspective.

Foster Receptiveness to Alternatives

While I like to think I'm pretty open-minded, I was recently reminded of how much I still need to work at growing my receptiveness to the alternatives that result from boundary spanning.

I was honoured to be invited to take part in what was billed as an "Aboriginal Thought-Leaders Forum" at the prestigious Banff Centre. Predominantly focusing on academic presentations, this forum explored "narrative inquiry" as a means or methodology that can be used to better understand and capture learnings. More than storytelling, narrative inquiry is a form of research this isn't just about what happened but also the meaning that people make of what happened.

To be honest, the first day of the forum didn't leave me feeling warm and fuzzy. My predominant reaction to presentations on case studies, ethnography, and other forms of community-based and applied research left me feeling mostly impatient and even somewhat sad and angry.

While I understood the value and importance of applied research as an important piece of the puzzle, the reality is that in some Aboriginal communities, there is a growing sense of urgency as they mobilize to respond to addictions, health issues, poverty, literacy, and leadership challenges.

Undeniably valuable, the information being shared by the talented presenters was almost drowned by the voice in my head saying, "Will those I've met in Aboriginal communities really care about this? Should this be the priority when people are dying?" I came looking for answers and solutions and found myself struggling to see how a focus on methodology was going to help.

But, just as I was about to admit I was a misfit and head home, we heard from Dr. Laura Brearly from Australia. Clearly colouring outside the typical lines of academia, she demonstrated how she brings multi-media, poetry, dance, and music into her research. In much of her work she has incorporated the Aboriginal concept of "dadirri" which is building community as the result of deep and respectful listening.

Another presenter, Sonia Ospina from the Research Center for Leadership in Action at New York University, provided practical examples of research that used a variety of methodologies to ensure new knowledge while also addressing practical challenges and enhanced practice. Additionally, she stressed the importance of offering immediate and tangible research products for those participating.

For me, those particular teachings reinforced that I could better acknowledge the importance of research in my work but still bend it somewhat in order to make it work more effectively for stakeholders. It also left me with a better understanding of how delivering a program or initiative on the ground could also be a form of critical research if learnings were captured using more academically trustworthy methodologies. It would mean our learnings could gain more of the credibility needed to ultimately shape policy decisions and priorities.

While I can't speak for the others who were in attendance, I don't think I was the only one who was pushed beyond their own views of what was deemed acceptable research. For some, there was also a growing recognition that research data could be more valuable if it were to be reflected in multiple and alternative ways rather than just those that might reflect our own learning preferences. Many acknowledged there are findings that can't be captured in written text yet must still be given a voice, and that more creative vehicles are needed if our learnings are to touch hearts and spirits as well as minds.

So while in the end I left with some answers as well as a much increased receptiveness to research, a lot of questions remained.

For example, how do we invite academic engagement that avoids intimidation, and how can we best integrate traditional and creative approaches to research? And, much as I'd like the simplicity of knowing there is one best way, we know that isn't likely to happen. As with so many other issues and situations these days, there isn't a best way. There are many ways. And, we'll never find them unless each of us is willing to stretch beyond our own assumptions, bias, prejudice, ingrained beliefs, and pressures to conform.

Even when we have our doubts, as I did, we must be patient and receptive to others who bring different viewpoints and alternatives. The nature and complexity of today's challenges in our communities means there has never been a more critical time or need for leaders to be open-minded about new directions and solutions.

Develop Partnerships and Collaboration

Partnerships are somewhat on my mind these days as our initiative continues to morph and grow. Over the past several weeks we've been approached by a number of government departments and organizations who see the value of our community-building work and the potential of the trusted networks we are nurturing across the province.

Given that we are committed to collaboration and its benefits, this is very good news. The more collaboration there is, the more opportunity there will be to view challenges holistically. Additionally, the neutral, collective space that sits between the organizations, businesses, or sectors involved in the partnership will provide a meeting place for the individual and organizational knowledge, expertise, and talents. This pooling of ideas, resources, and information is what often leads to innovation, as well as to the reduction of overlaps and duplication.

Like many others, I've learned about both personal and work-related partnerships by being part of some that were good and some I'd rather not think about. As with a good marriage, a good partnership has the potential to enrich who you are, what you do, and how you do it.

I've often thought partnerships could be compared to fabric. Even though one's existing fabric might be perfectly fine, it can be enriched and strengthened by the right partner who weaves, mixes, and mingles their own unique strands of thread and fibre with your own. The resulting mix has the potential to be synergistically rich and strong creating something that is greater than the sum of the respective parts.

For us it is especially timely to consider new potential partnerships and collaborations because we're at a point now where we have a better understanding of the outcomes we can deliver as well as what it is that makes us unique. However, before we can consider expanding to work with new partners, we have some work to do.

When an organization or business is considering the possibility of partners, just as with a marriage, they need to know not only who they are, but whether or not they're ready to partner. Questions for consideration could include: Why are we entering this collaboration? What value do we have to offer a potential partner? Do they bring value that could help us? Do we have the time and resources to work with a new partner?

My experience has shown that the most effective partnerships are those where all of those involved have determined they want to be part of the same vision. If that vision is compared to a pie, each partner will see their own unique and distinct piece of the pie. Most importantly, each partner will be happy with their particular piece of the pie and won't be as interested in each other's piece.

Unfortunately, assembling and baking that kind of pie will often take time and patience. Success will likely be determined by a number of factors.

In addition to the common vision, research shows that for a collaboration to be successful there must be a collectively-designed and owned plan. The collaboration must also allow the individual partners to utilize their respective strengths for the benefit of everyone involved. All partners will need to have the opportunity to contribute their expertise, ideas, and information to the implementation of the collaboration. Along the way, priority needs to be given to discussing values, principles, and policies that will address the practicalities of working together. Much of the focus will need to be placed on the development of strategies that will ensure open and honest communication.

Addressing the above issues will help your organization, business, or community determine the intensity of the potential partnership.

It could be that your collaboration is informal and short term with each partner retaining its own decision-making and responsibility. On the other hand, your collaboration could fall at the opposite end of the spectrum with a partnership that is more formal and long term with more decision-making and accountability to one another. Of course your collaboration could also fall on the continuum somewhere within those two extremes.

When it comes right down to it, any partnership will need to be about having the right people together at the right time doing the right things because ultimately partnerships are about people pulling together in the right direction. For sure it will be challenging but in the end it really is quite simple, collaboration means we do something better when we do it together.

Implementing Strategies to Facilitate Community Change

I'm not sure exactly who, but one of our staff posted a quote in our board room that captures the nature of the challenge faced by our ACE Communities initiative. The quote was from American jazz musician Charles Mingus who once said, "Creativity is more than just being different. Anybody can plan weird; that's easy. What's hard is to be as simple as Bach. Making the simple complicated is commonplace; making the complicated simple, awesomely simple, that's creativity."[96]

It is one heck of a challenge especially because ultimately our work is all about change. Not only are we charged with the task of attempting to enhance the quality of life across an entire province, we are responsible for being able to explain how we did it when we are finished.

Being blessed with previous learnings and some not-so-insignificant funding, we knew going in that we needed to focus on identifying and supporting local community leaders. We also knew that we'd be stressing collaboration and innovation by using recreation, parks, arts, culture and heritage as a catalyst. It is only now, three years into

---

96   Mingus, C. Retrieved Aug 2010. http://thinkexist.com/quotation/making_the_simple_complicated_is_commonplace/201908.html.

the initiative, that we believe we have finally landed on a way to describe a formula that seems to be working.

We know if a community—any community—wants to be stronger, healthier, and more vibrant, it must have citizens who are active, creative, and engaged. To make that change a reality, *three paths* or journeys within the community need to take place.

The *first path* is one that focuses on supporting the learning and growth of a local cohort of community leaders. Change and success simply doesn't happen without community leaders who can act as agents of change, ensure continuous improvement, provide big picture/system thinking, be catalysts for citizen responsibility, advocate for quality of life, and plan using a community development approach.

The *second path*, driven by local community leaders, needs to focus on a short term, cross-sectoral, grassroots initiative or project(s). It needs to be something that everyone in town agrees is important as well as be one that requires collaboration across sectors and silos. This contributes to the spirit and potential impetus within a community by illustrating what can happen when everyone works together. Think of it as a quick success or as "low-hanging fruit". Projects related to recreation, parks, arts, culture and heritage fit here very well because they are a safe, nonthreatening vehicle for a cross-sectoral collaboration to which everyone can relate.

> " Leisure, a setting to learn and practice public participation, contributes to democratic life. Leisure can help build bridges and build social networks."
>
> — World Leisure Congress, Quebec Declaration

Examples could include building or renovating a playground, park, skateboarding facility, community garden, or development of a recreational trail. It could also be something other than infrastructure such as a training event for volunteers, a conference for youth, or a festival. We've also worked with communities who have focused on putting a temporary floor in a curling rink so it can be used year round. Another built a nature park that had teens laying sod, and seniors and kids joining efforts to build birdhouses. Yet another town initiated a calendar that chose from hundreds of photographs submitted by residents to illustrate what they were most proud of in their community. The twelve photographs selected were unveiled at a spirited, well-attended launch.

The *third journey* involves the implementation of a longer term, community-driven plan that addresses the quality of life in the community from a big picture or systems perspective. This collective, community-owned plan and its vision, values, and action steps are essential for inspiring, engaging, and keeping citizens involved in the ongoing growth and development of their community.

Sounds simple now doesn't it? Three paths—the development of local community leaders, a short term project or initiative, and a longer term plan for quality of life. Strong leaders, low hanging fruit, and long term future direction. Who knew the complexity of facilitating community change could end up being so simple to describe?

Facilitate Consensus Building

I always knew that conflict was inevitable but no one ever told me how painful it could be.

Our work team is based in locations across the province and beyond. While we connect regularly using different technologies, face to face meetings aren't very common due to the costs in terms of time and money needed to get us all at the same location at the same time. Despite the challenges, we've somehow managed to become a community that values and enjoys our face time.

This week we participated in a meeting that finally put us all in the same room to share our respective learnings about the work we're doing to impact quality of life.

The first part of meeting was loud, spirited, and marked by howls of laughter that were prompted in part by introductions that had us sharing something that others in the group might be surprised to know about us. Suffice it to say the exercise involved the sharing of surprising stories as well as a show and tell of tattoos in unusual places. Who knew?

Anyway, after that we quickly hunkered down into some stunningly productive reflections. We listened intently to one another, asked questions to clarify, went deep into the learnings, and identified new answers as well as the tougher questions that still needed to be addressed.

By the end of the exercise, we were all feeling warm and fuzzy about our team and the productivity of the day.

At that point we were faced with the decision of either wrapping up the meeting or continuing to address a number of other, tougher issues that had created dissention and conflict during the previous few months. The issues seemed less important after the success of the day but they were still there bubbling under the surface. We could either ignore the issues or take advantage of being in the same room and press on.

We chose to press on.

The truth is that pressing on didn't really result in a happy ending—at least not yet anyway. It was painful and we didn't exactly leave on a high. However, even though we did leave with some regrets, in the end we knew it was good not to have ignored the situation.

Unfortunately, avoidance is the choice that many of us make when faced with conflict. Sometimes it does seem easier to withdraw, not act at all, or just give in. For others, conflict brings out their competitive side.

There's no doubt about it, conflict is hard. It's a tug of war, it's a debate, and it's messy. However, it's also something we need to embrace more because it's also an opportunity for constructive discussion, promoting change, high quality decisions, and stimulating creativity and innovation.

For us confronting the conflict meant we initiated tough conversations about change, accountability, and being true to our stated outcomes.

While we're not there yet, and although we did a fair bit to assess the situation, we'll need to do more to consider a variety of options and strategies before implementing the final consensual strategy to deal with the conflict.

For us, while definitely challenging, the process was easier than it might have been for others because we do share many of the same values. There would have been much more conflict if we had different values about what really matters in our work.

So what did we learn along the way?

Confronting conflict is hard, but it takes far less energy than it would to pretend it didn't exist. Acknowledging and managing the conflict, and working toward consensus makes us all better, stronger, and more effective.

Mobilize Resources

Some time ago a colleague forwarded me an email he had received that contained an insightful review of a book about community. Not only had the author of the review summarized the key messages within the book, he had also provided an analysis suggesting why it would be important to us in our day-to-day work.

Although I had never met the guy, there was something about that review that reflected a passion for the subject and made me flag it for follow up. While it did take me a while, I finally got around to connecting with him. The end result is that we may have recruited an incredible volunteer to write blogs for us on a regular basis.

So while it was a good result for both of us, in some ways the entire exchange left me a bit saddened. The truth is that this guy is a talented, passionate, and techno-savvy writer who had been lobbying his government employer for years to allow him to do the same thing within the scope of his job. After all, he reasoned, his employer had access to a lot of research and knowledge about policies, programs, and promising practices that would benefit the broader community. However, because those above him in the chain of command said "no", his talents were simply not being utilized as effectively as they could be.

This ability to understand individual passions and then connect them to possibilities is key to mobilizing resources in our communities.

Instead of trying to find bodies to fill positions, we need to personalize our approach. Maybe we need to find an individual's passion first, and then match them to the most appropriate volunteer or paid position. More time consuming for sure, but likely much more effective in the long run.

Supporting Investment in Volunteer Development

A number of years ago, a representative of Port CARES, a remarkable community building organization in Port Colborne, Ontario asked if I would be interested in delivering a keynote address at their annual volunteering recognition evening during National Volunteer Week.

I was a little hesitant at first as I'm much more interested in delivering interactive learning sessions rather than a stand-and-talk-at-you session. However, I did ultimately concede because who could resist the honour of addressing a room full of energetic and engaging volunteers? These volunteers were those involved as board members, in offering individual and job support, or in providing information, referrals, advocacy, crisis intervention, childcare, and so much more.

Preparing for the session made me think more about my own commitment to volunteering. In fact, volunteering is perhaps the most important legacy passed on by my maternal grandmother to my own mother, my generation, and now to our children.

At a time when stay-at-home moms were the norm, both my grandmother and mother looked to volunteering for opportunities to flex and grow. My mother kept busy with Parent Teachers Associations, a theatre group, and political campaigns. She remains active to this day and, as I write this, is making sure all is in order for the piano competition she organizes as part of the St. Catharines Kiwanis Music Festival. She is also a palliative care volunteer.

My grandmother was also always on the go. Her work as president of the Music Festival, Opera Guild, a theatre group, and local choirs led to her nomination as citizen of the year when she was well into her seventies.

Today it is much more difficult to paint a picture of the typical volunteer and the role they play in our communities. Even within the Port CARES meeting, the group was extraordinarily diverse in terms of age, personalities, and talents.

What we do know, is that Canadians volunteer 2.1 billion hours every year (equivalent to more than 1.1 million full-time jobs), fill 19 million volunteer positions and donate $10 billion annually, an average donation being $437. More than half of all organizations are run totally by volunteers and each Canadian, on average, has four memberships with a nonprofit or voluntary organization. Each volunteer contributes, on average, an astounding 166 hours per year.[97]

And while these statistics are impressive, they are only reflective of what has been found easiest to quantify or measure. What is perhaps even more important, but incredibly difficult to measure, are the qualitative but less tangible benefits of volunteering.

As the result of volunteering, people make contacts, learn skills, gain work experience, build self-esteem, improve their health, and sometimes even find paying jobs. I can personally vouch for that one as volunteering was a key factor in getting every single one of my jobs.

Research also shows that volunteering can help us to feel connected to others and to our community, experience a greater sense of health and well-being, perform more effectively at work, do better economically, and raise better adjusted children.

There is less research but a growing interest in how volunteering also leads to greater citizen participation and ultimately benefits that impact the broader community. Communities with high levels of citizen participation are safer, more democratic, more attractive to investment, have lower incidences of crime, homelessness, pollution, youth, and newcomer alienation.[98]

Perhaps more importantly this leads to greater trust. Trust in one another and trust in our ability to impact and shape our communities to be the best they can be.

Volunteers and other forms of citizen engagement are as essential to a community as government, industry, and infrastructure so we can't take their time and talents for granted. However, community organizations may need to find a way to measure the contributions of volunteers so they will be better understood, appreciated, and ultimately valued.

Managing volunteers within any organization requires implementing a process that ensures they are properly recruited, screened, placed, provided with an orientation, motivated, supervised, and evaluated. It doesn't just happen. Involving volunteers in meaning-

---

97   Statistics Canada. (2007). *Caring Canadians, involved Canadians: Highlights from the Canada survey of giving, volunteering and participating.* http://www.statcan.gc.ca/daily-quotidien/090608/dq090608a-eng.htm. Accessed February 2011.

98   Bowen, P. (March 2004). *Investing in Canada: Fostering an agenda for citizen and community participation*, www.policy.ca. Accessed March 2011.

ful and worthwhile activities requires an investment of time and resources but it is an investment with significant returns.

Typically, many organizations recruit to fit volunteers into positions that can be done by most people without any special skills or training. In the field of volunteer management this is typically referred to as *warm body recruitment.*

In some cases, they also use *targeted recruitment* geared to finding people who have specific skills or characteristics. With this approach you would try to track down someone who is suitable and might enjoy the job. It's a good process for getting involvement from new volunteers because it forces you to think about your organization's needs and interests and then proactively look for people who can address them.

For some initiatives these two techniques work very well. For instance, last week, I saw a group of almost one hundred volunteers who had been recruited using these two techniques come together to build a playground in one day. Most of those needed were "warm bodies" however there were some "specialists" required.

Concentric circle and *ambient recruitment*[99] are two additional volunteer recruitment strategies that should be considered.

Concentric circle recruitment moves out from the initial organizers, using their social connections. Consider it similar to tossing a pebble in a lake and seeing the concentric rings expand from the initial point of entry of the pebble. The basic reasoning behind this approach is that it is easiest to recruit potential volunteers from among the people we already know. All an organizer has to do is move out in concentric circles through an existing framework of family, friends, coworkers, and acquaintances. The disadvantage of this approach is that it doesn't always diversify the volunteer base.

Ambient recruitment, generally depends on geographic or organizational communities, such as a neighborhood. The idea is to promote a community atmosphere that values volunteerism.

Regardless of the approach used by community leaders to recruit volunteers, it is essential to know the needs and interests of each vol-

---

99   McCurley, S. (June 11, 1995). Volunteer recruitment campaigns. CASAnet. 1995. (June 11, 2009).

unteer and match them with the most appropriate and meaningful position.

Community leaders also have a responsibility to increase the awareness of the value of volunteers. Measuring the economic value of volunteer activity is one approach that can be applied. This approach involves assigning a dollar value to the hours that volunteers contribute to an organization.

Why measure the economic value of volunteer activity? By measuring the economic value of volunteer activity, it is possible to demonstrate to donors, funders, supporters, policy makers, the public, and volunteers themselves, how volunteer contributions extend budget, activities, and services. It can also be used to demonstrate the real costs associated with a volunteer program as well as the economic benefits of volunteer involvement.

The dollar value of volunteer time as a budget line item can be included and compared to the number of paid staff that would be required to do the same work. The out-of-pocket expenses that many volunteers incur but don't claim could also be included as an in-kind donation.

Above all, it is important to promote volunteering as our gatekeeper of democracy. Investing in their recruitment, screening, placement, orientation, motivation, supervision, and evaluation is one of the most worthwhile investments we can ever make.

Utilizing the Power of Information Technology

Not that long ago I had a chance to spend a significant amount of time with my good friend and oh-so-respected colleague, Dianne Renton Clark. While ostensibly we were working, we also spent a lot of time catching up, reminiscing, and brainstorming. As always, she pushed my way of thinking.

We were startled to realize that it's been almost fifteen years since she and I first worked together. Shortly after first connecting, we had jointly responded to a request for proposals and to our surprise were hired over much more experienced consultants to deliver community development training to staff within the City of Burlington's community services division.

Having identified an unmet and growing need for information and resources about community, we subsequently designed a concept for a magazine. A few days later, Dianne called me bubbling with excitement.

"I've got a great idea, I've got a great idea", she said. "Let's do our magazine as a BBS."

Not knowing what it was, I replied none too enthusiastically, "What the heck is a BBS?"

Turns out, a BBS was an electronic version of a bulletin board that allowed people to use their phone lines to dial in and connect with others.

If you keep in mind that this was prior to mainstream access to the Internet and I was a techno-peasant, it is significant that we dropped the idea of a traditional magazine and somehow managed to build an interactive, graphic, fun, and user-friendly interface that actually depicted a community.

Even more significant is that we got upwards of one hundred fifty people to connect online. No mean feat considering they had to pay a membership fee as well as struggle with the complexities of dial-in telephone modems.

In hindsight it's clear the driving force then, as it is today, was the significant number of people motivated and eager to share stories, resources, and meaningful conversations about their communities.

From this beginning and, despite our propensity to butt heads as the result of often differing approaches, Dianne and I are still working together all these years later.

It got me thinking about how much I value her gift of always providing a visionary and inspiring approach. While she doesn't describe herself as a geek, she definitely is one, having a broad-based understanding of many types of information technology. What makes her rare is that she is always grounded by a community development approach and intentionally works to empower end users by reducing their dependency on technology specialists.

I've learned a lot of other things from Dianne along the way about how to, and how not to, use technology.

For instance, I've learned that it's dangerous and irresponsible to leave decisions about information technology in the hands of one person or even an entire department of IT specialists. Where technology is concerned, everyone within an organization or business has a role to play in one or more aspects of planning, policy development, branding, communicating, relationship tracking, networking, storing resources, training, research etc.

I've learned there is rarely one best technology and that one of the greatest challenges these days is just determining the one that is the best fit. Even then it will need to be integrated with other technologies in order to meet what are often complex needs.

And, even though the look of the final result will always be important, making it all work together and function is critical and needs to be done first. After all, form follows function.

She has also been a role model for ethical leadership. While there were many times when the money would have been appreciated and she could have chosen to install a specific software solution at the request of a client, she wouldn't do it if it wasn't the most appropriate and sustainable choice.

Dianne taught me that everything involving technology is a work-in-progress because just when you get used to a specific product it's time to change.

The reality of technology is that it's much more complicated than everyone thinks it is. I learned from her that because of the many options, working in technology is a tough place to be. It's hard to get it right when there are so many options, so many people to please, and no quick fix. Additionally, if anything goes wrong it's the geek that gets blamed.

Most importantly, she taught me that building communities online is never really about the technology. Technology is secondary. The challenge is always finding ways to make it simple to build connections and relationships among people.

Generally though, it is somewhat easier these days as most people see the benefits of technology beyond pushing out information. Even my father is starting to come around after years of ranting against technology. When I called him recently he was a little distracted. It seemed he was trying to look up the phone number of his eye doctor.

Since I was at my computer, I simply googled the name and within seconds was able to give him the phone number. No big deal except that I was on the other side of the country and since he's a technophobe he was freaked out because he couldn't figure out how the heck I had managed to do it so quickly. He had to admit he was impressed even though he has absolutely refused to have anything to do with computers.

In another technology-related incident the same week, I received an email from a student I taught at Niagara College about ten years ago. He had managed to track me down through my Facebook page. I recognized his name because he was one I felt I had let down. He simply stopped coming to class, disappeared, and never did graduate.

He wrote, "I want to take this time to extend to you my thanks for all of your support and encouragement during my tenure at Niagara College. The freedom you extended to me with regard to my creative endeavours in the classroom is something that I have not forgotten. The learning environment you created was one in which I felt most comfortable and uninhibited. You truly created an atmosphere most conducive to self-exploration and self-realization."

It was such an unexpected and moving message that I put my head down on my desk and cried.

For sure it was good to know that both my dad and a former student felt I had done something valuable, but these stories are also examples of development that is moving beyond pushing information at us, to instead doing more to facilitate communication, information sharing, and collaboration on the web. So while it's true there are some legitimate concerns about how we're using technology, there still is much to celebrate.

Finding information is becoming simpler as keyword searches are improved, customized, and refined. The content available on the web is more meaningful as even those with little or no skill or experience are able to update, link to, and improve upon, the work of others.

Sharing is becoming simpler what with web-based, shared calendars, networking sites that make it easier to keep in touch, and improved capacity to bookmark sites and resources, and store documents. And, just as organizations, businesses, and even entire communities are working to integrate and converge, so too are those within the world of technology.

This emerging world will result in radically different opportunities for learning and growing together. Although often without seeing the full possibilities, many youth and young adults have embraced technology, there are still many others entrenched in bricks and mortar believing physical places are essential for accessing services and knowledge. But, as the song says, "It ain't necessarily so."

We all know that the bricks and mortar in our communities such as libraries, schools, and government buildings won't go away, they, like the web, instead need to have dual functionality as both warehouses and gathering places. These gathering places, often referred to as the previously described "third places"[100] (after the two other social environments of home and the workplace), are foundations of community life that facilitate and nurture broader, more creative interaction.

In the end, the information that we seek to share, and the services that we seek to provide, will have to be flexible enough to be available in many forms. We need to foster communities and a sense of connectedness online and on the ground.

Today our website at www.acecommunities.ca integrates a number of technologies that will facilitate learning and communications for the work we're doing to strengthen community leaders. Dianne and her team have researched, installed, tested, and pushed the limits of a number of different kinds of software to make them work together in a way that not only empowers us but will ultimately be sustainable.

As a result of her work, our website runs on a user-friendly, open source platform that allows everyone on our team to edit postings. The site pulls in feeds from our team of bloggers and from other sites as soon as it's posted so we always have fresh content.

We have an area for digital media so we all can upload video and photos, as well as our own google mini search appliance that scouts the sites we program it to search. In essence, this means we have created our own virtual library.

A CRM (customer relationship management database) means we are able to track individuals with whom we have relationships. We have the capacity for collaborative publishing that has allowed a team across the country to upload research in the same place.

---

100 Oldenburg, Ray (1991). *The great good place*. New York: Marlowe & Company.

Our intranet means we have productive online meetings, forums, and emails for connecting with one another, and an ability to view each other's calendars from the web.

For Dianne, it has been ridiculously challenging but also incredibly frustrating. Mostly it's because technology, like the foundation of a house, while understood to be important, is largely underground and not visible. And, while good technology is intuitive to use and enhances one's workflow, no one really seems to understand how difficult it is to make that happen. As a result it is too often taken for granted. Regardless, information technology provides community leaders with unprecedented opportunities to reach out, engage, and cultivate citizen responsibility.

 **Chapter 11**

Competency 5: Advocating for Quality of Life

Has the ability to work proactively to promote recreation, parks, sport, arts, culture, and heritage as services that deliver essential benefits to the community

COMPETENCY AREA		INDICATORS TO HELP YOU UNDERSTAND WHAT ENCOMPASSES THIS COMPETENCY	1 = I AM NOT AT ALL LIKE THAT	10 = I AM 100% LIKE THAT
5 Quality of Life Advocacy	5.1	I can describe concepts related to individual quality of life.	1 2 3 4 5 6 7 8 9 10	
	5.2	I can articulate the importance of investment in community quality of life.	1 2 3 4 5 6 7 8 9 10	
	5.3	I can describe approaches to measuring quality of life.	1 2 3 4 5 6 7 8 9 10	
	5.4	I can articulate the benefits of recreation and parks.	1 2 3 4 5 6 7 8 9 10	
	5.5	I apply knowledge of policy advocacy as relates to community change.	1 2 3 4 5 6 7 8 9 10	
	5.6	I collaborate with others to influence public policy.	1 2 3 4 5 6 7 8 9 10	
	5.7	I promote the importance of civility and kindness .	1 2 3 4 5 6 7 8 9 10	

Concepts Related to Individual Quality of Life

If community leaders are expected to advocate for quality of life, it is important they be able to describe it. Unfortunately, it's not as easy as it sounds.

For example, I'm blessed and grateful to have an excellent quality of life. If I was pressed to explain exactly what that means, I'm not sure I could do it. But I do know I've got it. Even if I did know exactly what it meant, it wouldn't be useful information for others as it is likely that what I consider as quality of life would be different for others. For example, work makes me happy. Not everyone relates working hard to quality of life.

What we do know is that when we have quality of life it seems to mean we have the ability to enjoy all that life has to offer.

So how does one determine whether or not they have "quality of life"?

Perhaps it's not as complicated as one might think. It might just mean stepping back a bit and asking yourself, "Are you happy? How happy are you with your physical health, your family, and your spiritual and community life? Do your personal relationships bring you joy? Do you have meaningful work?"

Good health is what most would agree is essential for us being able to enjoy quality of life. When our bodies, minds, and spirits are healthy we are able to enjoy our families, our work, and our leisure.

238

Typically we also see *stability* as being important to our quality of life. When our life is stable—meaning we have the basics of food, shelter, security, and income—we tend to make better decisions about our life and our future.

When we are more stable, we tend to be more responsible and more likely to find and embrace a *sense of purpose*. People who have this sense of purpose or meaning in their lives are more likely to have a high quality of life because meaning brings purpose and reasons for living.

Spending time and *enjoying family and friends* is also essential for meeting our natural social needs.

The term quality of life is used to evaluate the general well-being of individuals and communities in a variety of contexts. For instance, the Quality of Life Research Unit at the University of Toronto suggests quality of life is the degree to which a person enjoys the important possibilities of his/her life.[101] Possibilities result from the opportunities and limitations each person has in his/her life and reflect the interaction of personal and environmental factors. Enjoyment has two components: the experience of satisfaction and the possession or achievement of some characteristic, as illustrated by the expression: "She enjoys good health."

> "There are many things in life that will catch your eye, but only a few will catch your heart... pursue those."
>
> — Michael Nolan

Concepts frequently related to quality of life are *happiness, joy,* and *serving others*.

Happiness

Everyone in our family would agree that our youngest son is the fun factor in our lives. He brightens every gathering the moment he walks into the room and always, always makes us laugh.

He is creative and curious about all things and as a result carries an extraordinary amount of information that is interesting but rarely useful. Children are drawn to his enthusiasm and sense of playfulness and usually cry when it's time for him to leave, counting down the days until they'll see him again.

---

101   http://www.utoronto.ca/qol/. Accessed February 2011.

There isn't a lot of long term planning in his life and he drives me to distraction by his propensity for living in the moment. By his own admission, he is perhaps, too good at enjoying the immediacy of each day. For example, one time he almost ended up homeless even though he'd known for weeks that his rented living quarters had been sold and he needed to find a new apartment.

However, just when I am at my wits end, he shows a side that makes me realize he is going to be okay. One day as he was riding a bus, he watched a very cold and agitated man wearing only a short sleeve shirt talking animatedly with the bus driver. The bus driver kept shaking his head. To my son it was apparent that an unsuccessful barter was taking place as the man soon turned to exit the bus. My son intervened asking, "Hey man, how much do you need"? My son, who rarely has more than ten dollars in his pocket, didn't hesitate in handing over the dollar and a half the man was short for his fare.

What was even more telling was that as my son was exiting the bus, the driver leaned over to him and said, "Thanks a lot for making me look like a jerk, eh." Instead of feeling angry or sad, my son just laughed.

Despite having very little in terms of material wealth and often living precariously in the moment, my son has something a lot of people are looking for—happiness.

It appears there's a lot of interest these days in not only defining happiness but figuring out just how we are all supposed to get it. There's even a new branch of psychology founded by Dr. Martin Seligman called *Positive Psychology*.[102] His research has demonstrated that it is possible, regardless of one's circumstances, to be happier, feel more satisfied, be more engaged with life, find more meaning, have higher hopes, and even laugh and smile more.

One of the keys Seligman believes unlocks the door to happiness is being able to understand our own internal qualities and character strengths. His research has shown that there are twenty-four character strengths that contribute to happiness. These include creativity, curiosity, open-mindedness, a love of learning, and vitality—characteristics that describe my son. There are other strengths such as perspective, persistence, social intelligence, humility, and citizenship.

---

102   Accessed Sept 2010. http://www.ppc.sas.upenn.edu/index.html.

240

The research also suggests that happiness is strongly connected to characteristics Seligman describes as *heart strengths*—gratitude, hope, zest, and the ability to love and be loved. And, as he explains it, we can grow our heart strengths by deliberately practicing them. For example, an individual can strengthen their gratitude and thus their overall happiness by keeping a gratitude journal that recounts good things that happen each day.

Seligman has also concluded there are three paths to happiness and that the most satisfied people will practice all three.

One is the *pleasant life,* full of joy, pleasure, and good times. I think my son is definitely on track with this one.

The second is the *engaged life,* where one loses oneself in an activity or passion that is such a good fit with their interest and skill that they experience what Mihaly Csikszentmihalyi calls *flow.*[103]

The third is the *meaningful life*, one that is packed with purpose, meaning, and giving to others.

Maybe it's not all that complicated after all. Maybe we would all be a lot happier if we concentrated on the little things in life.

Perhaps it's also about taking the time to savour life's small pleasures. Often we are too busy getting ready for some future time when we will really be able to enjoy life. Too often we think, "When I retire", "when I get the kids into school", "when I get enough money". Before we know it, too many opportunities may have passed us by.

Maybe just maybe, happiness just might be about having more pillow fights, hugging more people, reading more books, sitting by more fires, watching more sunsets, going for more walks, eating more ice cream, and holding more hands.

Happy Work Environments

I often work from home as do many of those on our team. While many would question whether or not we are as productive as those who work from a regular office, we have found the exact opposite to be true. Part of it is the result of having time to focus.

Always available to staff via phone and email, I sometimes work in my pajamas, totally absorbed, and unbelievably productive. Yet, at

---

103 Csíkszentmihályi, M. (1996). *Creativity: Flow and the psychology of discovery and invention,* New York: Harper Perennial.

the end of the day, rather than being tired, I often feel so good it's almost like having a vacation day. A lot of it is just due to having time to concentrate.

Apparently, according to Mihaly Csikszentmihalyi, the director of The Quality of Life Research Center at Claremont Graduate University, "the opportunity to concentrate" is one of a number of factors that contribute to an organization's ability to build the "flow" that leads to success.[104]

Csikszentmihalyi calls flow that wonderful feeling one gets when one is in command, performing at the peak of their ability, often losing track of time. Action flows effortlessly from your thoughts because your skills are well matched to the challenge. If the challenge is too great, you get frustrated or anxious or, if the challenge is too easy, you get bored. Additionally, the task always needs to represent a continuing opportunity for growth.[105]

Csikszentmihalyi's interest in studying enjoyment began as a ten year old. Shortly after World War II, he and his family were interned by the Italians until they could prove they weren't Fascists. Although everyone worried constantly, he found that during his chess games against the grownups he forgot about everything. Later in his life he found the same kind of intense pleasure and absorption in rock climbing.

He further studied what he named flow by asking painters what they were thinking about as they worked. He expected they would talk about creating something beautiful. Instead, they talked about the process and how they got caught up and immersed in the experience.

Csikszentmihalyi believes organizations and businesses can use this understanding to be more successful and to have happier employees and volunteers by creating conditions that contribute to flow.[106]

For instance, flow is more likely to occur in physically attractive environments. In fact, he cites Cirque du Soleil is an example, explaining that they actually travel with disassembled sets of a village

---

104   Csíkszentmihályi, M. (2003). *Good business: Leadership, flow, and the making of meaning*, New York: Penguin Books.

105   Csíkszentmihályi, M. (1996). *Creativity: Flow and the psychology of discovery and invention*, New York: Harper Perennial.

106   Csíkszentmihályi, Mihály (2003). Ibid.

square which they erect wherever the circus stops in order to create a familiar and comfortable setting.

In work environments that produce flow, one often hears the voices of children. On-site childcare facilities are a convenience for busy parents but are also a return to a more natural way of living. Similarly, cheerful cafeterias, appetizing foods, and places to relax can decrease the often impersonal atmosphere of a workplace.

The environment can also be improved by policies like flextime that allow people to move and act with freedom, to have control over their tasks, and to have input into decisions affecting their work.

Additionally, Csikszentmihalyi suggests there are three common conditions that will determine the success of a team. First, workers must understand the company or organization's vision, mission, and goals, and see their own role in contributing to making it a reality.

In addition to knowing what needs to be done, workers need to know whether the goal is getting closer. In other words, how are *we* doing, in addition to how am *I* doing. Specific feedback about performance is one of the most effective tools for helping workers improve their performance.

Lastly, workers must be provided with opportunities for their skills to be used and refined to their fullest. In addition to ensuring an individual is a fit with an organization's goals, values, and culture, their skills must be matched to the challenges so they continue to grow. Conditions that contribute to this growth are opportunities to concentrate and reflect, and having control over one's job.

What it comes down to is that if as a community leader, you're ever in doubt about how to improve productivity and ensure happier employers, go for the flow.

Joy

A family connection resulted in me landing tickets to see Michael Bublé's sold-old concert.

The big band/jazz/pop crooner, often compared to Frank Sinatra and Tony Bennett, put on a magnificent show. His music literally had people dancing in the aisles. He was funny, irreverent, and surprisingly authentic—kind of made you proud that he was Canadian.

Of mostly Italian heritage, Bublé was born in British Columbia and grew up listening to his grandfather's collection of jazz records. In listening to the romantic and meaningful lyrics of those songs, it became clear to him that he wanted to be a singer who would sing that same kind of music.

Watching him on stage it was apparent he was doing exactly what he was put on earth to do. Absolutely in his element, Bublé exuded a palpable energy that filled the entire arena and drew everyone into the music. His child-like sense of glee, in combination with his more adult and sincere appreciation for the thousands of people who had paid to see him perform, made him absolutely irresistible.

It struck me that what we were witnessing was pure and unadulterated joy. It also occurred to me that while it's probably rare to have that kind of love for your job, the odds of success must surely increase where there is such a match.

For certain Bublé's passion, energy, and fun has led to success as a Juno and Grammy-winning international artist. Additionally his sense of joy was contagious, spreading not only to the audience but also to his musicians and to the performers in his opening act who also joined him in one of his final songs.

I'm guessing that those who have found this match of joy with their paid or volunteer work, know it and are grateful. But what do you do if you don't like your job and can't, for whatever reasons, make a move? Is there a way to bring joy, even in small doses to your work?

In asking that question, I am reminded of an administrative assistant I once worked with who made it a priority to create ambiance in her office. She had returned to the workforce as her children got older, vowing to make sure she wouldn't lose sight of that which brought her joy. As a result, she bought and displayed a fresh bouquet of flowers on her desk every single week. Another colleague of mine, managed to turn her cubbyhole of an office into a sanctuary with numerous plants and even a small water fountain.

When I find joy on the job elusive, I've found it important to get outside. Going for a walk always seems to help if I'm bored, antsy, or low-spirited. Something about fresh air, a change of scenery, and the exercise seems to open up new connections to joy.

I've also learned that joy is much more likely when you get more sleep. Going to bed even an hour earlier seems to increase the possibilities of waking up with a brighter outlook.

Another friend told me that she has managed to maintain a positive outlook in a challenging government environment by signing up for a number of listservs. One of them sends her an inspirational quote each day, another shares best practices from among her colleagues across the country.

A woman I work with now has her own, and encourages her staff to start, what she calls a sunshine file. In the file she keeps letters, notes, emails, and testimonials from clients and colleagues that have thanked her or acknowledged her work in some way. Whenever she needs a dose of joy, she flips through her file.

Sharing good news is also a strategy that can bring joy. I once had a boss who kept us focused on the difference we were making working with challenging kids by starting each staff meeting with everyone playing "new or good". Each of us would offer our own stories of what had happened over the past week that was new or good.

I took this same learning into my classroom when I was teaching by inviting students to share their good news at the beginning of the class each week. I once had a student who kept her news of winning a trip to Florida to herself for five days in order to be able to share it in that class for the first time.

Contributing to a student's or young employee's career can also help you find unexpected joy. While we typically think of mentoring as building someone else's future, there are surprising benefits young people contribute in terms of fresh outlooks and enthusiasm.

While it's likely each of us can find joy in small doses, our responsibilities as leaders are also to ensure we are planning for the big changes in communities that will ensure opportunities for everyone to work, play, and find a life they love.

Collective Joy

By the end of the week I'm generally tapped out. As a result, I'm more susceptible to the magpie syndrome and easily distracted by anything bright and shiny. This week it was a link to a YouTube video sent by my mother.

It was shot in the main concourse area of a busy train station in Brussels. As I watched, the classic version of Do-Re-Mi, sung by the indomitable Julie Andrews, was suddenly heard over the loudspeakers in place of the typical announcements of arrivals and departures. By the looks on the faces of those captured in the video, it wasn't quite what they were used to hearing.

Suddenly a tall, lanky young man started dancing. He was quickly joined by several young kids and before you could say "doe a deer", several hundred people of all ages had taken over the central area and were dancing animatedly to the iconic song from the Sound of Music in a series of choreographed, lively and funky moves.

The best part was watching the looks on peoples' faces as they went from initial puzzlement, to broad smiles, to clapping and bouncing, to what ultimately appeared to be total and unmitigated joy. Quite honestly as I watched it I too was smiling and laughing but also on some level, extraordinarily moved.

The images stuck with me and I found myself trying to figure out exactly what it was that touched me on such a deep level. There was just something about the rhythms, the music, and the happiness that struck a chord. I know it wasn't just the dancing because I watch "So You Think You Can Dance" and "Dancing with the Stars" and while I enjoy them, they are more about competition and therefore more intimidating and judgmental. This was something different because it was more of a communal celebration. It made me wistful and question why it is that we have so few, or perhaps even resist altogether, opportunities to have fun together?

Barbara Ehrenreich in her book, *Dancing in the Streets,* has explored the origins of this shared celebration as a history of what she has termed "collective joy".

Ehrenreich connects a growing epidemic of depression with our decline in group bonding rituals—think church, feasts, and carnivals. She also explains how throughout history, group celebrations have brought people together in a spirit of solidarity, joy, and union. These festivities have promoted not only human bonding but in some cases have been vehicles for change to fight oppression. Gay pride parades are a good example.

I'm not suggesting all our problems would be solved if we got out and danced together, but it is a classic, primeval way for people to bond together. But what's critical is that we don't do it anymore or, if we do, we aren't doing it enough.

So beyond encouraging more line dancing or circle dancing and less couples dancing at our parties, can we use collective joy to help motivate people and help promote our causes?

People who are working for change need to think about how they can design their events to create this spirit of belonging and joy just as spectator sports have done. In the case of sports, they've often using the traditional elements of carnival by encouraging the use of team colours, face painting, chants, and singing along to loud rock and roll music.

We can't forget that people do want to experience collective joy and cohesion in artistic and fun ways. Early in my career as a recreation practitioner, we brought the opportunity via cooperative games where everyone played and there were no winners and losers. Boomers experienced it during the rock rebellion of the 60s, when music invited and encouraged people not to sit still anymore. The ultimate message, literally as well as figuratively, was to get up and move with other people.

Bringing arts, culture, music, and dance into our politics can also be a way to express a vision for the kind of community, and ultimately the world, we're seeking. Additionally, it can teach the availability of joy that has nothing to do with material gain, and that it can be achieved in sustainable ways that don't impact the environment.

We have never lost the capacity for collective joy. It is part of our nature and being as humans. What we have lost are the opportunities for experiencing it. And that's the challenge for each of us—figuring out how to bring more opportunities for collective joy into our lives, organizations, and communities. It could be the best gift we ever give one another.

Serving Others

As I write this, I'm sitting on the deck of a cottage overlooking the appropriately named Paradise Lake. I have a lot of time to think.

The truth is that while no one is forcing me to write, somehow my overdeveloped work ethic and conscientiousness has meant I'm producing my regular weekly output even though I'm on vacation.

I'm also struggling somewhat, yet again, with the realization that I'm simply not very good at doing nothing. There's an Italian phrase, "Il bel far niete" that means the beauty of doing nothing. I'm not quite there, but then again, I'm not totally convinced I want to be.

Like many other baby boomers, though, I have realized that I have enough of everything.

I don't need another house or a bigger house, more shoes, or exotic vacations. Okay maybe a few more shoes wouldn't hurt. Nor am I going to be one of those obsessed with using creams and cosmetic procedures to stay young. After all, I've earned my wrinkles. I know too that being here relaxing at the cottage with our kids and extended families is as good as it gets.

I've also learned that happiness is far more likely when I focus on what I can give, rather than what I can get. I think that means I'm now a baby boomer in recovery. It's been an exhilarating ride for us boomers. Overwhelming in our numbers, we absorbed the spirit and optimism of the times and barreled through life.

Each phase we've gone through has shaped community priorities. When we were younger, boomers were the impetus for new subdivisions, schools, arenas, and swimming pools.

Today human services are wondering how they're going to deal with our numbers, not to mention our anticipated longevity, and developers are focused on designing and building retirement communities to meet everyone's needs.

As a generation that has become accustomed to being the centre of attention, perhaps though it's our turn to think about how we can expand our potential for happiness.

Hindu philosophy suggests there are four phases of life. In the first, we are students who are being educated and learning about life. In phase two we are busy making a living, raising a family, and being part of a community. Too often, we tend to do the first two and stop.

However, for Hindus phase three is a time for stepping back from life in order to question who you are and to think about life's deep questions.

Finally in phase four, the intent is to return to the world without attachment, to serve others.

While I'm not suggesting everyone embrace a Hindu lifestyle, perhaps middle age can hold greater adventures in addition to those offered by playing golf or planning the next cruise.

While I can't profess to being an expert on how exactly one goes about doing that, I do think it begins with getting in touch with what it is you're passionate about. Sometimes that may even mean doing something that scares the heck out of you.

Regardless, it is important that we as a generation spend time reflecting and figuring out how to give back.

Not sure about you, but I'd hate to think that boomers could go down in the history books as the generation that was too self-involved to leave the world in better shape than it was when they found it.

Benefits of Investment in Community Quality of Life

Some years ago our family moved to Welland because of Oprah.

I just happened to be watching an Oprah show when one of her guests suggested that everyone should ask themselves the deceptively simple question, *"What would make me happy"*?

Later, after discussing it at some length over dinner, my husband and I concluded that while we were both happy with our work, each other, and our children, our daily pace had become rather frantic. At the time I had moved from my teaching position in the Recreation and Leisure Services program at Niagara College to help establish the Centre for Community Leadership—a resource centre for the social-profit sector.

My husband carried the responsibility for the daily retail operations of an art gallery, his photography studio, and the custom picture framing end of the business. We shared responsibility for three sons, four cats, a large, high-maintenance house and yard, and a publishing and consulting company.

Our discussion led us to determine that one strategy for reducing our stress could lay in finding a building that would allow us to live in the same place as our business. With that, our hunt for a building began.

Seeking a larger population base, we first checked out possibilities in St. Catharines and Niagara Falls. We never really seriously considered Welland until I somehow ended up facilitating a townhall meeting. At the end of that meeting, I walked away with a totally changed perception of Welland.

I had discovered that the people in town were warm and friendly. There was a definite sense of spirit as well as amazing potential given the old Welland canal and its surrounding lands which had now been designated for recreational use. Not to mention the proximity to Niagara Falls and its millions of visitors each year, and the planned downtown development.

I went home that evening bubbling with enthusiasm. My husband didn't need much convincing as he had previously worked in downtown Welland and had always been a fan. With the help of a local realtor we soon found a property, tackled four months of renovations, and finally moved in.

Our new space allowed us to expand and grow our business as well as simplify our life. But even more importantly, we found a real sense of community in Welland.

My husband, who had always described himself as not being a *joiner*, became one. He was soon an active member of the local curling club and a local kite fliers association. I got involved as the co-chair of the city's recreation, parks, and culture master plan committee.

It is mostly this sense of being connected to the community that resulted in us never regretting our decision to move to Welland.

Interestingly enough, Robert Putnam, a professor of public policy at Harvard and author of a groundbreaking book called *Bowling Alone*,[107] shows that in far too many communities, people are increasingly experiencing quite the opposite. Many have become disconnected from family, friends, neighbours, and to community affairs. In some cases, they've even given up bowling leagues in favour of *bowling alone*. Putnam warns that our stock of social capital is in a dangerous decline.

---

107 Putnam, R. (2000). *Bowling alone: The collapse and revival of American community.* New York: Simon and Schuster.

The term social capital emphasizes not just warm feelings, but a wide variety of specific benefits that result from the trust, information, and cooperation that is associated with social networks.

So the next time a new club is formed, someone signs up as a volunteer, writes a letter to the editor, attends a concert or sporting event, or works on a community project, I hope community leaders will see it as a cause to celebrate. I also hope they will see that social networks have value. Where social capital is higher, the welfare of children is higher, schools work better, children watch less TV, violent crime is rarer, people are less pugnacious, health is better, tax evasion is lower, and tolerance is higher.

When people know one another, they help one another. The end result of investing in social capital is a culture of reciprocity, a stronger, healthier, and more vibrant community, and ultimately that elusive and hard to describe "quality of life".

Approaches to Measuring Quality of Life

My work means I often need to spend time thinking and talking to others about evaluation and measurement. Truth be told, there is usually some kicking and screaming involved in getting me to do it. While I do know it's important, there's just something about evaluation that makes me want to yawn and roll my eyes. Maybe instead of calling it evaluation we could make it more palatable by referring to it as reflections and learnings?

I do realize though that the reality is that what gets measured matters. What we count, quantify, measure, and evaluate influences public policy, decision-making, and investment.

However, community leaders haven't historically always measured that which matters most. We haven't emphasized assessments or report cards to measure what matters in a community. It just seems we don't have hard numbers for things that are soft. As a result, there's a lack of a comprehensive instrument that tells us how well we are doing—never mind whether we're getting better or worse.

Even the Gross Domestic Product (GDP) or Gross National Product (GNP) only measures economic consumption and not even whether it's good or bad consumption. It definitely doesn't provide an overall perspective on how we are doing in general.

And yet, GDP remains the most common measurement used among industrial nations to measure progress even though it's merely a gross tally of everything bought and sold with no distinction as to whether what's being bought and sold adds or subtracts from our well-being and quality of life.

As a vocal opponent of the use of GDP or GNP because he didn't see it as a measure of progress, the late Robert F. Kennedy Jr. probably wouldn't be too happy to know we're still using it as a predominant measure.

In one of his last speeches Robert Kennedy explained it this way, "The Gross National Product includes air pollution and advertising for cigarettes, and ambulances to clear our highways of carnage.

It counts special locks for our doors, and jails for the people who break them. GNP includes the destruction of the redwoods and the death of Lake Superior. It grows with the production of napalm and missiles and nuclear warheads…

And if GNP includes all this, there is much that it does not comprehend.

It does not allow for the health of our families, the quality of their education, or the joy of their play. It is indifferent to the decency of our factories and the safety of our streets alike.

It does not include the beauty of our poetry or the strength of our marriages, or the intelligence of our public debate, or the integrity of our public officials…

GNP measures neither our wit nor our courage, neither our wisdom nor our learning, neither our compassion nor our devotion to our country.

It measures everything, in short, except that which makes life worthwhile."[108]

While there are a number of movements afloat across Canada to develop an alternative form of measurement, none of them are quite there yet.

---

108 Kennedy, R. F. (March 18, 1968). Speech at the University of Kansas. Retrieved August 2010. http://www.jfklibrary.org/Historical+Resources/Archives/Reference+Desk/Speeches/RFK/RFKSpeech68Mar18UKansas.htm.

So what do we do about it in the meantime?

Perhaps we need community leaders who pay more attention to the quality rather than the quantity of growth in our communities. We need to measure the things that real people see as contributing to making their lives worthwhile.

Heeding this advice, ACE Communities has focused on the evaluation of some broader community outcomes that the GDP doesn't measure—knowledgeable decision makers, engaged communities, pro-active youth, responsive community initiatives, and informed communities.

We expect that communities keeping a watchful eye on these priorities are going to make different decisions than a community that is only paying attention to its economic activity.

In the meantime, a group of Canadian economists, statisticians, public health analysts, environmental researchers, and social scientists from universities and colleges, government agencies, and think-tanks across the country are working to create a series of objective standards to measure genuine social progress.

One of these is called the CIW—the Canadian Index of *Well-being*.[109] The CIW will track changes in eight quality of life categories or domains that include democratic engagement, living standards, healthy populations, time use, leisure and culture, education, and environment. The idea behind it is to provide community leaders and policy-makers with measurements to help them quantify quality of life.

Hopefully it will also mean we'll be "Measuring what we value rather than valuing what we measure."[110]

Articulate the Benefits of Recreation and Parks

While there isn't always a widespread awareness or appreciation for the field of recreation and parks, it taught me almost everything I know about community building and community leadership.

---

109   Canadian Index of Well-being. Accessed Aug 2010. http://www.ciw.ca/en/TheCanadianIndexOfWellbring/DomainsOfWellbeing.aspx.

110   Glaser Foundation. Accessed March 2011 http://www.ed4wb.org/?p=67.

That lack of appreciation for the field was reinforced for me again when I recently talked to yet another young person who is totally convinced that making money is the route to happiness. Despite working and doing a great job this past summer as a special event organizer for a social-profit recreation organization, he is also certain his path includes a university degree in business. In the ensuing conversation we talked about values, learning about what is important to one's self, and how money doesn't necessarily equate to happiness.

I also ended up sharing with him the reasons why I originally chose to work in the field of recreation and parks. Mostly I chose it because of what I didn't want. While understanding its importance, I knew I wanted my life's work to be about more than improving the bottom line of a business. I valued and wanted meaningful work that would make a difference in people's lives and the communities in which they lived.

I lucked into the field of recreation as the result of a job at the Niagara Falls Boys and Girls Club. It didn't pay a lot and it was hard work but there is no doubt in my mind that we touched kid's lives every single day.

In addition to looking out for kids to ensure they had opportunities to be active and creative as well as the self-esteem and skills to live a good life, I learned how to recruit and motivate staff and volunteers, fundraise, plan, design and implement programs, manage a facility, administer and budget, and organize outdoor activities. I was never bored.

Additionally, as the result of organizing support and services for club members who were financially, socially, or otherwise disadvantaged, I learned how communities worked, and sometimes didn't work, as the result of having to connect with schools, social service and health organizations, businesses, justice, service clubs, and different levels of government.

As my career progressed within municipal recreation and later to teaching recreation at Niagara College, I worked with other recreation practitioners to support and build the capacity of social-profit organizations to deliver recreation, sport, arts, culture, and heritage. We made sure there were programs, events, and festivals as well as pools, arenas, parks, playing fields, and trails for walking, jogging, cycling, and enjoying nature. Today my work is primarily focused on yet another key role of the recreation sector—community building.

Looking back, it's clear that while I may not have improved the bottom line of a business, I did contribute to the bottom line of a number of communities along the way. The recreation support and services were an investment yielding a different kind of return. Success was measured in how we were able to positively influence individual growth and wellness, enhance social inclusion and community development; protect and preserve natural environments; and enhance economic vitality.

And, while I like to think most would agree that's important, I still used to hesitate before putting up my hand to say I am a recreation practitioner. The truth is that recreation and parks is a field that doesn't always get a lot of respect from the general public or community leaders.

It makes me sad because what we do during our leisure time helps us enjoy and make sense of our lives, our families, our communities, and the world around us. It is a basic human need that contributes to our mental, physical, social, intellectual, and spiritual well-being and, ultimately, to our happiness. The positive use of our leisure time and the participation, relationships, and strengthening of our communities that results, are typically reliant upon the distinct and often under-valued contribution of recreation and parks practitioners.

66 During the 10th World Leisure Congress, held between October 6-10, 2008, in Quebec City, Canada, 4000 delegates from over 40 countries gathered to discuss leisure as a determining factor in the sustainable development of communities* and issued the Quebec Declaration.

At the end of their discussions, delegates declared the following: when individuals become players, leisure contributes to their quality of life and that of their community and requires a collective implementation of the values relating to quality of life; leisure is a powerful tool in the social capital development of communities and; leisure is a place for learning, the expression of public participation, and the heart of democratic life. Therefore, since leisure affects quality of life, contributes to social capital development and represents a place for expression and learning of democratic life, leisure plays an essential role in the social, cultural, political and economical development of communities." [111]

---

111   www.worldleisure.org/pdfs/quebec_declaration.pdf. Retrieved June 15, 2011.

Recreation and parks practitioners work in a variety of settings—community or municipal recreation, sports, fitness, outdoor recreation, aquatic, facility management, parks, natural environments, special events, heritage, arts and cultural or, in some cases, settings that combine a few or many of the above.

Increasingly, recreation and parks practitioners are also evolving, or perhaps returning to their roots, to play a key leadership role within their communities as the result of their holistic approach, knowledge, and understanding of communities and civic engagement.

Engaging communities for recreation often leads to a role as a "community connector" or "catalyst" who plays a bridging role in engaging multiple disciplines and sectors to tackle broader issues related to quality of life. Because recreation is a safe and non-threatening vehicle that impacts everyone from cradle to grave, each person can relate to it. As such it is a perfect vehicle for jumpstarting the collaboration necessary for building community capacity and resiliency.

This commitment to creating spaces and opportunities for quality of life, in combination with a passion and belief in the importance of work life balance, families, lifelong growth and health, and strong, vibrant communities, has resulted in recreation and parks practitioners who often tackle their work with an almost missionary zeal, seeing their work as a calling that allows them to make a difference, rather than simply doing a job.

So, as I wrapped up our conversation about values and my passion with the young man all set to major in business, I was gratified to hear him say that he would explore the field of recreation with a number of elective university courses.

For sure it's a start and a decision he'll likely never regret if he is at all interested in the work of the heart, the health, and the spirit of individuals and the communities where they live.

Experiencing the Benefits of Recreation

It's likely that my understanding of the benefits of recreation is the result of first-hand experience.

In my younger years, I was pretty much a jockette.

Growing up with three brothers and a younger sister I learned how to throw a football, stop hockey pucks—sometimes with my face—hit a baseball, and whip a lacrosse ball. And, while those activities were fun, the best of our sport and recreation activities took place at the local arena, swimming pool, and community centre.

During summer months we walked over a mile to the municipal pool almost every day, took part in morning swim and diving lessons and stayed until the pool closed for dinner. Sometimes we left so weary our knees would buckle as we stumbled home waterlogged and sunburned.

In the winter, all three of my brothers played hockey, my sister and I took figure skating lessons, and we all went to public skating on Saturdays.

The community centre was almost a second home. There we played floor hockey, basketball, and participated in hopscotch tournaments. Once, in a moment of lapsed judgment, I even took tap dancing lessons.

As part of the baby boomer generation, we had the benefit of playing in brand new facilities built during the 50's and 60's to accommodate the then burgeoning population. Later, during the 70's and 80's, provincial lottery dollars supported some additional building and renovations.

Today, the story is altogether different.

Many communities are struggling to maintain their recreation and cultural facilities. Arenas, community centres, swimming pools, museums, and theatres across the country are aging and new replacements are never guaranteed. Some are even being considered for permanent closure.

It isn't a stretch to say this lack of investment in our recreation infrastructure just might be a little shortsighted. We need more, not less, investment if we are to reduce health care costs and build healthier communities. Our recreational infrastructure is at-risk and it's sad that community leaders often fail to see there is a direct link between increasing physical activity levels and providing safe, affordable, and accessible community-based places for recreation, sport, and cultural activities.

In addition to ensuring we have activities, pools, arenas, parks and playing fields, we also need to have trails for walking, jogging, and cycling, fitness programs for children in our schools, employees in the workplace, and seniors in retirement homes, accessibility to schools for evening and weekend activities, and support to build the capacity of social-profit organizations to better serve youth and adults.

Ultimately I don't think it's all that complicated. We can pay now or we can pay much much more later.

The Benefits of Outdoor and Family Recreation

While the benefits of recreation are often the result of our municipal and social-profit delivery systems, community leaders also need to be aware of the many benefits gained from less formal outdoor activity.

As far as our family is concerned, one of the best things about summer is camping.

During a dinner with a couple who are good friends, my husband and I extolled the virtues of camping and suggested the two of them join us on a future trip.

Whereas Scott was absolutely receptive and ready, the same certainly couldn't be said of his wife Sandra. I could tell she wasn't too keen on the idea of pitching a tent and hanging out in the woods. As she summed it up a little more bluntly, "As far as I'm concerned, camping is one step away from homelessness and I'm not going there! My idea of roughing it is a hotel without room service!"

Okay, while camping, or "data fasting" as I now call it, may not be for everyone, I can tell you that some of our family's most vivid "Kodak Moments" or "Hallmark Memories" took place during our annual excursions.

My husband and I had what were likely our deepest and most meaningful conversations with our sons while sitting around the campfire or playing cards or board games. In addition to the fireside chats, we cycled, hiked, read books, and hung out at the beach.

In some respects, our camping trips weren't simply vacations. Perhaps more significantly, they were a tangible example of us conveying that family was important.

They were the times that allowed all of us to come together as a family without the distractions of work, chores, television, or video games. As such they signaled a sense of belonging.

Though today the traditional definition and structures of families may have changed, the need for having a sense of family remains.

There is still a need for stability within a family setting that an individual isn't always able to get on their own.

Additionally, many character traits and interpersonal skills are developed within the family unit and can be practiced and reinforced through recreation activities. Participating in recreation activities as a family provides examples of the personal interactions that ultimately teach life skills. For example, there's nothing like trying to set up camp an hour before dark to teach problem solving, cooperation, compromise, coping skills, perseverance, and a positive attitude.

An individual's lifelong leisure habits build on early experiences that contribute to a person's development and lifestyle. Many adults continue to participate in recreation activities they were introduced to as a child or will try a new sport or hobby after being inspired by a family member.

While camping may not be for everyone, there are other options to consider for family bonding.

Toss a Frisbee, play volleyball, fly a kite. Garden or cook together. Go for a hike, pedal along local bike paths, go horseback riding. Go fishing, go for a picnic, or for a scenic drive.

Volunteering as a family to plant trees or pick up trash also builds memories. Encourage collections. Even very young children love gathering rocks, shells, or wildflowers. As a child I remember being especially fascinated by my friend's rock tumbler that polished the stones.

In a time where kids are often over-programmed, "green hours" and a time for unstructured play and interaction with the natural world will be essential. Even fifteen minutes is a good start. Whenever possible, independent exploration should be encouraged.

Ultimately while we all benefit by being outdoors, it will be especially important for kids. Just as children need healthy food, sufficient sleep, and regular exercise, they also need unstructured contact with nature. After all, shouldn't every child have the experience of sleeping under the stars?

Recreating together as a family in activities that promote physical, emotional, mental, and social development and growth strengthens family bonds.[112]

---

112   Couchman, R. (1988). Leisure: A dynamic of family life. *Visions*, 1 (3).

Simply being outdoors can also be an antidote to stress.[113]

A while ago, some friends and I drove out to visit another friend who lives in a wonderfully restored rural home they lovingly refer to as "the ranch".

The view was spectacular, the weather was sunny and warm, and sitting on their front deck drinking lemonade and "activating"—as they called rocking in their wooden rocking chairs—was absolutely delightful. I could almost feel the stress ooze out of my body. Even more than the rest of us, my friend Carol just lapped up the ambiance, smiling like a Cheshire cat, savouring every minute we spent there. She almost had to be pried out of her chair when it was time to go.

It was clear to everyone that the quiet and peaceful outdoors just made us all feel good.

According to Pulitzer Prize winning biologist, Edward O. Wilson, we were experiencing biophilia. Even though it sounds like a disease, literally translated, biophilia means "love of living things".[114] It describes what Wilson believes is our innate need to connect with nature, plants and wildlife, and the great outdoors.

According to Wilson and a growing number of other scientists, the need for, and attraction to, natural environments is much more than the latest trend.

Research indicates our brain is programmed or wired to be receptive to nature. Over the past two million years, people existed in an environment where the sights, sounds, and smells of nature were crucial to survival. Those most in tune with nature were those who survived.

Today, our connections to the outdoors may be much more tenuous. It is quite possible to function without spending much time tuning in to nature. However, when we do take the time to commune with nature, it will have a positive impact on our health and well-being.

Even if you don't have time to hike, fish, garden, camp, or rock climb, simply viewing the outdoors can deliver benefits.

---

113 Alves, S., Bell, S., Hamilton, V., Montarzino, A., Rothnie, H., & Travlou, P. (2008). *Greenspace and quality of life: A critical literature review.*

114 Wilson, E. (1986) *Biophilia.* Boston:Harvard University.

One study found that workers whose office windows had natural views reported less job stress than those whose windows overlooked a parking lot. And while it may not quite be the same, the fact that my own kitchen window now overlooks a park does seem to take some of the pain out of washing dishes.

Another study concluded that people in hospitals heal quicker in rooms with a view of trees in a park-like setting.[115] Studies have also shown that patients in nursing homes or psychiatric hospitals are healthier amid plant and wildlife and that petting a dog or cat, talking to birds, or even simply watching fish swim in an aquarium can lower one's blood pressure and reduce the physical effects of stress.[116] That is why more and more caretakers in healthcare settings are turning to horticultural and pet therapy programs. Outdoor settings are especially important for children reducing their stress and increasing health, well-being, and socializing.[117]

While it may not be possible to visit friends in the country, fish, or take a hike every day, it may be possible to incorporate nature into our everyday lives.

Stop and admire the beauty of the fall foliage. Take a moment to watch Canada Geese fly south. Rake a pile of leaves and jump in, set up a bird feeder, move your office desk next to the window, play with your dog, buy a plant, or pick some apples.

If nothing else, wherever you are, open up those curtains and let the sun shine in.

Applying Knowledge of Policy Advocacy as it Relates to Community Change

Are we scared to change, overwhelmed, or do we really think the challenges in our communities will go away if we ignore them?

---

115 Ulrich, R. S. (1984). View through a window may influence recovery from surgery. *Science, 224,* 42-421.

116 Hartig, T., Mang, M., & Evans, G. (1991). Restorative effects of natural environment experiences. *Environment and Behavior, 23* (1), 3-26.

117 Munoz, S. (2009). *Children in the outdoors A literature review.* Forres, Scotland: Sustainable Development Research Centre.

In Thomas L. Friedman's book called *Hot, Flat and Crowded*,[118] he makes the case that post 9/11 Americans have shifted to a defense mode that has resulted in them exporting their fears rather than their hopes. And, as he points out, it's impossible to be visionary if you are in a defense mode.

It has also meant Americans have neglected such critical issues as their health care system, crumbling infrastructure, immigration reform, Social Security, Medicare, and dealing comprehensively with energy excesses. He also blames the mortgage mess that led to the 2010 financial crisis as being part of the same kind of overriding mentality—"We'll get to it when we feel like getting to it and it will never catch up with us because we're American."

Having now worked with over fifty different communities, I wish I could tell you Canadians are different. Unfortunately, albeit not to the same extreme, most of us are the same when it comes to change. The good news is that even if we haven't done anything about it yet, most do seem to know there must be a better way and are open and ready to consider options.

After all, we're living in a post-industrial, creativity-hungry era where quality of life is becoming an increasingly important measure of success. In smaller communities especially, there is also an understanding that quality of life isn't something we can take for granted as there are signs telling us it may be at-risk.

Unlike some politicians and corporate leaders, there are many who already get that this nexus of change demands huge shifts. They know we can't keep extracting natural resources or consume seemingly infinite resources. Nor can we be a homogenous society that values conformity or thinks only in terms of our local communities. While Canadians still want tightly-knit communities, they also understand the value of the creative capital that comes with more cosmopolitan regional communities.

The citizens I've met know our health care must shift from its current disease focus to one that is based more on wellness-focused holistic health. They also understand that recreation and culture is necessary for wellness.

---

118   Friedman, T. L. (2008). *Hot, flat and crowded*. New York: Straus and Giroux.

Canadians, unlike some Americans, are much further ahead in some regard because they do understand that the future needs us to move from "me to we" by balancing individual rights and interests with those of the broader community. Unlike our more traditional politicians, the average citizens we've met also understand that we need to move from top-down governing to governance as a shared accountability because it is too complex for any one leader to tackle on their own.

This time of change opens tremendous opportunities for positive action and an opportunity to shape a new environment as well as the kind of leadership that will use our resources to protect and enhance the quality of life in our communities. We can create a far more livable future than our current course is aligned to produce by advocating for policy change that will provide for higher quality of life and, in the long term, cost far less.

Typically, developing public policy is an activity carried out within distinct policy envelopes that involves research, analysis, consultation, and synthesis of information to produce recommendations. And, it generally involves an evaluation of options against a set of criteria used to assess each option.

Along with other issues in our communities, our approach to public policy needs to change because for the most part it isn't working. A new world needs a new, more integrated and collaborative approach to public policy if we are to better reflect our values and prioritize our resources.

My guess is that if we developed a quality of life framework based on the values held true by typical Canadians we'd be on the right track. If our collective values could serve as a filter or guiding policy, it would be much simpler for each of us to be part of the change that will result in an improved quality of life for all.

Perhaps it is as simple as framing our public policy decisions on doing the right thing just because it is the right thing to do.

Collaborating with Others to Influence Public Policy

It might not have been ankle-biting but it wasn't exactly an effective advocacy strategy either.

A number of years ago I was managing the Centre for Community Leadership at Niagara College during a period when the social profit sector was being subjected to a particularly brutal round of funding cuts. With little understanding of advocacy, we took it upon ourselves to challenge regional government as one of the sector's key funders. We asked for, and were granted, an opportunity to speak to a Committee of Council to present our concerns regarding the sector.

We presented a strong case including the results of a regional survey illustrating the impact of funding cuts on social-profit organizations and predictions that many were in a precarious position. As part of our pitch, we asked for funding that would help us to continue our work to strengthen the leadership and capacity within the sector.

Our request was denied and sadly much of what we had predicted has since come true. Some organizations have been forced to shut their doors while others continue to juggle the demands of serving the often increased public demands with declining resources.

Today I have a much better understanding of advocacy and the skills and practices needed to push for change. I'm also clearer that advocacy is core to ensuring active and engaged citizens and is, in fact, often how we learn to participate in decision-making at all levels. Advocating for what we believe and making ourselves heard teaches us how to identify priorities, plan a strategy, take action, and achieve results.

Knowing what I know now, I'd like to think I would be more patient and much more strategic in advocating for the social profit sector. After all, if we are to better understand and value the contributions of the sector, it will require a significant movement.

And, movements don't just happen. They require the marshalling of energy through a much larger advocacy effort that includes networks and coalitions that plan and coordinate their strategies, messages, and action plans. They don't bite at the ankles of their funders to meet their own needs but rather join forces to promote solutions for the greater good.

I've also learned that advocacy addressing public policy works best if we take time, careful thought, and planning as a team to be clear about what we want, and to figure out who needs to hear it, who they need to hear it from, the best mediums, what we need to put into place to make it happen, and how we will know that our advocacy strategies are working or not working.

Perhaps, though, my greatest learning has been about the importance of vision and values. If we spend time thinking, talking, and gaining consensus about what we value and the kind of communities we want, the public policy and decisions about where and how we invest will become clearer and hopefully simpler.

At the time we approached Regional Council, I'm not sure there was a clear vision and values in place addressing the quality of life in our communities. As a result, the predominant filter for decision-making was economic.

The lack of articulated values, together with a directive to maintain the status quo, meant we shouldn't have been surprised to have our request turned down. While one elected councilor did admit we had made them feel guilty about the state of the sector, they also felt their hands were tied because in effect we were asking them to change policy direction without clear indication of public support.

If I knew then what I know now, our advocacy would have been more about building a strong coalition and a movement that would have promoted a more balanced approached to decision-making that examined economic as well as quality of life values. After all, if and when decisions are made based wholly on money, we are at risk as a society for ending up with oil spills like the 2010 catastrophe in the Gulf of Mexico, companies moving jobs out of our communities, a social system that reacts rather than prevents, and an education system that prepares graduates for jobs but not for life.

In other words, even if we end up with communities that have jobs, there's a good chance they won't have the quality of life that will make people want to live there.

Advocating the Importance of Civility and Kindness

I recently watched American Gene Simmons, best known as the demonic, blood spitting bassist with a creepy waggling tongue in the 1970's hard rock band called Kiss, as a guest on a Canadian talk show.

Not being a huge fan, I wasn't paying a lot of attention especially when he ranted somewhat about the accumulation of money being

265

the only way to measure success. He did, however, get my attention when he waxed poetic about the warmth and friendliness of Canada. He also suggested that Canadians could teach Americans a thing or two about one of our greatest strengths—civility.

It wasn't until the next day, overhearing a conversation between an elderly woman and a sales clerk, that I thought more about it and realized civility is more than simply being nice or polite to one another.

As the woman purchased a pair of pants and socks at a ladies clothing store, the sales clerk learned that she and her husband had just recently moved back into the city after living for years in a small, more northern community. When the sales clerk asked the woman how they were enjoying the city, the woman shrugged, smiled somewhat sadly and said that while it meant they were closer to their daughter, they were lonely and missed all their friends back home.

> " We are on earth to do good to others. What the others are here for, I don't know."
>
> — W. H. Auden

While many would simply have smiled and hurried through the transaction in order to avoid spending more time in the woman's depressing presence, this salesclerk smiled and asked another question, "Do you live close to the mall"?

When the woman replied that they lived a block away, the clerk suggested they look into the Mall Walk program. As she pointed out, the popular early morning program was a safe way to get fit in a warm and safe environment. And, she went on to add, the post walk coffee club is a good place to meet new friends. She described the walking club community so vividly you could see the woman's interest was piqued and more details were subsequently exchanged.

As I thought about the conversation, I realized that I had witnessed what Gene Simmons had talked about as an exchange of civility. More than just being nice or polite, the salesclerk had extended a spirit of neighbourliness and a sense of caring. She was demonstrating social responsibility or, what my mother and grandmother repeatedly taught as, "Do unto others as you would have them do unto you."

For sure if it was my mother who had been uprooted and moved to a new city, I'd like to know there would be others reflecting the same spirit of civility and kindness as that salesclerk.

Sadly, I think civility is on the decline in today's often materialistic, time starved world. However, if we agree we want to see more of it, how do we go about it?

It seems to me that while we can encourage civility by teaching empathy to children, it's probably more important that we model it. For all of us, ensuring civility will be about conducting ourselves with integrity, courtesy, and respect toward fellow members of our community. We'll all need to hold each other accountable for our actions and promote an environment where individuals feel safe and supported.

Mostly though, it might be about behaving in a way that encourages connections. Perhaps we should all begin by ignoring our many distractions and work harder at paying more attention.

Real civility just might begin with us putting down what we're doing and simply being in the moment with one another. The moment of human connection begins with us doing what that salesclerk did—paying attention and listening with empathy.

When we speak of Canada as a country we are proud to call our own, and as a place where we want to raise our children and our grandchildren, it is in large part due to the civility and quality of life we have in our communities. As such, civility isn't just a value-added, it is perhaps who we are as Canadians. As such, it's worth fighting for, and something every community leader needs to make a priority.

It is also important to understand that we can advocate for kindness and compassion on a much smaller scale. That was reinforced during a recent trip to the grocery store.

While I'm the first to admit I'm a big fan of retail therapy, I don't consider shopping for groceries to be fun at all. For me grocery shopping is definitely a chore. However, as I was buying groceries one day, it seemed the clerk at my checkout was even less of a fan. She just looked so miserable I felt compelled to find something positive to say.

Glancing at her I smiled and said, "You're definitely a good packer."

Honestly, it's not as inane as it sounds. After all, she really was a good packer. I had noticed that she was scanning the pile and carefully selecting like-minded goods for each bag.

Well, the comment was no sooner out of my mouth then her face lit up with a warm and broad smile. From there we went on to have

267

a short but most interesting conversation about working intuitively and multi-tasking.

As I walked out of the store it seemed to me that she was happier. I felt better too even though I had managed to spend over two hundred dollars on what primarily amounted to fruit, vegetables, and assorted rice cakes.

The end result is that I felt good about having passed on a very small act of kindness. And, that was even before she pulled a coupon out of the drawer below her cash register that ended up saving me over five dollars.

Turns out that my dear and loving mother, who has always served as an exemplary role model for practicing acts of kindness, was right. Being kind brings its own rewards and when we give, we always get back more.

The researchers agree. Surveys show that participating in regular, small acts of kindness is beneficial to your health, longevity, and well being.[119] Being kind makes you feel good, useful, and alive. It somehow validates our humanness. We also know that being kind triggers a number of beneficial physical and psychological responses. The most obvious response is the "feel-good" sensation which has been officially titled the "helper's high".

When you do something good, your body rewards you by releasing endorphins. These morphine-like substances create the feel-good experience.

Being kind also has the capacity to reduce or even block pain signals to the brain. People suffering from physical or psychological pain actually experience relief when they carry out an act of kindness. Experts say this is because when you practice kindness you are focused on someone else and forget about yourself and your pain.[120]

The person who receives a kind act also experiences the feel-good response. Who doesn't like it when someone smiles, thanks, compliments, or helps you in some way? It bonds us and somehow seems to create a good feeling about one's self and people in general.

---

119   Luks, A. (2001). *The healing power of doing good: The health and spiritual benefits of helping others.* New York: iUniverse.com. Retrieved Sept 2010. http://www.actsofkindness.org/benefits/1.

120   Roland, C. and Van Puymbroeck, M. (2007). *Older adults benefit from volunteerism.* Ashburn, Virginia: National Recreation and Park Association.

Compliments are another form of kindness that we could all use more of.

Last week at the conclusion of a fascinating meeting with four people discussing how to capture community values, one of the participants shook my hand, thanked me, and told me it had been the highlight of his week.

He then proceeded to tell me that it was because I was "hot".

I squirmed uncomfortably as did the others in the room waiting for more explanation because for anyone who knows me personally it's definitely not an accurate adjective for describing my appearance.

Thank goodness he went on to clarify, "Don't get me wrong. I am a very happily married man with the best wife a guy could possibly have, but you're hot. You're hot because you have the first quality I look for in a woman—intelligence. I look for intelligence first and then secondly I look for heart. You've got both those qualities and that's what makes you hot."

Well that definitely made me sigh with relief, laugh out loud, and thank him profusely for one of the best gifts I've received.

It was an extraordinarily kind and personally meaningful thing to say.

Since that meeting I've thought a lot about that particular compliment...rolled it around in my head to savour it, shared the story with a few others, and repeated it to my husband. I must admit it was kind of fun watching his reaction when I told him that another man had told me I was hot!

So, while I'm keenly aware that I'm supposed to be a grown-up and shouldn't need external compliments, the result was that it made me feel good. It also made me realize I had been given an important gift that is far too rare these days.

Even though the experts say flattery will get you nowhere, I beg to differ. I would even venture to say that compliments are even more important today because they are so rare and unexpected.

Today's stress too often results in people being so wrapped up in their own work and personal lives, that they don't take time to recognize and validate others. And yet, it might just be that paying compliments is a key skill for personal success, and workplace and community leadership.

Whether you're dealing with your workplace colleagues, boss, friends, or family, an authentic, meaningful, and well-placed compliment will make both you and the recipient feel good.

Complimenting your boss works because they hardly ever get them. Complimenting your colleagues is effective because it will make them appreciate your attention to detail and want to work with you. Some studies even indicate that people who pay compliments are often perceived as being smarter. Family and friends will appreciate that you value them and aren't taking them for granted.

Keep in mind, though, that we're not talking here about generic, cliché run-of-the mill compliments. The cardinal rule of paying compliments is that they need to be distinguished, insightful, honest, and specific. It means paying attention and noticing something that is being done well by the other party.

Compliments also need to be timely. They are most effective if they are delivered immediately after someone has done something praiseworthy. On the other hand, sometimes timing is everything and if you see a friend, family member, or workplace colleague in a slump, a well placed compliment could have an uplifting and significant impact.

However, as with most things, compliments are also about balance so you also need to be careful about paying too many compliments or they won't be seen as valuable.

We can all try to be just a little kinder and more complimentary to one another. After all, the hot compliment I received is a gift that is still resonating. The cost of the gift? Zero dollars. The value to the recipient? Priceless.

 **Chapter 12**

Competency 6: Plan Using a Community Development Approach

Has the capacity to implement a community development planning approach

COMPETENCY AREA	INDICATORS TO HELP YOU UNDERSTAND WHAT ENCOMPASSES THIS COMPETENCY	1 = I AM NOT AT ALL LIKE THAT	10 = I AM 100% LIKE THAT
6 Community Development Planning	6.1 I can articulate the beliefs and philosophy of community development.	1 2 3 4 5 6 7 8 9 10	
	6.2 I promote the importance of planning in the development and implementation of all initiatives.	1 2 3 4 5 6 7 8 9 10	
	6.3 I advocate a community development approach to planning as typically the best approach for service delivery (helping people to help themselves).	1 2 3 4 5 6 7 8 9 10	
	6.4 I can facilitate the development of various types of plans. e.g. community strategic planning, municipal sustainability plans, master plans, feasibility studies, organizational strategic planning, operational reviews, land-use plans, project plans, event planning, funding proposals.	1 2 3 4 5 6 7 8 9 10	
	6.5 I apply a diverse and sophisticated set of facilitation models, skills, and techniques.	1 2 3 4 5 6 7 8 9 10	
	6.6 I can apply strategies for igniting and engaging others in the planning process.	1 2 3 4 5 6 7 8 9 10	
	6.7 I can implement appropriate research strategies.	1 2 3 4 5 6 7 8 9 10	
	6.8 I can apply strategies for measuring both outcomes and process.	1 2 3 4 5 6 7 8 9 10	
	6.9 I can apply a variety of facilitative techniques to assist in the development of a vision, purpose, values, outcomes, strategies, budgets, action plans etc.	1 2 3 4 5 6 7 8 9 10	

Articulate Community Development

A colleague of mine recently attended a national tourism conference. He had been especially excited because the program was focused on the leadership required for success within the tourism industry. Upon return, he shared that, despite their positioning of the leadership described in the sessions as being something new and innovative, in his mind it was actually more a case of "everything old is new again". As far as he was concerned, their leading-edge leadership was simply good old-fashioned "community development".

While I think he may be on to something, the challenge is that there isn't always a common understanding of what is meant by community development.

Understanding community development and its implications for how community leaders should approach planning is critical. As noted previously, the simplest way to understand the meaning of community development is to break down the two words—community and development. If *community* is about sharing, connecting, and belonging, and *development* means improvement or growth, then community development is simply "helping people to help themselves".[121] A more academic definition defines community development "as local empowerment through organized groups of people acting collectively to control decisions, projects, programs, and policies that affect them as a community".[122]

> ❝To lead people, walk beside them… As for the best leaders, the people do not notice their existence. The next best, the people, honor and praise. The next, the people fear; and the next, the people hate… When the best leader's work is done the people say, 'We did it ourselves!'❞
>
> — Lao Tzu

Applying this philosophy of community development to planning means leaders will need to fully engage their stakeholders in driving the process and the resulting plan. To do this, the emphasis must be placed on democratic procedures, voluntary cooperation, self-help, development of leadership competencies, education, and problem-solving by consensus.

What makes this approach different from what we are typically used to seeing in planning is that all of the stakeholders, not just hired consultants or senior staff, are perceived as the experts and as a potential source of strength and knowledge.

A community development approach is guided by a process based on collaboration, cooperation, leadership growth, and learning. It generally involves, identifies, and builds upon the assets within an organization, neighbourhood, or entire community.

It is more about engaging stakeholders in the process and supporting them to develop, support, and implement their own solutions. When this approach is used, those involved are much more likely to stay involved to implement the activities and programs they have determined will best strengthen their organization or community.

Ultimately though, community development is about power and control and who holds it. Therefore, real community development

---

121 Herchmer, B. (1996). *Creating community: A community development handbook for the recreation practitioner.* Edmonton: Grassroots Enterprises.

122 Rubin, H.J. & Rubin, I.S. (1992). *Community organising and developing.* NY: MacMillan.

273

and ultimately the "ownership" for change and growth, means power and control for the planning must be in the hands of the stakeholders who will be impacted by the decisions.

When a community development approach is used, it also means energy and resources are being directed toward removing the barriers that prevent people from participating in the issues that affect their lives in the first place. Good community development will validate people's experience and include approaches to delivery that facilitate involvement, equality, and empowerment. It will promote knowledge and skills for positive change at the individual, organizational, and community level and as such, will strengthen community capacity and resiliency.

The challenge of community development is that it takes time. It is about people. That means it can be simple or complicated, straightforward or muddled, and everything in between. It also necessitates an investment of time in having meaningful conversations, determining values and priorities, and building the trusted relationships needed for change and growth.

It also means understanding that the job of community leaders is not to solve the problems for their citizens but rather to design and support a *process* that will help *them* to find the solutions that work best for their community.

Importance of Planning

Today my husband and I are working hard to re-enter the real world as we've just returned from a fabulous vacation in Mexico. Having recently experienced a lack of life balance, simply anticipating the break had provided serious incentive for making it through my increasingly busy work weeks. However, being so busy also meant that while we had managed to book the flights and hotel, we hadn't done much else in terms of planning our itinerary. Or perhaps we had?

If planning is addressing the *gap* in between where one is *now,* and where one wants to *go,* we did have a plan. We were stressed and we wanted to be less stressed. As a result, to get from where we were (stressed), to where we wanted to go (not stressed), the plan was to do very little while we were away except relax. Sounds like a plan to me.

Although in our case our vacation plan was a plan not to plan, a plan typically could also be thought of as a list of actions arranged in the order that will best help you achieve your vision. Our holiday plan resulted in many books read while lounging poolside, good food found in out-of-the-way restaurants, good conversations, and walks on the beach. It was a good but ultimately simple plan.

Everyone plans. Whether it's jotting down a to-do list on a scrap piece of paper or developing a proposal for a new business, planning is an essential component of our lives. We work for businesses that depend on strategic plans to direct operations, we participate in clubs and organizations that rely on solid program plans and budgets, and we live in communities where priorities are often determined as the result of a strategic plan.

When I managed the Niagara College Centre for Community Leadership, January was always marked by a flurry of calls from organizations that, after finally getting a chance during the holidays to slow down and reflect, would get pumped up about organizing a strategic planning session.

Quite rightly they would see the beginning of a new calendar as a time to bring key stakeholders together to plan for the future by establishing a common direction, prioritizing their many competing demands, and determining financial requirements for the upcoming year.

Yet there were a number of organizations who never followed through on implementing their planning sessions. Mostly what we heard is that they didn't have time to plan, or they didn't see the value because plans are out of date before they're finished, or just gather dust sitting on a shelf.

However, my learning is that the real benefit of planning is as much about the process as it is the final plan.

The process of sitting down together as a team to have meaningful and thoughtful conversations and reflections is what is most important. The conversations allow opportunities to clarify, check assumptions, brainstorm, and harness the collective synergy of the group. The strategic planning process often provides a series of "aha" moments that contributes to doing the right things and being innovative while you're at it.

Planning as a team also provides an opportunity for cross-pollination among the team members. At our last team planning retreat, one of our team members who generally has very little to do with communication strategies, came up with an absolutely brilliant idea for how our annual report can be presented in a compelling and user-friendly way.

Another collective conversation made us rethink a decision that we all thought was carved in stone. Others brought ideas forward that had been put on the back burner. Of course, not all the ideas will be good ones but sometimes the best way to get good ideas is to make sure you get a lot of them and then just ignore the bad ones.

The planning process also allows you to establish common direction and determine priorities. One of our staff emailed me after our last planning session to say she was excited about everything and super pumped for the future. Planning also helps develop policies and to be clearer about financial requirements. Most importantly, those involved will be more confident, enthusiastic, and committed to implementing growth.

Even though planning will be time well spent, it won't be enough to guarantee success. Improvising after the planning session as new ideas and opportunities emerge will also be important. However, a good plan provides a basis for making decisions about those deviations by providing the right balance of framework and flexibility.

A focus on planning is always a great reminder for everyone of its value in terms of contributing to staying ahead. Planning is really about preparing ourselves for tomorrow and, as such, is essential whether we are planning for our own personal and career success, business, service club, sport group, organization, department, or an entire community.

Successful community leaders will be those who understand the importance of having a plan to inspire and motivate action by helping us determine what it is we want as our outcomes or goals and how we are going to reach them.

Despite this importance, planning is a subject matter to which we typically pay very little attention. Planning is rarely taught in our schools or likely to become a subject of media debate. Yet, in a world that is constantly changing, planning is becoming increasingly critical as we are often faced with more issues and responsibilities and not enough time or money to do everything we want to do.

This ability to plan is likely the main difference between being a manager and being a leader. The very essence of leadership is that you have a vision and a plan. As a wise man once said, "You can't blow an uncertain trumpet."

Even though it does seem rather simple, the reality is that there appears to be a shortage of visionary planners. As ancient Chinese philosopher Sun YatSen once said, "In the construction of a country, it is not the practical workers but the idealists and planners that are difficult to find."

Shortage of visionary planners aside, strategic planning remains crucial as a means of stimulating innovative thinking and clarifying future direction. The term "strategy" is derived from a Greek word meaning "the art of the general". Just as military commanders make day-to-day decisions with a larger plan in mind, a strategic plan is important for ensuring an orderly, thoughtful decision-making process that focuses attention on the most important issues and how they can best be achieved.

It is very easy to make planning more complex than it needs to be but over the years I learned that planning doesn't necessarily have to be all that complicated. Whether you're planning for your personal life, a business, an organization or community, it really can be quite simple.

You start by getting a good handle on just where your organization, business, or community is at. Secondly, determine where you want go. Then the plan simply becomes a case of sorting out the steps that have to be implemented to get you from where you are now, to the future where you want to go.

As a result I remain absolutely convinced that planning is an important priority. However, for a number of reasons we just may need to rethink how we've traditionally gone about doing it.

Advocate a Community Development Approach to Planning

Our approach to planning needs to change because challenges everywhere are much more complicated. Because the challenges are so complex, we too often continue to react to symptoms rather than dealing with the often multiple root causes. Even if we are able to wrap our thinking around the root causes, the fixes are daunting as they are often long term and involve multiple stakeholders and sectors.

This complex often chaotic environment has resulted in too many people retreating or hunkering down within their own bunkers assuming that someone else will tackle the big issues. Unfortunately, there aren't enough stepping up to the plate so we too often lose sight of what's really important.

Ultimately though, we all want our organizations, businesses, and communities to be happy, healthy, and highly functioning. We also know that this is determined by a complex mix of factors that include personal relationships, job satisfaction, physical environments, etc. Some factors are under our personal control, e.g. regular exercise, good eating habits but, we've let a lot of responsibility for the other factors sit with government and business.

However, we know that abdicating responsibility is not the answer. In fact, recent academic research shows that happiness and well-being are improved when stakeholders are empowered.[123]

This means that all our planning efforts need to answer three key questions.

Whether planning is taking place for an organization, business, or community, ask yourself, "Are we providing opportunities for our stakeholders to influence decisions that affect them? Their workplace? Their neighbourhood? Their community?"

Secondly, "Are we facilitating regular contact between stakeholders?"

And lastly, "Are we helping our stakeholders gain the confidence to exercise control over their circumstances?"

These three questions will be a sound starting point for the rich discussion necessary to initiate truly meaningful planning needed for happy and healthy organizations, businesses, and communities. They will also ensure a community development approach to planning rather than one controlled by consultants.

---

123   Hothi, M., Bacon, N., Brophy, M., Mulgan, G., (2008). *Neighbourliness & Empowerment=Wellbeing. Is there a formula for happy communities?*

Of course, we all still need plans that include a vision, values, goals, and action steps to get to where we want to go. But utilizing a community development approach will ensure we're headed in the right direction.

Types of Plans

It is important for community leaders to understand that plans come in a variety of shapes and sizes and vary from those that have a very broad focus like community strategic plans or municipal sustainability plans, to those that are much more narrowly defined like program or event plans. Who is involved in the planning and why it is being done will differ but the elements of each plan, as well as the approach, are generally the same.

Historically, most planning in community settings has taken place using one of three approaches or models. These include (1) *social action* (2) *social planning* or (3) *community development*.

While there is a time and place for each of these models, the more complex and innovative the solutions need to be, the more appropriate it will be to use the third or community development approach. However, understanding the first two approaches explains why many plans gather dust on a shelf rather than being implemented.

A *social action* approach is typically used when a segment of the population is overlooked or oppressed. The assumption is made that making a change will require an advocacy or activist role so conflict tactics, confrontation, and direct action are utilized. The community leader assumes the disadvantaged segment of the population needs to be organized if their resources or treatment are to be made more equitable. Examples typically include lobbying, picketing, or boycotting. Because social action approaches are usually about a perceived, unfair distribution of power and control, they are usually rooted in anger. Typically when social action takes place there is a winner and a loser so even if you end up on the winning side, you lose because stakeholders end up being so divided. On the positive side, social action does raise the profile of a situation or issue.

Social planning is utilized when there is an underlying belief that altering social conditions requires expertise and knowledge. Typically a paid consultant is hired to gather facts, analyze the information and make recommendations for appropriate programs, services, initiatives, facilities etc. Community members are viewed as *consumers* and the consultants are viewed as the *experts*. It is the experts and those who pay them who have the ultimate control and power to finalize the plans. For this reason, it is not unusual to find plans that have used a social planning approach end up as a home for dust bunnies.

A *community development* approach ensures stakeholder-driven and ultimately "owned" plans that identify and respond to their needs and interests. Because they are empowered and control the final plan, it's not unusual to find action being taken before the ink is dry on the paper.

Community leaders will be involved in initiatives that could use any of these approaches to develop plans that range from the very macro such as a community strategic plan, to those which are more micro such as a program or event plan.

The types of plans and who typically does them is outlined in the table that follows.

TYPE OF PLAN	WHO DOES IT
Community Strategic Plan or Community/Municipal Sustainability Plan	• Usually initiated by the municipality, region, or band council • Locally initiated and locally owned • Concerned with the future of the entire town or region and it's quality of life or quality of place e.g. social, economic, environmental, cultural • Ideally should be a cooperative effort involving a variety of sectors
Land Use Planning/Official Plan	• Elected councils of municipalities (ideally with input from citizens) • To help provide for the orderly growth and development of a community
Comprehensive/ Master Plan	• Usually by the municipality because it is typically concerned with the concerns of an entire sector • To help the municipality make rational, informed decisions about the development of programs, facilities, services etc.

Organizational Strategic Plan	• Any organization, department or agency concerned about the long term development and growth of their organization • Normally involves the board, senior staff, committees, and other stakeholders • To help the organization, department or agency revisit and reassess the effectiveness and relevance of the programs, services, facilities, supports etc.
Program/Project /Event Planning	• Clubs, community groups, recreation committees, departments • Those in an organization who are involved in providing program services • Groups or organizations interested in adapting to changing community needs • To improve the quality, quantity, and effectiveness of services based on defined community priorities
Operational Review	• When problem(s) or issue(s) are identified that threaten the effectiveness of the organization • As part of ongoing healthy management practices
Feasibility Study	• Any organization considering the development of a major facility • To help make decisions and to provide information and a comprehensive look at all of the alternatives involved in order to make the right decision.

Facilitation Models and Skills

Even though I didn't really want to go, I attended a full day session simply because I trusted and liked the woman who invited me as well as the facilitator who would be designing the process. The intent of the session was to bring together a number of organizations and individuals who were knowledgeable about board governance and have them help design a series of modules that would be made available for self-directed learning for board members of social profit organizations.

I know that board governance is important, and I've been lucky to have garnered a fair bit of knowledge about it over the years, but the truth is that it isn't a topic about which I am truly passionate. Regardless, I have to say I truly enjoyed the day. That was due in large part to the host organization being committed to working collaboratively in order to avoid reinventing the wheel. This is not always the case as in the past I have experienced organizations that despite often good intentions, talk collaboration but have a tough time walking their talk.

To better understand why it can be challenging, The International Association of Public Participation has developed a spectrum[124] that illustrates five different levels of public participation and shows how each type garners different results. It is an excellent model for determining the most suitable types of engagement and to effectively facilitate and manage participation.

There really is no right or wrong choice among the five levels described in the spectrum as it is simply a case of determining how much power and control the host government or organization wants to share. The process is then designed accordingly.

Public participation is an essential part of encouraging change and ensuring community and other stakeholders have ownership of a direction, course of action, or decision, and having it implemented. The more control stakeholders have, the more likely they are to support it being put into place. What's most important is being clear and transparent about the level of participation you are promising and the power that is (and isn't) intended to be devolved.

The five levels begin with *inform* which provides the least power and also the least potential for public impact. It sends the message that "we will keep you informed." The next levels are *consult, involve,* and *collaborate.* The one at the far end of the continuum and the one providing the most public impact is *empower.* This clearly conveys to stakeholders that "we will implement what you decide."

The session I attended this week was pretty close to empowering those in the room by landing at the fourth or *collaborate* level. We worked together to design the curriculum for board governance and were assured they were looking to us for advice and direction. They also suggested that they would incorporate our recommendations into the curriculum to the maximum extent possible.

So why is it important to understand these different levels of participation? Community challenges are complex these days and often require the complex thinking that is the result of collaboration. We all need to be able to implement facilitative strategies that will engage and empower stakeholders. Effective facilitation makes it easier for stakeholders to do their best thinking because they are guided through a process that enables them to define and reach their goals.

---

124 http://www.iap2.org/associations/4748/files/IAP2%20Spectrum_vertical.pdf.

The basis of effective facilitation reflects a belief that people are intelligent, capable, and want to do the right thing, many heads are better than one, each person's opinion is of equal value, people commit to ideas and plans when they are part of the development process, and people can, and will, act responsibly when offered true accountability for their decisions.

It is also important to understand the role the facilitator plays in contributing to successful collaborative efforts. In this case, we had a good facilitator who understood her role was to manage the process—not the content—and ensure everyone was heard. In this situation, the facilitator also had a great deal of knowledge about the content but disciplined herself to stay focused on process. She remained neutral, listened actively, asked questions, paraphrased to clarify, and synthesized ideas.

An important part of community leadership, facilitators play an essential role in helping groups work together more effectively when a collaborative consensus-building process is made the priority.

Truth be told, working collaboratively on the board governance learning modules made for a long day that involved very hard work for everyone involved. However, there is no doubt the curriculum will be richer and more meaningful as a result.

But perhaps even more important is that because we were all involved in the design we will all become ambassadors for the training module and promote its use among our respective stakeholders. The scenario would have been much different it had simply been handed to us.

Strategies for Engaging Others in the Planning Process

While planning terminology often differs, it is generally accepted that a traditional planning process includes:

1) Needs Assessment
2) Vision and Values
3) Mission/Purpose/Mandate
4) Outcomes
5) Goals/Deliverables/Strategies

6) Objectives, Action Steps, Timelines, Costs

7) Evaluation

While these elements of a plan remain important, ensuring a community development process will require the inclusion of five preliminary planning steps. These include:

Step 1: Ignite and invite others to participate

Step 2: Share strengths and successes

Step 3: Research your community

Step 4 Define priorities

Step 5 Engage others who need to be involved[125]

In addition to making these first five steps in the planning framework different from the more traditional forms of planning, they are what will ensure a meaningful and relevant plan that is successfully implemented.

Implementing Appropriate Research Strategies

It has become so mainstream to our way of life that yesterday I heard a four year old say, "Just google it, Daddy."

Google just might be one of the best as well as one of the worst things ever invented. While it is without question the most powerful research tool ever put into our hands, the sheer volume of the data can also be totally overwhelming. For sure it has changed our approach to research.

Research is any investigative activity or search for knowledge that is carried out by a person or a group, with the goal of discovering something new, at least to them. We can conduct research on existing published information, history or promising practices, or by making new observations.[126] It can be *scientific research* that relies on the ap-

---

125 Herchmer, B. (2009). *A toolkit for community leaders*. Edmonton: Alberta Recreation and Parks Association.

126 Charitable Research Reserve. *Why research and why is it important?* Retrieved http://www.raresites.org/cms/en/Research/WhyResearch.aspx?menuid=12.

plication of the scientific method or *applied research* that discovers, interprets, and develops methods and systems.

Research is important for community leaders as it helps develop vision and direction, assists us to better understand, define, and solve problems; determine priorities; surface public opinion; develop community support; and stimulate action.

While we often think of research as needing to be formal, sometimes it can be informal and serve more us a "pulse-taking". Before doing a keynote, ACE Ambassador Ian Hill, typically gathers the names of ten stakeholders from the organizers and calls them to get a better handle on how his keynote can best address their issues and opportunities.

When dealing with community-wide issues he often employs a strategy he calls "100 Cups of Coffee". He simply sits down and has a cup of coffee with key stakeholders—one at a time—to better prepare him to work with the community to develop relevant recommendations and strategies.

There are also numerous facilitative techniques that can be used to gather feedback such as *Open Space Technology,* focus groups, *Six Hats of Thinking, Future Search, World Café* etc.[127] On the other hand, formal research involves a more stringent process and greater attention being paid to survey design and sample sizes and numbers. This is necessary to ensure there will be confidence that the results speak for the entire population being surveyed.

Regardless of the type of research, it is always important to invest time in the beginning to clearly articulate, test, and refine the purpose and outcomes of the results. Time also needs to be spent determining the research methods, reviewing time and cost factors, designing and administering the research tools, and presenting the information.

One of my most important learnings about research happened in one of my first volunteer positions. I was chair of a committee that was working to establish recreation opportunities for adults with developmental challenges.

---

127 Herchmer, B. (2009). *A toolkit for community leaders.* Edmonton: Alberta Recreation and Parks Association.

Being cognizant of the importance of research, I thought it best to begin with a survey of the adults and their families to gather more about their leisure interests. The survey response was excellent but the results were somewhat puzzling.

Despite the wide variety of options posed by recreation and sport options, the respondents were unanimous in their desires to pursue swimming, dancing, and skating. Turns out, those were the activities they had all been exposed to during their school years. And, therein was the learning—you don't know, what you don't know. Research is critical, however sometimes facts may need to be combined with more intuitive learnings.

Outcome Measurement

Like many others, I was drawn to the field of recreation and parks because I saw it as an opportunity to make a difference. It wasn't until several years later that I learned more about outcome measurement and how recreation, sport, parks, arts, culture and heritage had the potential to play a key role in developing healthy individuals, vibrant communities, and a strong economy and environment.

> Not everything that counts can be counted, and not everything that can be counted counts."
>
> — Albert Einstein

Often from our own experience growing up, we knew that recreation helped us grow our confidence and self-esteem, learn more about ourselves and our values, and increased our sense of belonging and ultimately, our quality of life. This leisure literacy,[128] or ability to use our leisure time wisely, pumped vitality, creativity, and positive energy into our lives and our communities.

Despite these contributions, the profession of recreation doesn't always get a lot of respect. Over the years I've often spent time explaining and documenting that the field is much more than someone carrying a clipboard and a whistle—much more.

Passionate about wanting to make a difference, I entered the field in the late 80's at a time when diminishing local government resources meant that recreation and parks were absorbing major funding cuts. Yet, in some ways, it was a major wake-up call because even

---

128   Petersen, C. (March, 2011). *Leisure Literacy.* ACE Communities Webinar.

though we intuitively knew recreation was important to individuals, communities, the economy and the environment, it wasn't something we were able to measure or prove.

It was, and remains, especially challenging because recreation and parks, like a lot of other fields, contributes more to the *public benefit economy* and the intangible social and community benefits than the *market economy* which measures worth based on monetary return.

Determined to help prove its worth, I got involved in a pan-Canadian movement that collected evidence and research that documented the benefits or outcomes delivered by recreation and parks.[129]

What I ultimately learned is that *outcomes* are the *desired results or impact of a process, program, project, or activity*. Outcomes are about individual, organizational, or community change and can include change in our *knowledge, status or condition, behaviours, attitudes, values, or skills.*[130]

But probably what was most helpful for me, as well as potentially any community leader, was eventually seeing that *an outcome is what stakeholders will have that they didn't have when they started*. It was also important to learn how outcomes could be used to generate better performance and accountability measures, and to illustrate their essential role in both individual, organizational, and community growth and development. The regular, systematic tracking of the extent to which stakeholders experienced the benefits or outcomes also became a priority.

We learned that what gets measured gets done, if you can't measure results you can't see success or measure it, and if you can't demonstrate results you can't win public support.[131]

Having a clearer handle on the outcomes that could potentially be delivered by parks and recreation meant the field was better equipped to conduct surveys that would measure the delivery of those outcomes. Surveys of the general public conducted in both Ontario[132]

---

129 http://benefitshub.ca/.

130 United Way. (1996). *Measuring program outcomes: A practical approach.* United Way of America.

131 Osborne, D. & Gabler, T. (1993) *Reinventing government: How the entrepreneurial spirit is transforming the public sector.* New York: Penguin Books.

132 Parks and Recreation Ontario (2009). *Recreation and parks services: An Ontario perspective.* Toronto: http://www.prontario.org/index.php/ci_id/3674.htm.

and Alberta[133] showed that the majority of the general public see their leisure as being more important than their work. Additionally, the average citizen clearly sees the link between recreation and parks and their personal satisfaction, reduced social problems, a reduction in unnecessary spending in health, social services, and justice, and protected environmental spaces.

Although I came into the field intuitively understanding the outcomes and benefits delivered by the field, outcome measurement confirmed that parks provide a sense of place in the community, allowing for escape, contemplation, discovery, access to nature, interpretive education, and recreation. They also provide shelter, wildlife habitat, improved air quality, and serve as buffers between residential and industrial areas. Parks enhance aesthetic quality, increase property values, and improve the image and livability of communities.[134]

Additionally, recreation, through physical, social, and artistic expression, provides opportunities for us to improve our health, socialize and interact with others, learn new skills, have fun and find life balance. Sport and recreation events, festivals and the visual and performing arts provide opportunities for self-expression, social interaction, and are a source of civic pride and economic impact. They contribute to human happiness, and to the resiliency and adaptive capacity of our communities.

> " The future is not some place we are going, but one we are creating. The paths to it are not found but made, and the activity of making them changes both the maker and the destination."
>
> — John Schaar

Just as outcome measurement helped the field of recreation and parks, so too will it assist community leaders in determining what their stakeholders consider to be most important, their fit within the pursuit of broader community goals and priorities, and what needs to be done so programs, services, events, facilities etc. can be prioritized within the context of the broader public good.

Outcome measurement can be used to clarify direction, communicate powerful results to stakeholders, motivate staff and volunteers,

---

133   Parks and Recreation Ontario (2009). *Recreation and parks services: An Ontario perspective.* Toronto: http://www.prontario.org/index.php/ci_id/3674.htm.

134   Harper, J. (2008). Summary Report: *Public perceptions on use and benefits of local government recreation and parks services.* Edmonton: Alberta: Alberta Recreation and Parks Association (ARPA).

288

identify successful practices, improve performance, strengthen accountability, encourage innovation, identify training needs, ensure a continued focus on delivering outcomes, and support necessary change.

Community leaders will need to ensure outcomes that reflect noticeable impact and yet are realistic and achievable. They will also need to be outcomes that inspire commitment and action particularly at a cross-sectoral or cross-agency level.

Outcomes can also be considered in terms of being *short term, mid-term,* or *long-term.* For instance, short term outcomes typically focus on awareness, knowledge, attitudes, opinion, and motivation. Mid term are about action and are therefore more likely to be about behaviour, practice, skill, decision-making, and policies. Outcomes for the longer term are about social, environmental, civic, and economic conditions.

Longer term broad community outcomes could potentially include:

- communities are stronger—capacity is increased
- people live longer
- people know and help their neighbours
- independent living is prolonged
- residents express pride in their community
- lowered healthcare costs
- enhanced overall well-being
- reduction in costs of social service intervention
- contributions to child and youth development are increased
- risk of coronary heart disease and stroke is reduced
- reduced police, justice, and incarceration costs
- adults are helped to develop to their full potential
- improved work performance
- life-long learning promoted
- community viewed as attractive to businesses
- spirituality explored
- tourism increased
- individual self esteem and positive self image improved
- employment generated

- satisfaction levels enhanced
- perceived quality of life improved
- property values increased
- reduction in self-destructive behaviour
- ecological integrity protected
- reduction in crime
- air quality improved
- racism reduced
- environmental education embraced
- reduction in isolation and loneliness
- protection against environmental disaster
- families are strengthened
- energy is saved
- more leaders are produced
- environmental stewardship is encouraged
- social skills are improved

In addition to the specific outcomes, community leaders will also need to ensure consideration is given to developing specific indicators related to each of the outcomes, who will evaluate, when and how often, how, and with which tools.

> ❝ A strong passion for any object will ensure success, for the desire of the end will point out the means."
>
> — William Hazlit

It is critically important work that United Way perhaps put best when they said, "It's not how many worms the bird feeds its young, but how well the fledgling flies."

Develop Vision, Values, and Purpose

I have this fabulous brother who my sister and I often refer to as a renaissance man. Growing up in a somewhat dysfunctional family, we didn't know each other all that well even though we were only three years apart in age. The only thing I really knew for sure was that he was the brother who tormented me less than the other two.

When he ended up as the single parent of a daughter, he made a decision to go back to university to become a teacher and lived with us for awhile as he got on his feet. It was then I got to know him better. I learned he was kind, caring, and considerate. He was also a great cook, doting father, hardworking student, gifted athlete, and sensitive listener.

Somewhere along the line, he got diverted from his path to teaching, and began to work with adults who were developmentally challenged. Eventually he became the Executive Director of Mainstream Services in St. Catharines which, until a number of years ago, was housed in a maze of main floor and basement rooms in a commercial building in Port Dalhousie.

There he continues to work with staff and volunteers to "improve the quality of life for people with a developmental challenges by providing a supportive environment that strives to empower individuals with the necessary skills and confidence for lifelong learning and growth."

A number of years ago when he was relatively new on the job, I helped him out by volunteering to facilitate a planning session for his staff team. As he and his team were keen to develop an exciting and compelling vision that would "grow" Mainstream, I took a somewhat risky step as a facilitator and took them on a guided tour of what Mainstream might look like five years into the future.

Guided imagery, a technique that has existed for years, can help individuals more readily develop ideas and visualize images that stretch their existing concepts and problem solving abilities. The resulting vision for Mainstream was indeed inspiring and much of what they envisioned on

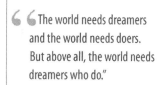

> The world needs dreamers and the world needs doers. But above all, the world needs dreamers who do."
>
> — Sarah Ban Breathnach

that day was gradually put into place. As they continued to grow and serve, I pretty much forgot about that day of planning until my brother called me several years later to thank me.

As he explained it, he got a call from a church member who was a relative of one of their clients. Apparently his church, faced with a dwindling congregation, had made a decision to close down. As a result he was calling Mainstream to come and see if any of their furnishings would be of use.

My brother walked into the church thinking about tables and chairs but was struck immediately by an unexpected and overwhelming sense of familiarity. Although it took him a while to figure it out, he finally realized that what he was seeing was what he and his staff had envisioned a number of years before in that planning session.

During that exercise, he and his staff had envisioned themselves right out of their maze of basement offices and into a bright and spacious facility. They had seen the large expanse of property where clients could be taught horticultural skills, the welcoming entrance, the large common room, a kitchen that could be used for training, classrooms, and so much more.

As a result of understanding the building was familiar because of the vision he had been carrying around in his brain for years, my brother spun toward the church representative and said, "Forget the table and chairs, what are you going to do with the building?"

And that, was the first of many discussions that led to Mainstream Services buying and renovating Glenview United Church as their wonderful new home.

I can tell you that I felt pretty good about the small role I had played in Mainstream's long journey. But more importantly, it reinforced for me the necessity of spending time thinking and dreaming about the future.

A positive, meaningful vision of the future helps set direction, make decisions, and motivate action. While some shy away from the use of vision, seeing it as fluffy and impractical, it ultimately is intensely practical because while it reflects our values and principles, a good vision is also built on facts as well as the intangibles of intuition and imagination.

> "If you have built castles in the air, your work need not be lost, that is where they should be. Now put foundations under them."
>
> — Henry David Thoreau

The vision for Mainstream Services worked because it reflected the key elements of a vision. It was a complete and recognizable picture of their future, it reflected what was best for all of their stakeholders, and it was inspiring and yet achievable.

The learning is that if you don't like your life, your organization, your business, or your community, it is critical to take the time to envision how it could be.

But what happens if you find yourself with a less than perfect vision?

292

A number of years ago, I had a rather lengthy conversation with our youngest son trying to provide more explanation for why I had moved across the country. He was genuinely perplexed and likely feeling somewhat abandoned, even though he's been living on his own for several years. After all, as he reminded me, hadn't I always said, "Family first"?

I struggled to find the words but started by assuring him that my family is, and always will be, my most important value. I then went on to explain that for years I had quite willingly put my family first even though my personal vision had always involved wanting to make a difference in my field.

When, as an empty-nester, an opportunity opened up for me to focus on my career in community development and community leadership, I was really interested. I explained to my son, however, that I wasn't convinced I was ready to move across the country to do the work.

After all, it wasn't a perfect vision.

The offer put before me was for two years of part time consulting work that equated to slightly more than I was currently making full time. While that was well and good, there was no safety net, benefits, or pension. Yet, my instincts were also telling me that if I was ever going to let go of the trapeze, it needed to be now. Fortunately, I was also blessed with a generous and trusting husband who felt it was "my turn".

I've since learned the experts were right. It is true that when you do what you love, the money will follow. Challenging and rewarding consulting opportunities seemed to fall into my lap so my fears about financial security were never an issue.

The reality, though, is that I can't really take much credit. I think it has much more to do with the fact that I've also been blessed with a gene that makes it easy for me to live with uncertainty.

Regardless, this time of uncertainty and complexity has also meant I'm working with those who are practicing a very different kind of leadership. For the leaders I'm now working with, it means being okay with not always having the answers. It also means it is much more about facilitating a process that will lead to accessing the wisdom among our colleagues and communities.

It means moving ahead even when the vision is less than perfect knowing that the majority of initiatives are never implemented exactly as planned. Sometimes there is as much, if not more, learning in the mistakes we make along the way.

In times of complexity, which is definitely where we are at these days, we all need to focus on building a vision that is good enough to get the work started. As the work progresses, the vision can be more finely tuned and adjusted. That kind of vision will ensure the work is grounded but also flexible. In other words, as written in "Getting to Maybe", "We build the road as we travel, but we never travel without a map."[135]

Strategies and Action Plans

Yesterday I overheard a customer ask a young sales clerk about her plans for school. She replied that she was majoring in arts until she could get a handle on what she wants to do with her life.

With a deep sigh she went on to say, "There are just so many options."

> "Without a deadline, baby, I wouldn't do nothing."
>
> — Duke Ellington

While I don't plan to go back to school this year, I too often flounder as the result of the many options that present themselves to me each day on my never ending work to-do list. Even though I know it is somewhat irrational, I sometimes put things on the list even though I've already done them, just so I can have something to cross off.

Just as with planning for organizations or communities, some items on my list are straightforward and easy to check off, whereas others are far more complex. No one will be surprised to learn that generally it is the complex items on the list that I'm more apt to ignore.

This is a significant learning for community leaders to absorb when developing strategies and action plans. Quite simply, when directions aren't clear, the items on the to-do list won't get done. As a

---

135 Westley, F., Zimmerman, B. & Patton, M. (2007). *Getting to maybe: How the world is changed.* Vintage Canada.

rule we humans don't like ambiguity. When there are too many options or things are too complex, we move into overload mode.

This means effective leaders need to work really hard at making things simple. Simplicity begets action.

We live in a complex and often chaotic world. If our direction is not clear, decision-making is hampered. Despite the best of intentions, we might just head in the wrong direction, lose our sense of initiative, or place too much emphasis on gathering more research and studies to reduce the ambiguity.

Albert Einstein addressed this need for simplicity in one of his more famous quotes: "Three Rules of Work: Out of clutter find simplicity; From discord find harmony; In the middle of difficulty lies opportunity."

Simplicity is the leader's responsibility—both for themselves and for their organization. If you want clear and simple strategies and action plans, make sure the vision and outcomes are clear, ensure open and honest communications, and minimize distractions and diversions that could get in the way and detract from clear thinking and simple action.

Keep reinforcing the key priorities, because if everything is important, nothing is important. Do fewer things but do them really well.

Ensure the strategies and action plans are written down, reviewed on a regular basis, and assigned with deadlines. Think about the action plans as a to-do list for each strategy. Ensure they have the potential to be achievable within the next year, build on strengths, address challenges, and capitalize on opportunities.

A leader devoted to the successful implementation of the strategy and action plans needs to ensure they are supported with people, resources, time, systems, and above all, communication. Communicate the plan to everyone in your organization. Hold a monthly or quarterly strategy meeting to report on the progress taking action as well as to adapt to changes in the environment.

Strategies and action plans need to be seen as a work-in-progress. It doesn't have to be perfect or one hundred percent complete. Think of it instead as making a list and determining priorities.

 **Chapter 13**

... Next Steps

It will be Challenging and Amazing

Chances are, if you are reading this book, you are likely already demonstrating many of the competencies for community leaders presented here. If not, it may be that you're looking for a path to a new and different kind of leadership.

Either way, it is hoped this will contribute to helping you recognize and strengthen the leader within you. That's not to say that applying these community leadership competencies is going to be easy. Ensuring leadership that will result in the kind of communities where we want to live, work, and play will no doubt be a challenge.

It will require leaders who are incredibly diverse in their thinking, experience, and skills, and yet are willing to come together to help advance the quality of life in their communities.

No one individual, organization, or business will have all the answers so an emphasis will need to be placed on working together to make a difference.

There will be tense moments along the way. And there will definitely be times when our intent to replace top-down leadership with something shared across communities will be questioned by everyone involved. It will sometimes be as challenging as nailing Jell-O to the wall. Yet, a more shared and collaborative approach will ultimately produce remarkable results as amazing things happen when we follow the trail of energy and passion.

We will need to be patient. Of key importance will be taking the time to ensure those involved share and embrace a collective vision. It also means being patient as each person prods and shapes the original vision in order to embrace it as their own.

We will also have to be tolerant and respectful of one another if we are to truly appreciate different perspectives.

The importance of values will also have to be recognized. Just as marriages, organizations, and even communities can reflect very different personalities, they will be more apt to flourish when grounded by similar values.

We will need to park our egos and be reminded that a brilliant idea is a brilliant idea regardless of who puts it on the table. Supporting and expanding on an idea even if it is someone else's, and not caring about who gets the credit, will lead to greater success.

Even those who have been around for a while will need to value and appreciate just how much opportunity there is to learn from one another. Participation needs to be welcomed and invited within a culture that celebrates curiosity, a willingness to embrace experimentation, exploration, idea generation, and risk taking. When that takes place it will be a much simpler matter to connect the dots in order to create a cohesive and synergistic direction that everyone will support. It is only then that the differences that often create tension can be invitations to learn and grow, rather that separate and divide.

The only real training for leadership is leadership."

— Anthony Jay

We will also have to realize that even things we thought we knew for sure will be rattled by new information and perspectives.

Most importantly, we need to shift our perspective that leadership is top down, and become more comfortable and practiced with it being much more about building, nurturing strong relationships and trust, holding the big picture of a collective vision and plan, and then making sure it is implemented.

Large scale community change and growth will happen when community leaders are able to facilitate support for building on our assets and alleviating many of our most serious and complex community challenges by bringing together social profits, governments, businesses, and the public around a common agenda that will create collective impact.

While definitely achievable in any community, it will require leaders like you—even if you've never thought of yourself as one—who can be an agent of change; promote a commitment to continuous improvement; be an optimistic, proactive, big picture thinker; act as a catalyst for encouraging citizen responsibility and for engaging and cultivating community ownership; serve as an advocate for quality of life promoting an understanding that the most important investments we can ever make will be in our children, our families, our health, our environment, and our social infrastructure; and know how to plan effectively to ensure visionary, yet pragmatic plans, that are owned and implemented by the communities we serve.

Best of luck on your journey—may your leadership grow and your communities prosper.

24362739R10185

Made in the USA
Lexington, KY
17 July 2013